Routledge Cavendish

Q&A series

Equity & Trusts

4th Edition

TITLES IN THE Q&A SERIES

Routledge
Cavendish

series

Equity & Trusts
4th Edition

Mohamed Ramjohn, LLM, CIOT, JP
Principal Lecturer in Law at Thames Valley University

Routledge·Cavendish
Taylor & Francis Group

First published 2006
by Routledge·Cavendish
2 Park Square, Milton Park, Abingdon, Oxon, OX14 4RN

Simultaneously published in the USA and Canada
by Routledge·Cavendish
270 Madison Ave, New York, NY 10016

Routledge·Cavendish is an imprint of the Taylor & Francis Group, an informa business

© 2006 Routledge-Cavendish
1995, 1998, 2001 Martin Dixon

Typeset in Palatino by Newgen Imaging Systems (P) Ltd., Chennai, India
Printed and bound in Great Britain by TJ International Ltd, Padstow

British Library Cataloguing in Publication Data
Ramjohn, Mohamed
Equity & trusts. – 4th ed. – (Q&A series)
1. Equity – England 2. Trusts and trustees – England 3. Equity – Wales
4. Trusts and trustees – Wales
I. Title
346. 4'2004

Library of Congress Cataloging in Publication Data
A catalog record for this book has been requested

ISBN10: 1-859-41741-8 (pbk)
ISBN13: 978-1-859-41741-6 (pbk)

FOR ALFRED WILLIAM AND WILLIAM ALFRED JAMES

Contents

Table of Cases

Table of Statutes

1 The Creation of Trusts

Introduction

It might be thought prudent at the very start of any book on the law of trusts to attempt to define exactly what a 'trust' is. Unfortunately, that is not as easy as we might hope. Of course, the essential ingredients of a trust are well known: there is a 'trustee', who is the holder of the legal (or 'paper') title to property, and this person holds the trust property 'on trust' for the 'beneficiary' (or *cestui que trust*). The beneficiary is the equitable owner of the property and this is the person (or persons) to whom the real or 'beneficial' advantages of ownership will accrue. The interest enjoyed by the beneficiary is proprietary or 'in rem'. Thus, he is able to trace his property and recover it from any intermeddler with the exception of the *bona fide* transferee of the legal estate for value without notice. Further, although, as just indicated, the trustee usually holds the 'legal' title and the beneficiary holds the 'equitable' title, it is perfectly possible for an equitable owner to create a trust of *that* interest. In such cases, the first equitable owner is the trustee (as well as the beneficiary under the first trust!), holding an equitable interest on trust for a beneficiary. Sometimes this is known as a 'subtrust'. However, whatever the precise configuration of legal and equitable ownership, necessarily there is a relationship between the trustee and the beneficiary – sometimes referred to as a 'fiduciary relationship' – and it is clear that the former has certain responsibilities and duties to the latter. Furthermore, sometimes the property which is the subject matter of the trust – and this can be any property, tangible or intangible, real or personal – will have been provided by a 'settlor' or a 'testator' and it is they who have set up the trust either during his or her lifetime (settlor) or on death (testator). Indeed, in the case of a trust established by *inter vivos* gift (that is, not by will), the settlor and the trustee may be the same person and, in such cases, the settlor is said to have declared himself or herself trustee of the trust property. Finally, it should be noted that a trustee may also be a beneficiary under a trust. This quite often happens with trusts of co-habited property where the man may hold the property on trust for himself and his lover in some defined shares.

This, then, is a very simple picture of a trust and beyond this it is not easy to make general statements about the nature of a trust without also explaining the one or more exceptions that exist to nearly every rule. The law of trusts is not something that can be neatly dissected nor can its principles be safely pigeon-holed. Perhaps the best way to understand it is through an analysis of the substantive law without recourse to *a priori* definitions and assumptions that may prove wholly inadequate in explaining how the unique legal concept of the trust actually works in practice. With that in mind, the first topics to consider are the requirements imposed by general statute law and general principles of common law for the creation of a valid trust.

There are two sets of formal requirements which must be met before a valid trust can exist. On the one hand, there are those rules imposed by statute – principally the Law of Property Act 1925 – which establish formality requirements for the creation of trusts of certain kinds of property. These are requirements of writing and the like which are not inherent in the concept of the trust *per se*, although failure to comply with them will render the trust unenforceable. Rather, they are 'external' requirements imposed in order to ensure the proper working of the trust concept, especially the prevention of fraud by the trustee. Secondly, there are those rules of common law and equity which require the declaration of trust and/or the transfer of ownership of the trust property to the trustee to be achieved in specific ways according to the particular type of trust property. Examples include the need for a deed or registered disposition for the transfer of land to the trustee and entry in the company's register for the transfer of shares. These rules are not peculiar to the law of trusts, but given that the property which is the subject matter of the trust must pass into the hands of the trustee before the trust can exist (if it is not already there), the mode of transfer appropriate to each particular kind of property must be used if the trust is to be regarded as properly constituted. Failure to constitute the trust because of a failure to transfer the trust property to the trustee by the appropriate method has serious consequences.

Thus, the issues covered in this chapter require an understanding of the following matters:

(a) the different formality requirements for the creation of trusts of land and those for the creation of trusts of other property;

(b) the distinction between the creation of a trust and the 'disposition' of a 'subsisting' equitable interest under an existing trust and the reasons why an accurate distinction must be made;

(c) the necessity of properly constituting a trust and the manner in which this may be achieved relative to specific types of trust property; and

(d) the consequences of failure to constitute the trust properly.

Question 1

In order for a settlor to create a valid *inter vivos* trust of property he owns absolutely, it is necessary both to constitute the trust perfectly and to meet certain statutory requirements.

Discuss.

Answer plan

- Brief summary of the concept of a trust;
- the need for title to the trust property to be effectively conveyed to the trustee, if not already present (*Milroy v Lord* (1862));
- the statutory requirements for the validity of trusts of certain kinds of property (s 53 of the Law of Property Act 1925); and
- the consequences of imperfect creation (briefly).

Answer

The trust is a unique creation of the common law and one of its most versatile concepts. Moreover, when the trustee holds property on trust for the beneficiary, the trustee is submitting to one of the most powerful forms of legal obligation known to English law. A trustee may well find himself bound by onerous duties, either imposed by the trust instrument, by statute or by general principles of equity and there are serious consequences awaiting any trustee who neglects his duties or breaches the terms of the trust. Likewise, the trustee is only the mere 'paper' owner of the property and, unless he is also a beneficiary, will derive no benefit from the trust property. The trustee holds the trust property 'on trust' for the beneficiary for *the beneficiary's* use and benefit, and the trustee may even be prohibited from being paid for his labours (although this will be rare for professional trustees: see ss 28–30 of the Trustee Act 2000). Necessarily, therefore, there must be clarity and certainty when establishing a trust. It is vital to be clear that the person to whom title to the property is transferred (or who already possesses it) is indeed bound by a trust and so may not use the property for himself. Similarly, the rights of the beneficiaries must be established with certainty so that they may be allowed to enforce the trust should the trustee fail to carry out its terms. In other words, the need to determine where the real ownership of property lies and the need to be certain about the nature of the ownership of the trustee and beneficiary requires trusts to be created and evidenced with some measure of formality. Of course, that is not to say that all trusts must fulfil the same requirements of form before they can be recognised and enforced. After all, it is common in English law for there to be different levels of formality when dealing with different types of property. For example, transactions concerning land – an immovable asset – have traditionally required a higher degree of formality than dealings with other kinds of property. Thus, it should come as no surprise to learn that the nature of the property which is to be the subject matter of the trust is relevant when considering how trusts may be validly created.

In considering the creation of trusts, it is important to realise that there are two distinct and separate issues which must be addressed. First, it is inherent in the concept of a trust that the trustee be invested with title to the trust property, either because he is already the owner of that property or because such title has been effectively conveyed to him by the settlor. Unless that is the case, the trust is said to be incompletely constituted and the beneficiaries will have no claim on the trust property under the failed trust (*Milroy v Lord* (1862)). A recent innovation created by the Privy Council involves the occasion where the settlor appoints multiple owners as trustees, including himself. If he manifests an irrevocable intention to create a trust, his retention of the property will be construed as one of the trustees thereby constituting the trust, whether with or without a transfer to the other trustees. The maxim, 'equity regards as done that which ought to be done' will be applicable, see *Choithram v Pagarani* [2001] 1 WLR 1. In cases where the trust property needs to be conveyed to a trustee, it is necessary to examine the particular type of trust property in order to determine what must be done in order effectively to transfer the title. The requirements will be different for each type of property. Secondly, there are 'external' formality rules, imposed by statute, which regulate the way in which trusts *per se* can be created. These are to be found in the Law of Property Act (LPA) 1925 and they are designed to ensure that the creation of trusts of certain kinds of property is not open to doubt and to minimise the potential for fraud by the trustee. Failure to fulfil these requirements renders the trust unenforceable, even if title to the property is effectively vested in the trustee (s 53 of the LPA 1925).

The first issue is the creation of a trust by establishing that the trustee has title to the property. Once again, a distinction needs to be drawn at the outset between situations where the existing owner of the trust property declares himself to be a trustee (self-declarations) and situations where the existing owner of property wishes to transfer the property to someone else as trustee (transfer and declaration). In the former case, the person who is to be the trustee already has title and, therefore, there is no need to transfer the property. Consequently, there is no need for any formality for this aspect of trust creation. All that is needed for an effective declaration of trust – or rather, a declaration by the current owner of himself as trustee – is some clear evidence of a present and irrevocable declaration of trust, as in *Paul v Constance* (1977), and this evidence may take any form. Indeed, there is no requirement that the declaration of trust ever be communicated to the intended beneficiary (*Middleton v Pollock* (1876)). So, for example, if A, the owner of a book, declares that 'I now hold this book on trust for B', a trust will be created even if B is unaware of the fact, provided that there are no external formality requirements imposed by statute for the creation of trusts of books (which there are not). It is important to note, however, that for a declaration of trust by the present owner of the property to be effective, the circumstances of the case must not reveal a failed attempt by that owner to create a trust by the transfer of the trust property to another as trustee. In other words, declaration of oneself as trustee requires no formality, because the declarer already owns the property; but such a declaration will not be validly made if the owner had tried and failed to create a trust by the other method – transfer of property to a trustee – especially if that failure is due to a defect in the formality requirements for the transfer of that property (*Milroy v Lord* (1862)). The intention to declare oneself a trustee is very different from the intention to transfer property to another as trustee and they are mutually exclusive.

The second way in which trusts may be created is the effective transfer of property to the trustee. As noted at the outset, unless the trustee has title to the property, the trust is incompletely constituted and the beneficiaries have no enforceable claim to the property under the failed 'trust' (*Jones v Lock* (1865)). Thus, if the owner of property decides to create a trust by transferring that property to someone else as trustee, it is essential that the intended trustee obtains title to the property in the manner appropriate to the type of intended trust property. So, if S (the owner and 'settlor') decides to create a trust of his book by transferring the book to A on trust for B, legal title to the book must be effectively transferred to A if the trust is to be constituted and B is to have enforceable rights to it. In reality, then, it is essential to know how title to different types of property may be transferred. Indeed, there is nothing special about the rules we are about to consider, as they are the normal rules applicable to the transfer of title to property whenever and whyever it is conveyed. It is just that, with trusts, the trustee is receiving the property on behalf of someone else and not for his own use. Typical examples of the formality requirements for the transfer of title in property to a trustee are: a deed or registered disposition for land (unregistered and registered respectively); execution of a share transfer form and registration as owner for stocks and shares; written assignment for choses in action; and delivery of possession or a deed of gift for personal property. It is clear, then, that the particular requirements for the effective transfer of title to a trustee depend upon the nature of the property being transferred and, in this sense, the formality requirements for the creation of a trust are really the formality requirements for the effective transfer of ownership of property generally.

Finally, before considering the 'external' formality requirements for the creation of a trust, it is necessary to consider briefly one or two exceptions to the general principle just considered. First, a trust may be held to have been validly constituted, despite the fact that the trustee has not formally received title, if failure to be invested with that title is because of non-compliance with some condition outside the control of the settlor or trustee. Thus, in *Re Rose* (1952), a trust of shares in a private company was held to be perfectly constituted despite the fact that the legal title of the trustee had not been formally confirmed at the relevant time by entry in the share register of the company. This was because transfer of legal title was by registration in the company's register but its directors had a discretion to refuse such registration and registration had not yet taken place. Given, then, that complete transfer of legal title was outside the settlor's (and trustee's) control, lack of compliance was not destructive of the trust. Similarly, in *Mascall v Mascall* (1985) title to registered land was taken to have been effectively transferred by completion of the relevant land transfer form even though registration of that title by the registrar had not yet occurred. Likewise, in *Pennington v Waine* [2002] All ER (D) 24, the Court of Appeal decided that the execution and delivery of share transfer forms to an intermediary for the purpose of registering the new owner was sufficient to transfer the equitable interest. However, it is unclear whether legal title will be taken to have been effectively transferred if subsequent registration (of the private company's shares or registered land) does not take place and so the exception really allows the trust to be constituted in advance of the time that it technically occurs. Secondly, according to *Re Ralli* (1964), it may be immaterial that the trustee acquires title to the trust property in a manner different from that which the settlor originally intended. So, even though the settlor has failed to transfer title to the trustee during his lifetime, if the intended trustee is also the settlor's executor under his will, when the settlor dies, the executor (and trustee) will obtain legal title by virtue of his position as executor and the trust will thereby be constituted, albeit in a different manner from that which was intended. Thirdly, there are several other methods by which title to property may be effectively transferred from one person to another without the normal formality rules for that type of property being satisfied. However, these are usually relevant when the transferee obtains the property absolutely and not as trustee – that is, they are used to make gifts, not to perfect trusts. Examples include the principles of *donatio mortis causa* and the law of proprietary estoppel.

We shall look now at the other major requirement for the valid creation of a trust: the external formality rules imposed by statute. In essence, these rules are necessary to ensure certainty in dealings with certain kinds of property, especially land. In fact, the position in respect of trusts of property created *inter vivos* is relatively straightforward. First, assuming that title to the property is with, or has been transferred to, the trustee, there are no further formal requirements for the creation of trusts of personalty (that is, not land or interests in land). So, trusts of property other than land may be created orally or in writing and all that is needed is a declaration of self as trustee or an effective transfer of title to another as trustee. In the case of land, however, the creation of a trust must be 'manifested and proved' in writing. Although the trust does not have to be *in* writing, there must be written evidence of it, even if that evidence is not contemporaneous with the date of the creation of the trust (s 53(1)(b) of the LPA 1925 and *Rouchefoucauld v Boustead* (1897)). Failure to comply with this evidential requirement renders the trust of land unenforceable, although there are exceptions for resulting or constructive trusts of land (s 53(2) of the LPA 1925 and *Pettitt v Pettitt* (1970)). Likewise, the court may, in exceptional circumstances, allow oral evidence to prove the existence of a trust of land if this is necessary to prevent fraud by the trustee, as where the trustee dishonestly claims that there is no trust and that he may keep the property *because* of an absence of the necessary writing (*Rouchefoucauld v Boustead*).

These, then, are the necessary formalities which must be met before a settlor can create an *inter vivos* trust of property which he owns absolutely. Of course, if the trust is by will, then different considerations apply (see s 9 of the Wills Act 1837, as amended) and if the subject matter of the trust is itself an equitable interest (so that the trustee holds an equitable title on trust for another), there may be further formality requirements springing from the requirements of writing found in s 53(1)(c) of the LPA 1925. Finally, it is relevant to note that, in some circumstances, it may be difficult to distinguish between, on the one hand, the creation of a trust of pure personalty (no writing) or of land (evidenced in writing) and, on the other, the transfer of an equitable interest in personalty or land under a trust which already exists. The difference is, however, crucial, for the transfer of any equitable interest under an existing trust – be it of personalty or realty – must actually be *in* writing under s 53(1)(c) of the LPA 1925. As the cases of *Grey v IRC* (1960) and *Vandervell v IRC* (1967) demonstrate, such a distinction is not always easy to draw.

Note

This question is quite specific as it does not require consideration of trusts by will (testamentary trusts) or where the settlor has only a purely equitable interest. Understanding the distinction between creation of trusts by declaration and by transfer of property is important, especially as the methods are mutually exclusive. The consequences of a failure to constitute the trust are not dealt with here (but see below, Question 4).

Question 2

Is it possible to say with certainty when any potential dealing with trust property will amount to a 'disposition' within s 53(1)(c) of the Law of Property Act 1925. Why is it important to have some measure of certainty in this area?

Answer plan

- The distinction between the creation of a trust and a 'disposition' of a 'subsisting equitable interest' under a trust (s 53(1(c) of the LPA 1925);
- cases where the courts have established that a proposed transaction amounts to a 'disposition' and therefore requires writing (especially *Grey v IRC* (1960), *Oughtred v IRC* (1960) and *Neville v Wilson* (1996)); and
- cases where the courts have established that a proposed transaction does not amount to a 'disposition' and therefore does not require writing (especially the *Vandervell* cases).

Answer

Section 53 of the Law of Property Act (LPA) 1925 lays down certain requirements of formality which must be satisfied for the successful creation of certain types of trusts *inter vivos* and for the effective disposition (that is, transfer) of equitable interests under trusts that already exist, ie 'subsisting trusts' ... In the case of the creation of trusts other than by will, the requirements of formality are quite easily stated. Thus, assuming that the trust property has been effectively vested in the hands of the trustee (or is already owned by him), the creation of a trust of pure personalty requires no formality at all; simply a clear intention to establish the trust. This intention may be made manifest orally or in writing, but is effective in both cases. For trusts of land the position is different, mainly because of the overwhelming need for certainty when dealing with 'real property'. Consequently, s 53(1)(b) of the LPA 1925 requires that trusts of land be manifested or proved in writing, and although this does not require the actual trust instrument to be in writing itself, it does require some document in order to prove the trust and its terms.

This is all quite straightforward, but the position becomes more complicated when s 53(1)(c) of the LPA 1925 is examined. According to s 53(1)(c), 'a disposition of an equitable interest ... subsisting at the time of the disposition must be in writing'. This means that if a trust already exists, so that there is a beneficiary who has an equitable interest, any attempted 'disposition' (that is, transfer) of that equitable interest must actually be in writing. Such a rule is, of course, designed to ensure that the location of the equitable interest is clear and manifest, not only to provide certainty *per se*, but also to prevent fraud on the part of the trustee and to ensure that the proper person (that is, the current holder of the equitable interest) may enforce the trust and receive the benefit of the trust property. It ought to be noted that s 53(1)(c) of the LPA 1925 is applicable to both personal and real property. This is the position despite the definition of 'equitable interests' in s 205(1)(x) of the Law of Property Act 1925. The statutory definition refers to equitable interests in the context of land. Despite this definition, the effect of the decisions of the courts, including the House of Lords, has been to construe s 53(1)(c) as incorporating both realty and personalty. However, as far as this essay is concerned, there are two important issues to be considered. First, although the creation of trusts of land must be *evidenced* in writing, any disposition of an equitable interest under an existing trust of land must actually be *in* writing. Secondly, although the creation of trusts of personalty requires no writing at all, once again the disposition of an equitable interest under an existing trust of personalty must actually be *in* writing. Consequently, it is vital, in the cases of both trusts of land and trusts of personalty, to be able to distinguish between the creation of a new trust and the transfer of an equitable interest under a trust that already exists. Moreover, if we realise that written documents (for example, those within s 53(1)(c)) attract *ad valorem* stamp duty – that is, a percentage of the value of the property transferred by the written document must be paid in tax – it is clear that some beneficiaries will attempt to avoid the need for writing (and thus avoid stamp duty) by claiming that their dealings with the trust property amount to a creation of a trust and not a disposition of an interest under a trust that already exists. In short, there is a penalty of voidness for dispositions of equitable interests that are not in writing and this helps to prevent fraud and to allow the trustees to discharge their duties effectively and in favour of the appropriate persons. Unfortunately, there is also an incentive to avoid compliance with the section so as to minimise stamp duty which is why so many of the important cases in this area concern the Inland Revenue.

In order to examine what may amount to a 'disposition' within s 53(1)(c) of the LPA, we could attempt to define our terms *ab initio* and judge each transaction involving trust property by this standard. However, such an abstract approach does not guarantee success, not least because s 53(1) of the LPA 1925 is not the most clearly drafted statutory provision. Although it is clear that 'disposition' is to be given a wide, natural meaning, such as it would enjoy in everyday use (*Grey v IRC* (1960)), it is also clear that its meaning within s 53(1)(c) of the LPA 1925 is not the same as its meaning within s 205(1)(ii) of that Act, where it is defined generally for the purposes of the Act (*Re Paradise Motor Co Ltd* (1968)). Therefore, it may be more profitable to examine various practical situations, especially those covered by case law, in order to determine what will, and will not, amount to a disposition so as to require writing under s 53(1)(c) of the LPA 1925. The starting point for this empirical analysis can be the judgment of Romer LJ in *Timpson's Executors v Yerbury* (1936), where he identified four different ways by which a beneficiary might dispose of an equitable interest. In addition, there are other circumstances, not covered by Romer LJ, which should also be considered.

First, there are a number of situations where it is clear that an intended dealing with an equitable interest does indeed amount to a disposition within s 53(1)(c) of the LPA. Most obvious of all is when the beneficiary wishes to transfer (or 'assign') his equitable interest directly to another person, as where B, the beneficiary, wishes to give her equitable interest to C (*Timpson's Executors v Yerbury* (1936)). Likewise, if a beneficiary is able, under the terms of a trust, to direct her trustee to deal with the trust property in any manner she (the beneficiary) chooses, as is the case in a 'bare' trust, a direction by the beneficiary to the trustee to hold the property on trust for another person is a disposition of that interest within s 53(1)(c) (*Grey v IRC* (1960)). The point is simply that the bare trustee must carry out the original beneficiary's wishes and the net result of the beneficiary's direction is that the equitable interest has passed to a third person. Again, if the beneficiary under a trust declares herself trustee of her own equitable interest for another – as where T (trustee and legal owner) holds on trust for B (original beneficiary), and B then declares herself trustee of that equitable interest for C – this may well amount to a disposition if the original beneficiary (B) 'drops out of the picture' thus leaving the trustee effectively holding on trust for C. A beneficiary who declares this 'subtrust' will drop out of the picture when she has no active duties to perform in relation to the new beneficiary, so effectively disposing of her interest to C (*Grainge v Wilberforce* (1889) and implicit in *Neville v Wilson* (1996)). Although this view of a subtrust is not necessarily adhered to by all commentators, it is consistent with the policy behind s 53(1)(c) of the LPA, as it prevents hidden (that is, purely oral) dealings with equitable interests. Of course, if the original beneficiary (subtrustee) does not drop out of the picture, then a new trust has been created and no disposition of a 'subsisting' equitable interest has occurred. A contrary view was expressed by Brian Green to the effect that the sub-section makes no distinction between a declaration of trust of part of, or the entire, equitable interest and in addition, the inelegant distinction between declarations within s 53(1)(c) and declarations outside the sub-section is at odds with the House of Lords decisions in *Grey v IRC* and *Oughtred v IRC*. Fourthly, it is consistent with the policy of s 53(1)(c) that a surrender of the equitable interest by the equitable owner to the trustee should also count as a disposition. This was not considered by Romer LJ in *Timpson's Executors v Yerbury* (1936) and we might argue that a surrender of the equitable interest merely extinguishes the trust and does not 'dispose' of an interest. However, if a surrender did not fall within s 53(1)(c), a beneficiary (B) could orally surrender her interest to the trustee (T), who then might orally declare a new trust in favour of a third party (C) (assuming the property is not land). This amounts to a direct transfer of the equitable interest from B to C and, if writing were not required, would be a simple method of evading s 53.

The last example of a transfer of an equitable interest considered by Romer LJ in *Timpson's Executors v Yerbury* (1936) may, or may not, amount to a 'disposition' so as to bring it within s 53(1)(c) of the LPA, although the balance of authority is now that it does not. The case where the issue arose (*Oughtred v IRC* (1960)) was primarily concerned with whether stamp duty was payable on a written document and not whether that written document was actually necessary to transfer the equitable interest under the trust. The facts of the case suggest that, where T holds on trust for B, but B orally agrees by contract to sell his equitable interest to C, if that contract is specifically enforceable, it appears that B holds his equitable interest on constructive trust for C (because, under a specifically enforceable contract, 'equity treats as done what ought to be done'). Furthermore, when B drops out of the picture on payment of the purchase price by C, no writing is necessary to confirm the transfer of the equitable interest because s 53(1)(c) does not apply to the 'operation of ... constructive trusts' (s 53(2) of the LPA). In essence, B has transferred his interest to C without the need for writing, because of the protective umbrella of the constructive trust, and any written agreement that is drawn up later merely confirms the new situation and does not transfer the interest. Hence, its value for tax purposes is nil. This was the position argued in *Oughtred v IRC* (1960) although, in the case itself, the majority decided that stamp duty was payable on the later written document. However, although this implies that the oral contract did not effectively transfer the equitable interest (that is, that writing was necessary), the judgments are not conclusive. The matter turns on the difficult question of what exactly has been passed to the purchaser by the specifically enforceable contract. So, if the equitable interest of the original beneficiary passes under the constructive trust, then writing is not necessary because of s 53(2); if, however, the purchaser merely obtains a right to that equitable interest which cannot be denied by the original beneficiary but which, nevertheless, has not been transferred to him, then any later transfer of that interest will need to be in writing because it will be a disposition within s 53(1)(c). Admittedly, this seems complicated, but the essence of the matter is whether the constructive trust which arises from the contract (if the contract is specifically enforceable) actually passes the equitable interest to the purchaser so as to negate the need for writing because s 53(2) is an exception to s 53(1)(c). In *Neville v Wilson* (1996), the Court of Appeal accepted specifically that the equitable interest of the vendor can pass to the purchaser under a constructive trust and this appears now to have confirmed that no writing is needed in such cases: that is, that s 53(1)(c) does not apply. As far as the payment of stamp duty is concerned, however, the later case of *Pariny (Hatfield) Ltd v IRC* (1997) suggests that, irrespective of whether writing is actually needed, any subsequent writing will still attract duty. Clearly, the dichotomy of *Oughtred* (writing not needed, but *ad valorem* duty still payable) has been maintained.

Finally, we come to those cases where dealings with existing equitable interests under a trust clearly do not amount to a 'disposition' within s 53(1)(c) of the LPA and, therefore, do not require writing to be carried into effect. This may be so for a variety of reasons, but the point is that even though the equitable interest has changed its form or passed to another person, the circumstances are not caught by s 53(1)(c) of the LPA. First, as noted above, there are those cases where the beneficiary declares herself trustee of her equitable interest but does not drop out of the picture. This is a new subtrust and not a disposition of a subsisting equitable interest (*Grainge v Wilberforce* (1889)). But note also the agreements revised by Brian Green (see above). Secondly, according to *Vandervell v IRC* (1967), if a beneficiary (B) under a bare trust (that is, where the beneficiary controls the beneficial interest and the trustee is a mere nominee) directs the trustee (T) to transfer the legal title of trust property to a third person (C), with the intention that the equitable interest should also pass from B to C, no writing is required to pass the equitable interest to C. The reason for this is that the third party (C) is now the absolute owner of the property, both at law and in equity. In other words, the mischief which s 53(1)(c) was intended to prevent is not present and the case is different from *Grey v IRC* (1960) because, now, the legal and equitable titles are unified in the recipient. Thirdly, no writing is required for disclaimers of the equitable interest, as where the intended beneficiary orally disavows acceptance of the interest (*Re Paradise Motor Co Ltd* (1968)). This is despite the fact that a disposition is defined as including a disclaimer in s 205(1)(ii) of the LPA 1925 because disclaimers do not represent hidden dealings with equitable interests of the type which s 53(1)(c) is intended to prevent. Fourthly, nominations by beneficiaries under staff pension funds, whereby the staff member indicates to whom the benefits of the pension should be paid, do not require writing under s 53(1)(c) and nor, incidentally, do they require writing as testamentary dispositions within the Wills Act 1837 if the nomination is made on death (*Re Danish Bacon Co Ltd Staff Pension Fund* (1971); *Baird v Baird* (1990)) and *Re Gilbert* (1998)). Fifthly, variation of trusts made by virtue of powers under the Variation of Trusts Act 1958 do not require writing even if they involve a reshuffling of the beneficial interests (*Re Holt* (1969)). Sixthly, and most controversially, it appears from *Re Vandervell's Trusts (No 2)* (1974) that a declaration of new trusts *by the trustees* with the consent of a beneficial owner who is absolutely entitled to the property does not have to be in writing, even if the result is that the trustees now hold the trust property on the same terms for different beneficiaries. To many, this will look like a transfer of the equitable interest from the original beneficiary to a new equitable owner and the only apparent difference between this case and *Grey v IRC* (1960) is that, in the latter, the directions were given by the beneficiary, whereas in *Re Vandervell* they were given by the trustee with the consent of the beneficiary. Alternatively, the principle in *Re Vandervell Trusts (No 2)* [1974] Ch 269, may be vindicated on the grounds of equitable estoppel as laid down in the *High Trees* case [1947] KB 130. The directions of the trustee company, with the consent of the beneficiary (Mr Vandervell), amounted to a voluntary promise by the beneficiary which had been relied on by the new beneficial owner to his detriment. This promise may be used as a 'shield' by the new owner against a claim by the original beneficial owner (Mr Vandervell) or his estate. However, be that as it may, *Re Vandervell* is a highly complex case and perhaps the best that can be said for it is that it was decided with reference to its own special facts and should not be regarded as laying down any general principle.

In conclusion then, it is apparent that the most effective way to discern whether any given transaction falls within s 53(1)(c) of the LPA 1925, so as to require it to be in writing, is to examine the many varied factual circumstances that may arise. Of course, failing to achieve an *a priori* definition of 'a disposition' may make it difficult to determine whether there has been a 'disposition of an equitable interest ... subsisting at the time of the disposition' in novel cases, but at least this has the merit of preserving the flexibility which so many of the cases discussed in this essay seem to require. It is also revealing that s 53 of the LPA is currently being reviewed by the Law Commission with a view to its replacement by a clearer provision.

Note

For further discussion of *Re Vandervell (No 2)*, see Harris (1975) 38 MLR 557, Green (1984) 47 MLR 385.

Question 3

Billy is the sole beneficiary under two trusts: the Tulip Trust and the Daffodil Trust. Thomas, his trustee, holds shares in Bulb plc and Garden Centres Ltd on trust for him absolutely under the Tulip Trust, and various antique items of furniture on trust for him absolutely under the Daffodil Trust. On 12 January, Billy writes to Thomas, telling him to hold all the shares on trust for Frederick, but on 30 January, he telephones saying that his previous instructions are not to be carried out and that he should transfer the shares absolutely to Gloria. Thomas readily agrees, and executes a share transfer form for both companies and sends them off immediately. The same day, Billy orally agrees that he will transfer his interest in the antique furniture to Paul (his brother) for a nominal sum and is especially pleased because the furniture belonged to their mother. Unfortunately, on 1 February, Billy dies, and it transpires that he has left all his property, legal and equitable, by will to Norman. It also transpires that the share registration forms were not received for registration until 8 February.

Advise Norman as to his rights to claim Billy's property under the will. Would the position in respect of the shares have been any different if, on 20 January, Billy had orally surrendered his equitable interest to Thomas with the intention that Thomas should declare a new trust of the shares for Gloria or if Thomas (with Billy's consent) had orally declared himself trustee of those shares for her?

Answer plan

- The importance of distinguishing between creation of new trusts and the transfer (disposition) of equitable interests under new trusts;
- the disputed dispositions (*Grey v IRC* (1960), *Vandervell v IRC* (1967), *Oughtred v IRC* (1960), *Neville v Wilson* (1997), *Re Vandervell's Trust* (1970));
- the need for conveyance of the legal title (*Re Rose* (1952)).

Answer

This question concerns the formalities that are required for both the creation of trusts and the transfer of equitable interests under trusts that already exist. Such formalities are found in s 53 of the Law of Property Act (LPA) 1925, although they are supplemented by various common law rules concerning the measures necessary to vest title to trust property in the hands of the trustee. In general, the creation of trusts of personalty do not require any special degree of formality other than the effective declaration of the trust by the settlor or the effective transfer of the trust property to the intended trustee with a clear intention to establish a trust. In particular, with personalty (as in this question), no writing is needed to create a trust. However, it is also clear that the transfer of an equitable interest under an existing trust from the original beneficiary to another person will require writing, even if the trust property is personalty. This is because s 53(1)(c) of the LPA stipulates that 'a disposition of an equitable interest ... subsisting at the time of the disposition, must be in writing signed by the person disposing of the same, or by his agent thereunto lawfully authorised in writing or by his will'. Thus, for the purposes of this question, where Billy has attempted to deal in certain ways with his interests under the Tulip and Daffodil Trusts, it will be necessary to determine whether he has created new trusts of personalty – which may be done orally – or whether he has transferred any of his subsisting equitable interests – which may be accomplished only in writing. We shall examine each attempted disposition in turn.

First, there are the dealings with the equitable interests under the Tulip Trust on 1 January: the shares in Bulb plc and Garden Centres Ltd. Billy, the beneficiary and equitable owner of the shares in the two companies, attempts to transfer his equitable interests by writing a letter to his trustee instructing him to hold the shares on trust for Frederick. As Billy is the sole beneficiary under the Tulip Trust, we can assume that he is absolutely entitled to the shares and does, in fact, have power to dispose of his equitable interests in this way. However, dispositions of subsisting equitable interests may be made only if they are in writing, or else they will be void and the interest will remain with the original beneficiary (s 53(1)(c) of the LPA 1925). Moreover, it is clear from *Grey v IRC* (1960) that a direction to a trustee by the equitable owner to hold on trust for a third person (here Frederick) does, in principle, amount to a disposition within s 53(1)(c) and must be made in writing. In our case, Billy has not simply orally instructed Thomas to hold the shares for Frederick but has, rather, written to his trustee to this effect. The case is, therefore, distinguishable from *Grey* on this point, but it still remains to be seen whether Billy's form of writing complies with the terms of s 53(1)(c). According to the section, a disposition of the equitable interest must be *in writing* and signed by the person making the disposition. There is no requirement that the writing be directed towards the intended recipient of the equitable interest and, indeed, for the policy behind s 53(1)(c) to be fulfilled, it is often better that it be received by the trustee as well as the new beneficiary. Unfortunately, however, it may well be that Billy's letter to Thomas does not comply with the section. We may assume – given that Billy has sent a letter – that the letter is signed, thus fulfilling one of the requirements of s 53(1)(c). However, the disposition must be in writing, not merely be evidenced by writing, and it is doubtful whether this letter can be construed to be the actual disposition of the equitable interest to Frederick. Rather, it is merely evidence of an intention that a disposition should take place. Of course, the matter is debatable and a sympathetic court may take a different view of the letter. That aside, if there has been no effective writing within s 53(1)(c), the purported disposition is void and Billy's later telephone instructions are unnecessary since he had never parted with the equitable interests in the shares. For the sake of completeness, it should be noted that, if Billy's letter is taken to have complied with s 53(1)(c) of the LPA, and so to have effected a transfer, then no later oral (or indeed written) communication on his part may change this since the disposition would by then have taken effect and the equitable interest in the shares passed out of his hands to Frederick.

Secondly, there is the instruction on 30 January to transfer the shares absolutely to Gloria. On the basis that Billy still retains power to deal with the shares on 30 January, it is necessary to consider the effect of his oral instruction that the shares should be transferred absolutely to Gloria. Once again, there is a prima facie problem in that, if Billy is attempting to transfer his equitable interest in the shares to Gloria, this should be done in writing pursuant to s 53(1)(c) of the LPA. However, the problem makes it clear that the shares are to be transferred to Gloria 'absolutely' and this suggests that Gloria is to be the sole owner at law and in equity. Thus, Thomas is to transfer the legal title to Gloria and Billy is to transfer to her his equitable interest. This is within the ambit of *Vandervell v IRC* (1967), where the House of Lords decided that, if a beneficiary under a bare trust (as here, Billy being absolutely entitled) directs his trustee to transfer the legal title to another, with the intention that the equitable title should also pass, that equitable title may pass without writing and s 53(1)(c) is therefore not applicable. Accordingly, if Gloria is to be able to claim the shares, it is vital that the legal title to them should have been properly conveyed to Gloria before Billy dies: otherwise, the shares will pass under Billy's will to Norman. Here, then, is a problem because legal title to the shares in both companies will not pass to Gloria until she is registered as such in each company's share register. This does not take place until 8 February, some time after Billy's death. In normal circumstances, failure to pass legal title to property in the proper manner at the relevant time is fatal to the gift – it will not pass to the intended recipient. However, in *Re Rose* (1952), the transfer of legal title to shares in a private company was regarded as effective even though it was not completed by entry in the share register of the company. This was because registration of new ownership in the company's register was at the directors' discretion and thus outside the control of the parties attempting to deal with the shares. Following this analogy, Gloria may be regarded as legal owner (and hence equitable owner under *Vandervell v IRC*) of the shares in Garden Centres Ltd (a private company). The shares in Bulb plc are, however, those of a public company, and registration as owner occurs automatically and is not subject to external confirmation. Consequently, *Re Rose* is not entirely pertinent and the shares may not have been effectively transferred by the time of Billy's death. However, *Mascall v Mascall* (1984) suggests that the true rationale in cases such as these is that registration is merely a technical matter that needs to be completed before legal title is perfected in the transferee and should not be regarded as fatal to the transfer of the legal title if registration subsequently takes place (but see *Brown & Root v Sun Alliance* (1997) to the contrary). In the more recent case, *Pennington v Waine* [2002] All ER (D) 24, the Court of Appeal decided that the execution and delivery of share transfer forms to an intermediary for the purpose of registering the new owner was sufficient to transfer the equitable interest. The issue is not whether the transferor did everything required of him short of registration but simply whether he had done all in his power to transfer the property. If this is the true ratio of the cases, it can be argued that legal title to the shares in Bulb plc did effectively pass on completion of the share transfer form, although this was not formalised until their later registration. Consequently, Gloria may claim the shares in both companies absolutely, utilising *Vandervell v IRC* and *Re Rose*.

Thirdly, there is the attempted transfer of the interest in the antique furniture under the Daffodil Trust. Once again, Billy attempts to deal orally with his equitable interest under one of the trusts, this time by orally agreeing to transfer his interest (presumably his equitable interest) under the Daffodil Trust to his brother. Again, s 53(1)(c) of the LPA is in issue, but this time Billy has not actually transferred his interest: rather, he has agreed to do so for a nominal consideration. In other words, there is a contract between Billy and his brother for the transfer of an equitable interest. In these circumstances, whether Paul can claim an interest in the antique furniture depends on the validity and effect of this oral contract. The matter appears to be governed by *Oughtred v IRC* (1960) and *Neville v Wilson* (1996). Thus, if the contract between Billy and Paul is specifically enforceable, it may be that the subject matter of the contract – Billy's equitable interest – can be regarded as having passed to Paul under a constructive trust by virtue of the equitable maxim that 'equity treats as done that which ought to be done' and, of course, constructive trusts are exempt from the requirement of writing in s 53(1)(c) of the LPA 1925 by virtue of s 53(2). In our case, there is some evidence that the contract is specifically enforceable because, first, damages for breach of contract would be an inappropriate remedy due to the special nature of the property (antique family property); secondly, valuable consideration appears to have been paid (even though it may be merely nominal); and thirdly, there is no evidence that Paul has behaved inequitably, so requiring the remedy of specific performance to be denied. On this basis, assuming *Oughtred* and *Neville* to be correct, then Paul may claim the equitable interest in the shares even though there is no writing, only an oral contract. However, another view of *Oughtred* is that the effect of the specifically enforceable contract is merely to prevent the vendor (Billy) from denying the interest to the purchaser (Paul). It might not be effective to defeat the claim of a third party (here Norman, under the will) unless the transfer of the equitable interest to the purchaser had been completed by being in writing under s 53(1)(c) of the LPA. The answer depends on the view one takes of *Oughtred*, although its adoption by *Neville* suggests that Paul may indeed be the new owner of the equitable trust.

Fourthly, there is the attempted surrender of the shares on 20 January. The purpose behind Billy's potential surrender of his equitable interest in the shares to his trustee, knowing that the trustee will then declare a trust of those shares for Gloria, is to avoid the provisions of s 53(1)(c) of the LPA. *Prima facie*, a surrender of an equitable interest to a trustee does not amount to a 'disposition' of a 'subsisting' equitable interest, because the trust may be terminated by the trustee becoming absolutely entitled to the property. Thus, the surrender would not have to be in writing. Similarly, a subsequent declaration of new trusts of personalty by the former trustee and now absolute owner would need no writing since there are no formality requirements for the creation of new trusts unless land is involved. Yet, when one takes together the surrender of the equitable interest and the subsequent declaration of 'new' trusts by the trustee, it is clear that the net effect is a transfer of the equitable interest from one equitable owner (Billy) to another (Gloria). This is little different from the issue in *Grey v IRC* (1960) and, for the same reasons that s 53(1)(c) was applicable then, it should be applicable in this type of case. Consequently, in the absence of writing, this attempt to give the equitable interests to Gloria is void.

Fifthly, there is Billy's oral declaration of himself as trustee of the shares for Gloria. The purpose behind this manoeuvre is to avoid a 'disposition' of a subsisting equitable interest under a trust within s 53(1)(c) of the LPA and the need for writing, and to institute instead the creation of a new trust of personalty which needs no such formality. Whether Billy will be successful depends on the nature of the subtrust he creates when he declares himself trustee. If he retains no duties under the subtrust he will drop out of the picture, effectively making Thomas the trustee of the shares for Gloria. This will be taken to be a disposition of a subsisting equitable interest and so writing will be necessary. Conversely, if Billy does retain some active duties under the subtrust, a genuinely new trust of personalty will exist and the oral declaration thereof will be effective to invest Gloria with an equitable interest in the shares, albeit one distinct from that held by Billy originally (*Grainge v Wilberforce* (1889)).

Note

The issues raised here represent practical illustrations of the problems discussed in Question 2. As is apparent, a knowledge of the case law is invaluable.

Question 4

To what extent has the Contracts (Rights of Third Parties) Act 1999 ameliorated the position of the volunteer under an imperfect trust?

Discuss by reference to decided cases.

Answer plan

- The significance of a perfect trust;
- the distinction between volunteers and non-volunteers;
- the extent to which a volunteer may enforce an imperfect trust before the introduction of the Contracts (Rights of Third Parties Act) 1999;
- the nature and effect of the Contracts (Rights of Third Parties Act) 1999.

Answer

Under a perfect trust the beneficiary, who may be a volunteer, is entitled to enforce the trust. He acquires an equitable interest *in rem* and is entitled as of right to protect his interest. However, if the trust is imperfect (ie the principles in *Milroy v Lord* (1862) have not been complied with) the status of the claimant is of paramount importance. If the claimant is a non-volunteer he is entitled to assert a right to the property as if the trust is perfect and may be able to obtain specific performance of the promise to transfer the relevant property. Thus, at the instance of a non-volunteer the imperfect trust will be treated as equivalent to a perfect trust. On the other hand, if the trust is imperfect the claimant is, subject to the Contracts (Rights of Third Parties Act) 1999, required to establish that he had furnished consideration. A volunteer will not be entitled to any equitable remedies.

A volunteer is someone who has not provided valuable consideration. Valuable consideration at common law is money or money's worth or, in equity, marriage consideration.

The position before the Contracts (Rights of Third Parties) Act 1999 was that an intended beneficiary under an imperfect trust was not entitled to an equitable remedy because he was a volunteer. The maxim in this context was, and remains, that equity will not assist a volunteer, subject to limited exceptions. In addition, there was a conflict of authorities as to whether the volunteer, who is a third party to the agreement to create a trust (such as a deed or a covenant), was entitled to the common law remedy of damages.

In *Re Pryce* (1917) the High Court decided that the volunteer (third party) was not entitled to directions, the consequences of which would have entitled him to force the covenantee (intended trustee) to sue the covenantor for damages. The reason put forward as justification for this rule was to prevent the volunteer obtaining indirectly a remedy that he could not obtain directly. In effect, there is some justification for the decision, as opposed to the reason for the decision. The volunteer third party's position ought not to be elevated to allow him to force the covenantee to sue for damages. As a volunteer he is not entitled to any equitable assistance and by seeking the directions of the court to enforce an imperfect trust he was attempting to enhance his position. However, the reason for the decision seems to be excessively broad based.

In *Re Kay* (1939) the court went further and decided that the covenantee (intended trustee) will be prevented from bringing an action at law for damages against the covenantor. In this case the court applied the principle laid down in *Re Pryce* in positively preventing the covenantee from succeeding in such a claim. It was as if the court was attempting to frustrate the covenantee's claim to pursue his common law remedy. The principle in *Re Kay*, as distinct from *Re Pryce*, was based on two implied assumptions namely:

(a) if the covenantor pursued his claim for damages, he would have been entitled to substantial damages, measured by reference to the failure on the part of the covenantor to fulfil his obligations;

(b) the substantial damages received by the covenantee would be held on trust for the volunteer, third party.

Accordingly, the covenantee was prevented from pursuing his claim in order to prevent the volunteer becoming a beneficiary under a perfect trust.

On the other hand, in *Re Cavendish Browne* (1916) the High Court decided that the covenantee was entitled to pursue his common law remedy and awarded the claimant substantial damages. The additional issue as to whether the damages were to be held on trust for the volunteer third party was not considered by the court. This case seems to be in direct conflict with *Re Kay*. Strained efforts have been made to reconcile the decisions on the ground that in *Re Cavendish Browne* the property was in existence namely land in Canada. Whereas in *Re Kay* the subject matter of the covenant was after acquired property. This distinction lies with the facts of the case only and cannot be supported in principle.

In *Cannon v Hartley* (1949) the High Court decided that where the volunteer was a party to the covenant he was entitled to bring a claim for damages for breach of covenant. The decision is justifiable on the ground that he is a party to the covenant and has suffered loss personally. He does not seek any equitable assistance and pursues his common law remedy for damages only.

In *Beswick v Beswick* (1968) the House of Lords decided that a non-volunteer and party to a covenant was entitled to enforce a covenant in favour of a volunteer. Accordingly, on the death of the non-volunteer, the volunteer (and executor of the deceased) was entitled to enforce the covenant in his favour. In this case the volunteer was able to obtain specific performance.

The Contracts (Rights of Third Parties) Act 1999

The 1999 Act introduced a long overdue reform of the law. Its purpose is to reform the rule of privity of contract under which a person may only enforce a contract if he is a party to it.

Entitlement to sue

Section 1(1) of the Contracts (Rights of Third Parties) Act 1999 sets out the circumstances when a third party to a contract will have a right to enforce the agreement. These are that the contract was made expressly or impliedly for the benefit of the third party (ss 1(1) and (2)). The third party is required to be identified by name or description, although he need not be in existence at the time the contract was made, (s 1(3)).

This provision will be satisfied if A covenants (or makes a simple agreement) with B to transfer property to him upon trust for C. Assuming that A has not transferred the property to B and that C is a 'volunteer' then, as a third party, the requirements above will be satisfied. The effect is that the third party (C) is entitled 'in his own right to enforce' the contract, s 1(1). This is the typical case with regard to an incompletely constituted trust.

The remedy

Section 1(5) of the 1999 Act declares the remedy which will be available to the third party (C in the above example).

Section 1(5) of the Contracts (Rights of Third Parties) Act 1999 declares that for the purpose of exercising his right to enforce a term of the contract, there shall be available to the third party *any remedy that would have been available to him in an action for breach of contract if he had been a party to the contract* (and the *rules* relating to damages, injunctions, specific performance and other relief shall apply accordingly.

The effect of the provision is to treat C, the volunteer and third party, as if he is a party to the agreement and to grant him such remedies as would be available to him as a party to the agreement. There is no doubt that s 1(5) gives C a claim for damages, but subject to the rules regarding the quantification of the damages. Under the Act, C's position is treated as similar to the claimant in *Cannon v Hartley* [1949] Ch 213. Alternatively, if C has provided valuable consideration for the promise, but is not a party to the agreement, (ie he has provided marriage consideration) he would be entitled to damages, if this remedy is appropriate (as declared by the Act). But if the remedy of damages is not appropriate the third party, non-volunteer, would be entitled to an equitable remedy such as specific performance as in *Pullan v Koe* [1913] 1 Ch 9. This principle has not been changed by the Act but is simply confirmed by the provision.

Is the volunteer entitled to an equitable remedy?

The contentious issue is what remedy would C, a volunteer and third party to the contract, be entitled to in an action against A for breach of contract? The remedy that C (the claimant) is entitled to, save for damages, has not been altered by the Act. It is submitted that C, as a volunteer, will only be entitled to damages for four reasons.

First, the policy of the Act was to reform the privity rule and treat the third party in the circumstances laid down in the Act as if he is a party to the contract. On this basis the third party (who is now treated under the Act as though he is a party) is entitled to bring an action against the party in breach *in his own right* ie the claim is not dependent on the means of another. In our example C may sue A directly without joining B as a co-claimant or a co-defendant.

Secondly, the reformation of the privity rule does not automatically change the law with regard to equitable remedies. These remain discretionary, but damages are obtainable as of right, subject to the rules regarding the quantification of damages.

Thirdly, s 1(5) confirms that the *rules* regarding damages ... and specific performance shall apply. The rules regarding damages are well known. In particular the rules concerning remoteness of damage and the duty to mitigate the loss. These rules remain the same after the Act. In addition, the equitable concept that 'equity will not assist a volunteer' is applicable with equal force after the Act. Since C is a volunteer he should not expect an equitable remedy, such as specific performance, for he was not entitled to such a remedy prior to the passing of the Act and the Act has not changed this rule. The normal rules of law applicable to those remedies, including the rules relating to causation, remoteness and the duty to mitigate one's loss, apply to the third party's claim. Thus, it follows that since the volunteer non-covenantee (ie C) is now treated as though he is a party to the covenant, his status remains a volunteer and as such will not gain any equitable assistance.

Fourthly, a volunteer in the eyes of equity is treated as not having lost anything under the contract and, without more, is not entitled in his own right to gain any benefits under the contract. The position is not the same at common law with regard to damages, which is obtainable as of right. Thus, it makes no difference whether the subject matter of the contract to transfer property to B for the benefit of C involves land, shares in a private company or cash. As a contract as opposed to a trust C has lost nothing in the eyes of equity.

In conclusion, the 1999 Act has effected the following changes:

(a) a reversal of *Re Pryce* [1917] 1 Ch 234 – where a volunteer, non-covenantee (C), was not able to force the covenantee (B) to bring an action for damages;

(b) a reversal of *Re Kay* [1939] Ch 329 – where a covenantee (B) was prevented from bringing an action for damages on behalf of a volunteer non-covenantee (C);

(c) an endorsement of *Re Cavendish-Browne* [1916] WN 341 – where a covenantee (B) successfully brought an action for damages on behalf of a non-covenantee (C);

(d) an approval of the principle in *Cannon v Hartley* [1949] Ch 213 – the volunteer covenantee is entitled to claim substantial damages for breach of covenant, but is not entitled to the equitable remedy of specific performance.

Question 5

A young couple, Wendy and Harold decided to get married. On the happy occasion, Wendy's father, Frank, who was a pioneer heart surgeon, covenanted with his friends, John and Smith (who were also the executors under his will) to transfer to them £200,000 and a house in Chelsea, to hold on trust for the benefit of Wendy and Harold for their respective lives, thereafter for their children and thereafter for their grandchildren. Failing issue, the trust properties were to be conveyed to Norman, his next-of-kin absolutely.

The day after the wedding, Frank, who had made a fortune from his practice at Harley Street, received the shocking news that he had an inoperable brain tumour and that he was unlikely to live longer than 12 months. Frank then decided to sort out his affairs. He called the trustees of the above settlement and told them that he would shortly be transferring the house and cash to them. He also executed a further covenant with the trustees to transfer to them his portfolio of 20,000 shares in Lazerdot.com. At the same time, Frank informed his solicitor that, if he should die within 12 months, he wanted his son, Sam, to have his antique Rolls-Royce motor car. He did this by letter enclosing a spare ignition key to the car.

Later that night, Frank executed the necessary documents relating to the various properties, except for the cheque for £200,000, which he had filled in but forgotten to sign. He gave the documents to his solicitor to effect the transfers. When he went to the door to see the solicitor off, a bolt of lightning suddenly struck and killed both men instantly.

Consider the issues raised by the events above and advise the executors whether any of the intended beneficiaries and donees are entitled to an interest in any of the properties.

Answer plan

- Whether the requirements for the creation of trusts of the various properties were complied with;
- whether the covenant to create trusts is enforceable;
- effect of the Contracts (Rights of Third Parties) Act 1999;
- Donatio Mortis Causa.

Answer

This problem concerns the fundamental principles for the creation of an express trust and the consequences of a perfect and imperfect trust.

A trust is perfectly created when the trust property is 'at home', that is, the trustees have acquired the property subject to the terms of the trust as declared by the settlor. There are two modes of creating an express trust. A transfer of property to the trustees, subject to a declaration of trust by the settlor. This is the transfer and declaration mode. The second mode of creation requires the settlor to declare himself a trustee for the beneficiaries. This is a self-declaration of trust. In order to create a valid express trust one of these modes is required to be complied with. This is the test laid down by Turner LJ in *Milroy v Lord* (1862).

One of the primary issues in this problem is whether a trust attaches to each of the properties specified.

Cheque for £200,000

Frank had forgotten to sign the cheque that would have transferred the funds to the nominated trustees, John and Smith. Accordingly, there is no transfer of the funds to the trustees. In any event, a cheque is a revocable mandate which is revoked on death, see *Re Beaumont*. The effect is that Frank had manifested an intention to settle funds specified in the cheque without a transfer of the funds.

At the same time an imperfect transfer will not automatically be construed as a self declaration of trust with the effect of imposing a trust obligation on Frank, for otherwise all imperfect transfers will be treated as perfect, *Richards v Delbridge* (1874). In any event Frank did not declare an intention to make himself a trustee. On this basis *Re Ralli* (1964) and *Choithram v Pagarani* (2001) could be distinguished from the facts of this problem.

In accordance with the principle in *Fletcher v Fletcher* (1844), the covenant to transfer £200,000 may be treated as a transfer of a chose in action (ie the benefit of the covenant) provided that the cash existed (or its equivalent) at the time of the covenant, and Frank intended the chose to be the subject matter of the trust. Whether Frank intended to create a trust of a chose in action would depend on the circumstances of each case. This involves a question of fact to be construed by the courts. There is very little evidence that Frank intended the subject matter of the trust to be the right created under the covenant, as distinct from the cash sum of £200,000.

On the assumption that there is no transfer of property to the trustees (either as funds in a bank account or a chose in action), the intended trust of the covenanted sum will involve an imperfect trust and the maxims that are applicable are 'equity will not assist a volunteer' and 'equity will not perfect an imperfect transfer'. The consequences of such an omission by Frank will be considered later.

The house in Chelsea

The transfer of the legal title to the house has not been completed by Frank because he died after 'executing the necessary documents' but before the same were sent to the Land Registry. Indeed, Frank delivered the documents to his solicitor for the purpose of securing registration of John and Smith as the legal owners. Unfortunately, the solicitor also died in the same tragedy and presumably before any steps could be taken to transfer the property. The issue here is whether Frank had done everything required of him? This is a question of degree, but if he had, a constructive trust (involving Frank holding the property as constructive trustee) would arise transferring the equitable interest to the trustees, John and Smith, on trust for the named beneficiaries, see *Re Rose* (1952), *Mascall v Mascall* (1985). In the recent case of *Pennington v Waine* (2002) the Court of Appeal introduced an alternative basis for resolving the dispute namely, whether it would be unconscionable for the transferor to deny the transfer. This is a question for the court to decide on the facts of each case. The fact that in *Pennington* the subject matter was shares in a company, as opposed to land (as in the present case), is not material. On the facts of the problem Frank may have been motivated by the marriage of Wendy, he executed a covenant with the intended trustees, John and Smith and after receiving the tragic news of his medical condition called the intended trustees to inform them that he will shortly transfer *inter alia* the house. He also informed his solicitor of his intentions and executed the transfer document to the house. Drawing the evidence together it would appear that there is strong evidence to suggest not only that Frank felt that he had done everything required of him to transfer the house, but that it may be unconscionable for Frank's estate to deny the transfer.

In respect of the *Fletcher v Fletcher* rule (1844) it had been decided in *Re Cook* (1965) that that rule is restricted to debts enforceable at law. This limitation restricts *Fletcher* to one type of chose only, namely covenanted obligations to transfer money. Thus the principle would not be applicable to a covenant to transfer the house.

20,000 shares in Lazerdot.com

Lazerdot.com appears to be a private company. The significance of this is that the directors of the company have a right to refuse registration of new owners of shares. At the same time the legal title to shares is only transferred if the new owner is registered in the share register of the company. Frank has an obligation to comply with sections 182 and 183 of the Companies Act 1985 and the Stock Transfer Act 1963 in order to transfer the legal title to shares. The requirements under these Acts require Frank to execute a share transfer form and send the share certificates, along with the form, (personally or through his agent) to the company at its registered office in order to secure registration. Frank had 'executed the necessary documents' and delivered these to his solicitor (his agent). Has he done everything required of him? This is a question of fact – see *Re Rose*; *Pennington v Waine* (above) contra *Re Fry* (1946). If he has, the transfer would be effective in equity and he (or his executors) would become a constructive trustee of the shares. In *Pennington v Waine* the court decided that the delivery of the executed transfer documents to an intermediary to secure registration was sufficient compliance with all that was required from the transferor.

The car

Frank has communicated his intention to his solicitor to give the car to Sam, but without delivering the same to the donee unconditionally. Thus, the gift is imperfect inter vivos and 'equity will not perfect an imperfect gift', and 'equity will not assist a volunteer'. On the facts Sam is a volunteer, see later.

Could there be a *Donatio Mortis Causa* of the car? A DMC involves a transfer of dominion over property during the lifetime of the transferor in contemplation of, and conditional on, death, see *Re Craven's Estate* (1937). The requirements of contemplation and conditional on death are subjective questions of fact and on the facts there is some evidence that these requirements are satisfied. However, the controversial question is whether Frank has transferred control of the car to Sam during his (Frank's) lifetime? This is a question of degree. The car is tangible, moveable property and title may only be transferred by delivery accompanied by the relevant intention to transfer. Frank may deliver the car constructively by delivering the symbols of control accompanied by an intention to transfer control. On the facts, Frank has delivered the spare key to his agent (the solicitor) but there is little evidence that the solicitor is an agent for Sam. In any event, delivery of the spare ignition key is not fatal to Sam's claim, see *Woodard v Woodard* (1991).

It is evident that the intended trust of some of the properties may be perfect. Much depends on the view taken by the court. However, if the trust of any of the properties is imperfect the question that arises is whether the respective claimant is entitled to enforce the covenant to create a trust.

It was stated earlier that the two equitable maxims are applicable with regard to imperfect trusts. A volunteer would not be entitled to equitable assistance if the trust is imperfect. The issue therefore is whether the respective claimants are volunteers and if so, what claims may they pursue?

A volunteer is one who has not provided valuable consideration, ie money or money's worth or a person who does not come within the marriage consideration. The latter requires a marriage settlement, ie an ante-nuptial settlement made in consideration of marriage or a post-nuptial settlement made in pursuance of an ante-nuptial agreement, see *Re Park (No 2)* (1972). The persons within the marriage settlement are the parties to the marriage as well as the issue of the marriage, including grandchildren. In respect of the facts it would appear that Wendy and Harold are non-volunteers. The effect is that Wendy and Harold are entitled to enforce the covenant in equity as non-volunteers. Thus, they are entitled to claim specific performance of the agreement as if they were beneficiaries under a perfect trust, see *Pullan v Koe* (1913).

The next of kin is a volunteer and unable to enforce the covenant in equity, *Re Plumtre* (1910). But under the Contracts (Rights of Third Parties) Act 1999, the next of kin (third party) is given the capacity to bring an action in his own right. Effectively, this is only in respect of damages, for the rule remains that equity will not assist a volunteer. The volunteer therefore does not have a claim in priority over the non-volunteers.

In any event, John and Smith as the intended trustees are the executors of Frank's will. It is tempting to argue that the rule in *Strong v Bird* (1874) will perfect the imperfect gifts, see *Re Ralli*. But on reflection Frank's intention was to make future transfers to the trustees. This has the effect of excluding the rule in *Strong v Bird*, see *Re Freeland* (1952).

2 Secret Trusts

Introduction

Secret trusts are a peculiar animal. They are special because they allow the creation of valid trusts even though the normal formality rules for the creation of trusts by will have not been met. In this sense, they are an exception to the principles discussed in Chapter 1. However, as we shall see, although 'secret' trusts arise out of testamentary dispositions (that is, wills), there is often little that is secret about either their existence or their terms. Originally, the doctrine of secret trusts was developed to allow testators to make provision for beneficiaries whose identity, or even existence, was best kept quiet, such as illegitimate children or mistresses. Today, however, they are more likely to provide an indecisive testator with a means of avoiding the strict forms required by the Wills Act 1837 (as amended).

Secret trusts are of two types: 'fully secret' trusts and 'half secret' trusts. In essence, the difference between the two is that nothing of the existence of the trust is revealed in the will of a testator with a fully secret trust, whereas with a half secret trust, the fact of a trust, but not the identity of the beneficiaries, is revealed in the will. This difference in purpose is reflected in the somewhat different conditions which must be met before the existence of each type of secret trust can be recognised and enforced by the 'secret' beneficiaries. In addition, because both forms of secret trusts do not meet the strict requirements of the Wills Act, there is considerable academic interest in the theory behind the validity of secret trusts, especially how they gel with statutory and common law rules which would otherwise require their invalidity.

There are two general issues which may face a student dealing with secret trusts. First, there are the conditions for the existence of both types of trusts and the manner in which they operate. This requires a knowledge of substantive law and some appreciation of the requirements of the Wills Act and general equitable principles concerning the validity of trusts. Secondly, there is the largely theoretical argument about the rationale or theory behind secret trusts. While not necessarily of great practical importance, this is fertile ground for examination questions.

Question 6

Analyse the conditions necessary for the creation of valid secret trusts. Are there any significant differences between fully and half secret trusts?

Answer plan

- The context of the Wills Act 1837 (as amended) and the need for writing for testamentary trusts;

- secret trusts as an exception to these formality requirements;
- fully secret trusts: apparently absolute gifts and acceptance of the trust obligation;
- half secret trusts: the trust but no beneficiary; communication and acceptance rules; and
- differences between fully secret and half secret trusts.

Answer

According to Pennycuick J in *Re Tyler* (1967), the 'particular principles of law applicable to secret trusts are really concerned only with trusts created by will'. By virtue of s 9 of the Wills Act 1837 (as amended), no will shall be valid unless, *inter alia*, it is in writing and signed by the testator and properly witnessed. Further, all wills are public documents and any bequests and devises contained therein may be on view for all the world to see. Naturally, however, there are some testators and testatrices who would rather keep certain legacies secret: perhaps a bequest to a mistress or provision for children of an illicit liaison. The equitable doctrine of secret trusts allows shy testators to make 'private' bequests and so avoid embarrassment to many parties. In essence, secret trusts are those trusts which, although contained in a will, are valid without the need to satisfy the conditions laid down in s 9 of the Wills Act. They allow the testator or testatrix to make such dispositions as he or she pleases without the details being made public, save only to the person who is bound to put into effect those wishes.

Secret trusts fall into two categories: fully secret trusts and half secret trusts. In a fully secret trust, property is given by will to a legatee absolutely without mention of any trust: the gift appears to be absolute and there is no trust on the face of the will (*Thynn v Thynn* (1684)). However, at any time during the testator's lifetime, the details of a trust and the intended beneficiaries thereof may have been communicated to the legatee – orally or in writing – and, if the legatee agrees, he will hold the property on trust for the 'hidden' beneficiaries when the testator dies. Both the very existence of the trust and the identity of the beneficiaries are 'secret'. Of course, the onerous trust obligation cannot be imposed on a legatee of an absolute gift without that person's consent, and so it is essential that the fact of the trust and the details thereof are communicated to the legatee/trustee and accepted by him during the testator's lifetime (*McCormick v Grogan* (1869)), although either before or after the date of the will is acceptable (*Wallgrave v Tebbs* (1855)). Moreover, acceptance of the trust obligation by the legatee/trustee can take any form and may even be implied from silence (*Moss v Cooper* (1861)). Once the trustee has accepted the trust obligation, he is usually barred from receiving any personal benefit from the legacy, even though it appears to have been given to him absolutely. Thus, if the testator has communicated the fact of the trust to the legatee/trustee, but not the identity of the beneficiaries, the trustee will hold the property on trust for those entitled to the residuary estate or the next of kin, as the case may be (*Re Boyes* (1884)). The only exception to this is where the fully secret trustee can prove that he or she also was intended to be a beneficiary under the secret trust, a difficult, though not impossible, task (*Irvine v Sullivan* (1869)).

Turning now to half secret trusts, it will be apparent that they are quite distinct from fully secret trusts, both as to the conditions for their validity and in the way they operate. In a half secret trust, the bequest or legacy is given in the will 'on trust' to a trustee, but the identity of the beneficiaries is not disclosed (*Blackwell v Blackwell* (1929)). In other words, it is clear that the recipient is not entitled to take the gift absolutely, although for whom the trustee holds the property is secret. Crucially, in order for a half secret trust to be valid – that is, enforceable by the beneficiaries – the details of the trust must be communicated to the trustee and accepted by him before or contemporaneously with the execution of the will (*Re Bateman* (1970)). It is not enough that the identity of the beneficiaries be communicated at any point prior to the testator's death, although it is sufficient if the trustee is given exclusive access to this information before the will is made, as where he is handed a sealed envelope or key to a safe at the relevant time, even if this is not to be opened until after the testator's death (*Re Boyes* (1884)). Similarly, because the actuality of the trust is declared on the face of the will, a half secret trust will be invalid if the information communicated to the trustee contradicts the will (*Re Keen* (1937)).

At first sight, then, both fully secret and half secret trusts appear to offer the testator two different routes to achieve the same end: viz the distribution of testamentary property to unnamed persons. Of course, the fully secret trust offers more secrecy because there is no written evidence of a trust at all, but this is not the only difference between the two concepts. We have seen already that there is a major difference in the communication rules for each type of trust, with the half secret trust suffering from a more stringent requirement. For the fully secret trust, however, the fact that communication may be at any time before or after the date of the will has important consequences. For example, it is often the case that a testator executes his will many years before his death but the law of fully secret trusts allows him to redirect his property by gaining a legatee's consent to the imposition of a trust for another person at any time after that. It is obvious that this is not at all consistent with the policy of the Wills Act 1837 – after all, the testator could have executed an amended will or codicil – and there is a strong case for preventing the misuse of the principles of fully secret trusts in this way. Similarly, there is no *Re Keen* rule in fully secret trusts that requires the terms of the will and the details of the trust to be consistent although, given that the will says nothing about a trust in the first place, there will always be an inconsistency if the legatee is holding the property for someone else.

In addition to these differences concerning the circumstances in which fully secret and half secret trusts may come into existence, there are differences in the way they operate, not all of them logical or justifiable. Thus, if a fully secret trustee does not accept the trust obligation, the property remains his under the will because the absolute legacy takes effect. On the other hand, a half secret trustee, being declared a trustee in the will, is forever barred from taking the property and must hold it for the residuary estate (*Re Keen*). Nor may a half secret trustee qualify as a beneficiary under the trust (*Re Rees* (1950)), whereas this appears possible under a fully secret trust (*Irvine v Sullivan* (1869)). Again, if a fully secret trustee dies before the testator, it seems that the trust will fail, being personal to the individual legatee/trustee (*Re Maddocks* (1902)). This is not so with a half secret trust, where equity will intervene on the ground that 'a trust will not fail for want of a trustee' (*Sonley v Clock Makers Company* (1780)), although it is not clear why equity cannot intervene to save a fully secret trust in like manner. The same difference in result appears to exist if the trustee dies or revokes his acceptance of the trust before the testator's death, with the fully secret trust failing (although possibly the fully secret trustee cannot keep the property for himself) and the half secret trust being supported by the appointment of a new trustee. Similarly, whereas a fully secret trust can be revoked *and replaced* by a new fully secret trust by the testator at any time up to his death, a half secret trust can only be revoked prior to death (thus leaving the property held on resulting trust) because it is impossible to communicate details of new beneficiaries after the will has been executed.

Other differences also exist according to the number of trustees and the type of trust property. Thus, legacies to two or more persons in the will as trustees (that is, a half secret trust) will usually be to them as joint tenants and, therefore, a valid acceptance of the trust obligation by any one of them will bind them all (*Re Stead* (1900)). However, in fully secret trusts, if there are two legatees/trustees, the gift in the will may be to them as tenants in common or as joint tenants because they are not declared trustees. If it is to them as tenants in common, only those who actually accept the trust are bound and the others may keep their own share (*Tee v Ferris* (1856)). If, on the other hand, the gift is made to the legatees/trustees as joint tenants, an acceptance by any one before the will is made will bind all, irrespective of the wishes of the others, although acceptance after the will binds only those so accepting (*Re Stead*). Finally, there may well be differences in respect of the additional formality requirements necessary to establish secret trusts of land, although the issue is shrouded in doubt. So, while it has been suggested that fully secret trusts of land do not need to comply with s 53(1)(b) of the Law of Property Act (LPA) 1925, and, thus, do not need to be evidenced in writing (*Ottaway v Norman* (1972)), there is clear authority that half secret trusts of land must meet this requirement (*Re Baillie* (1886)). It is uncertain whether this is a justifiable distinction between fully and half secret trusts of land and there is much to be said for the *Ottaway* approach, as it seems illogical that a half secret trust will be valid despite non-compliance with the formalities of the Wills Act 1837, but then fail because of lack of compliance with s 53(1)(b) of the LPA 1925. Indeed, it may well be that a half secret trust of land can avoid being caught by s 53(1)(b) on the ground that 'equity will not permit a statute (s 53) to be an instrument of fraud'. Be that as it may, the point was not fully argued in *Ottaway v Norman* and an apparent distinction remains.

In conclusion, then, although fully secret and half secret trusts share the same general characteristic of being exempt from the formalities of the Wills Act, they are not so similar when it comes to the conditions necessary for their existence, nor the way in which they operate. Whether this be right or wrong, it is reason enough to require a distinction to be made between the two concepts.

 # Question 7

To what extent is it possible to develop a coherent theory to explain the validity of so called secret trusts?

 ## *Answer plan*

- The context of secret trusts: their special status with respect to formalities for the creation of trusts;
- fully secret and half secret trusts briefly distinguished;
- theories based on fraud: using a statute as an instrument of fraud or disregarding the intention of the testator (old fraud and new fraud);
- the declaration and constitution theory; and
- views on the different communication requirements.

 # Answer

Fully secret and half secret trusts have a special place in the law of trusts. Not only are they a relic of the days when society frowned on mistresses and illegitimate children, so that a testator had to make provision for his illicit dependants in secret, they are also very difficult to justify within conventional norms of the law of equity. The starting point must be to state the obvious: that is, that both fully secret and half secret trusts may be valid and enforceable despite lack of compliance with the formalities laid down by s 9 of the Wills Act 1837 and other statutes. Fully secret trusts are not declared in the will at all, with the trustee apparently taking the property absolutely, while in the case of half secret trusts the fact of a trust is declared in the will, so bringing partial compliance with s 9, but the identity of the beneficiaries is not.

The lawyer's natural instinct when faced with the exceptional situation of secret trusts is to search for (and expect) a rational, coherent theory which will explain why the normal rules of statute and common law do not apply. As we shall see, it may be that such a search is fruitless, or that such theories as do exist are not coherent or all embracing. Nevertheless, it should not be thought that the exercise is entirely academic, for the great merit of a theory is that it enables a dispassionate observer to judge novel situations as and when they arise and thus to reach sensible and justifiable practical solutions to new practical problems. With that in mind, what can be said about the rationale for secret trusts? There are a number of different views.

Perhaps the most prevalent theory, when the doctrine of secret trusts was in its heyday, was that secret trusts would be enforced by a court of equity in favour of a secret beneficiary on the ground that 'equity will not permit a statute to be an instrument of fraud' (*McCormick v Grogan* (1869) and noted with approval in *Box v Barclays Bank* (1998)). That is, if a fully secret trust was declared unenforceable because it did not comply with the Wills Act, the legatee/trustee would be able to keep the trust property for himself despite the fact that he had accepted the trust obligation during the testator's lifetime. Indeed, the real problem was not so much that the fully secret trustee *could* keep the property if the trust were not enforced, but that he would *try* to keep the property in defiance of the trust by pleading its invalidity for non-compliance with the Wills Act 1837. To accept this could be to accept that the Wills Act would assist the trustee in his fraud.

Certainly, this rationale has the attraction of simplicity and, indeed, the equitable maxim used here is familiar and well established (see, for example, *Rouchefoucauld v Boustead* (1897)). However, a moment's thought will reveal that this rationale cannot explain the validity of half secret trusts. In half secret trusts, the testator leaves property to the legatee 'on trust' for unnamed beneficiaries. There is thus no possibility that the half secret trustee may commit fraud, as he or she is forever barred from the property. At the very least, the half secret trustee must hold the property on trust for the residuary estate and cannot even claim to be a beneficiary under the trust (*Re Keen* (1937); *Re Rees* (1950)). Simply put, there is no possibility of fraudulent gain by the trustee with a half secret trust.

The impossibility of explaining both fully and half secret trusts on the basis of *McCormick v Grogan* type fraud has led to the development of theories that secret trusts are founded on a redefinition of what 'fraud' actually means. Traditionally, 'fraud' would mean the trustee taking a personal benefit when he or she was meant to hold the property for another and this is what is meant by the *Grogan* rationale. However, some commentators have argued that this is a far too narrow definition of 'fraud' and that a wider view might be taken, which can then be used to justify both fully secret and half secret trusts. Taking this approach, we might say that secret trusts of both types should be enforced because, otherwise, a 'fraud' would be perpetrated on the testator or the beneficiaries. The testator would be defrauded because he would have parted with his legacy on the understanding that his wishes in respect of it would be carried out (*Re Fleetwood* (1880)). After all, had the secret trustee not agreed to the plan, the testator may have changed his will and made alternative arrangements. This was the view of Lord Westbury in *McCormick v Grogan*. Here, however, lies the flaw in this theory, because it amounts to no more than the bald assertion that a testator's wishes should be respected even if he has put them into effect in a manner that is not acceptable (that is, not in compliance with the Wills Act). Yet, if this is an acceptable justification for secret trusts, the next logical step is to repeal the Wills Act altogether, since the Wills Act often defeats a testator's intention. Likewise, the argument that the beneficiaries would be defrauded (for example, as put by Lord Buckmaster in *Blackwell v Blackwell* (1929)) if secret trusts were not enforced is equally flawed. Beneficiaries are routinely deprived of property which testators and settlors would desire them to have, for the simple reason that the trust or gift has not been put into effect in the proper manner. In essence then, both these variants on the 'new fraud' theory are circular and amount only to the argument that the testator's wishes should be respected. There is nothing here to explain why the formalities prescribed by statute for facilitating that intention can be ignored.

A final theory seeks to prise secret trusts away from its link with the Wills Act altogether and to explain them as ordinary trusts created *inter vivos*. According to this view – sometimes called the declaration and constitution theory of secret trusts – both fully secret and half secret trusts operate outside the testator's will and should not be regarded as dependent upon it (*Blackwell v Blackwell*). They are trusts within the normal, equitable jurisdiction, to which the Wills Act 1837 does not apply. The evidence for this is, apparently, provided by *Re Young* (1951), where a witness to a will was permitted to be a beneficiary under a secret trust and *Re Gardner (No 2)* (1923), where a beneficiary under a secret trust died before the testator but, nevertheless, his interest passed to his estate. Both of these results would have been impossible if the trust was governed by the Wills Act because witnesses to wills may not take a legacy and beneficiaries who predecease testators lose their interests.

Assuming, then, that the Wills Act is not central to the whole matter, how are secret trusts formed under this theory? The rationale is that the communication by the testator to the trustee of the trust and/or its terms amounts to a normal *inter vivos* declaration of trust which is then completed on the testator's death when the property passes in to the hands of the trustee. The will is simply the mechanism by which the trustee obtains the property and the trust becomes constituted.

This declaration/constitution theory of secret trusts does have its attractions. It justifies secret trusts on the same basis as other trusts and, in effect, classes them as express *inter vivos* trusts. It means, of course, that the trust does not come into existence until the testator dies, that being when the property passes and the trust becomes constituted. Yet, as ever, there are difficulties. If secret trusts are express trusts, this should mean that such trusts of land must be evidenced in writing as required by s 53(1)(b) of the Law of Property Act (LPA) 1925. However, at least with fully secret trusts, *Ottaway v Norman* (1972) suggests that writing is not required and it would be strange for written evidence to be necessary for compliance with s 53 of the LPA when none such was required for compliance with the Wills Act. Nevertheless, *Re Baillie* (1886) is unequivocal that writing is needed for half secret trusts of land. There are other problems, too. If the secret trust does not come into existence until the testator's death, *Re Gardner (No 2)* (1923) must be wrongly decided, as the trust did not exist when the beneficiary died! More importantly, if the relevant date for constitution of the half secret trust might be the testator's death, why is the date of the will so important for communication purposes? Why is it necessary to declare the trust before the will is made if the will is only a trigger for the constitution of the trust? It is difficult to answer this criticism, save only to say that the communication rule for half secret trusts is wrong and that post-testamentary communication should be possible. Support for this radical proposition comes from other common law jurisdictions where the distinction between fully secret and half secret trusts has been abolished (for example, Australia). Nevertheless, there are other explanations of why there is a difference in this respect between the two types of secret trust, although none is altogether convincing. Two of the more cogent theories are, first, that the rule allowing acceptance after the will in fully secret trusts was originally procedural, viz that evidence of events occurring after the will (that is, acceptance of the trust obligation) could be admitted by a court to prove a fully secret trust in order to prevent fraud by the legatee/trustee, whereas with half secret trusts, where the legatee is clearly stated to be a trustee, there is no possibility of fraud and therefore no need to examine events (for example, acceptance) occurring after the will. Secondly, it may be that the half secret trust rule is a mistake because of confusion with the law of incorporation of documents. A will may be said to 'incorporate' another document if the will makes reference to that document and if that document was in existence at the time the will was made. It is easy to see how this rule could have been carried over to require acceptance of the half secret trust at the time the will was made. Of course, it is clear that neither of these theories (nor any other) is wholly satisfactory, and they do not help in finding a rationale for secret trusts generally. What they do illustrate, however, is that any theory concerning any aspect of the law of secret trusts is not watertight.

So, after examining all the relevant theories, we are only a little more aware of a consistent rationale for the validity and enforcement of secret trusts. Indeed, the true answer may well be that there is no coherent theory, no logic and no golden thread that links all the cases. After all, we are dealing with the court's equitable jurisdiction and perhaps the best we can say is that the law of secret trusts has developed organically, with judges solving practical problems in real cases according to the needs of the parties at the time. That they may have had no real theory in mind is not in itself a serious criticism.

Note

The previous two questions are typical 'bookwork' questions on the law of secret trusts. It is imperative when answering such questions to avoid a lengthy repetition of the rules concerning the validity of secret trusts – they are straightforward – and to concentrate instead on addressing the precise issues raised by the question.

Question 8

Thomas executed his will on 1 April, which contained a legacy of £5,000 to Arnold, a legacy of £10,000 to Betty and a legacy of £20,000 to Clive, his brother. In his will, Thomas directed Betty to hold her legacy 'as a matter of trust for such persons as I have communicated to her'. On 1 May, Thomas told Arnold that he wished Arnold to pay his legacy to Thomas's illegitimate son, Zeus. One month later, after a quarrel with Zeus's mother, Thomas told Arnold to keep the money for himself. On 30 March, Thomas telephoned Betty and asked her whether she would be prepared to be a trustee of the money he would leave her in his will. Betty said she would think about it, and received a letter on 2 April enclosing a key to a safe where Thomas said he had deposited instructions as to the destination of the money. Betty immediately telephoned Thomas to assure him she would carry out his wishes. After Thomas's death, a letter was found in the safe directing Betty to pay the money to Lucy. On 1 August, Thomas told Clive that he wished his legacy to be paid to the London Dogs' Home, a registered charity. Clive agreed, but just before Thomas's death, Clive telephoned his brother to withdraw his consent, and indicated his desire to spend 'his legacy' on a world cruise. Thomas died soon afterwards without altering his will in any way.

─Answer plan

- Fully secret trusts: communication and acceptance, validity of revocation of trust and substitution of trustee/legatee as sole legatee;
- half secret trusts: date of communication and acceptance, method of communication and acceptance, possible contradiction of the will; and
- fully secret trust: trustee disclaiming trust, whether possible and consequences thereof.

━━━━ Answer ━━━━

This question concerns the law of secret trusts. In essence, secret trusts are those trusts which operate in relation to a testamentary disposition but where either the very fact and details of the trust are not declared in the testator's will (fully secret trusts) or where, although the fact of the trust is declared in the will, the identity of the beneficiaries is not (half secret trusts) (*McCormick v Grogan* (1869); *Re Keen* (1937)). The peculiarity of secret trusts is that they are regarded as valid and enforceable despite the fact that they do not comply with the strict requirements of formality found in s 9 of the Wills Act 1837. Under this section, dispositions in wills must be in writing and signed and witnessed by the appropriate persons; yet, as we shall see, secret trusts may be valid where either or both the fact of the trust and its details are declared orally or by post-testamentary writing. In this question, there appear to be issues concerning the validity of fully secret trusts and half secret trusts. Each attempted disposition will be discussed in turn.

First, we shall consider the legacy to Arnold, with oral instructions to hold the property for another under a potential secret trust.

In his will, Thomas makes a bequest of £5,000 to Arnold without any limitation on the way in which Arnold may use his gift. On the face of the will, this is an absolute gift to Arnold. Consequently, any claim that Zeus may have to the money may arise only under a fully secret trust. A fully secret trust will arise where, despite an apparently absolute gift, the testator has communicated a desire to the legatee that the property should be held for another, which expressed desire has been accepted by the legatee (*Thynn v Thynn* (1684)). In our case, there is no doubt of Thomas's intention to create a trust (contrast *Margulies v Margulies* (2000)) and, providing that the legatee/trustee accepts the obligation at any time before the testator's death, there is every chance that the secret trust will be enforced in favour of the intended beneficiary. Arnold's acceptance of the trust obligation is clear enough and, *prima facie*, a fully secret trust seems to have arisen. However, before his death, Thomas attempts to revoke this secret trust and revert to the position as it is expressed on the face of the will; viz, an absolute gift to Arnold. This poses a far reaching question about the time at which a fully secret trust comes into existence. If, for example, the secret trust comes into existence the moment the legatee/trustee accepts the trust obligation, then clearly Arnold will hold the property on trust for Zeus, as once a trust is created, the beneficiaries' rights become perfect (see *Milroy v Lord* (1862)). If, on the other hand, the secret trust comes into existence at the testator's death, then clearly the intended trust can be revoked at any time prior to that event and alternative arrangements can be made.

The former view, which would enable Zeus to claim the £5,000, is superficially attractive because it prevents the testator from using fully secret trusts to alter his testamentary dispositions without making another will. It is one thing to allow secret trusts to avoid the Wills Act 1837 in their formation, but should they also be used to circumvent the requirements of writing by giving the testator a power of unattested disposition right up to his death? Moreover, if the rationale for enforcing secret trusts is to prevent the trustee/legatee perpetrating a fraud by agreeing to accept a trust obligation and then claiming the property himself because of non-compliance with the Wills Act, this policy can be upheld by deciding that the trust becomes constituted at the date of acceptance of the obligation. Such a view of secret trusts is implicit in the decisions in *Re Gardner (No 2)* (1923) and *Sonley v Clock Makers Company* (1780), although *Sonley* was a half secret trust and *Re Gardner (No 2)* has attracted considerable academic criticism.

The alternative view sees the secret trust as arising on the testator's death and therefore revocable until then. The judgments in *Blackwell v Blackwell* (1929) and *Re Maddocks* (1902) support this view. The logic of this approach is that the communication to the trustee during his lifetime, and acceptance thereof, is simply an *inter vivos* declaration of trust and that the trust becomes constituted when the property passes into the hands of the trustee on the testator's death. Thus, the trust may be revoked by the settlor prior to his death. If this is the better view (despite the fact that it allows oral post-testamentary dispositions of property), then clearly Thomas can revoke the trust in favour of Zeus. Further, it seems from the facts that Arnold is to revert to being the beneficiary of an absolute gift as stated on the face of the will and, if the revocation is effective, this will be the final position. Indeed, even if one were to argue that Arnold is to be the new beneficiary under the secret trust (that is, holding on trust for himself), *Irvine v Sullivan* (1869) is clear authority for the proposition that a fully secret trustee can be a beneficiary under his own trust. Arnold may claim his legacy.

Next, there is the gift on trust to Betty, holding for Lucy.

There is a clear intention in respect of the bequest in the will to Betty that she is to be a trustee. Hence, whatever conclusion we come to about the persons ultimately entitled to the £10,000, we know that Betty will not be able to claim the gift. At the very least, she will hold the money on resulting trust for Thomas's estate (*Re Keen* (1937) and *Re Rees* (1950)). However, in order that Lucy may claim the property, she must establish a half secret trust, wherein the details of the trust were communicated to Betty and accepted by her prior to, or simultaneously with, the execution of the will (*Re Bateman* (1970)). Here is Lucy's first problem as the facts make it clear that, although Thomas asked Betty to be a trustee before the date of the will, acceptance thereof was not made until after the will was executed on 1 April. There are four possibilities. First, the communication rule is applied strictly and the half secret trust is invalid, with Betty therefore holding on resulting trust for Thomas's estate. Although a perfectly defensible result on the authorities, this seems harsh in the circumstances. Secondly, it might be argued that Betty had impliedly accepted the trust at the date of the initial telephone call. This seems untenable on the facts and *Moss v Cooper* (1861) is not applicable. Thirdly, we could take the robust view that the communication rule for half secret trusts is wrong and that the proper approach is that of other common law jurisdictions where the rules for fully secret trusts and half secret trusts are assimilated. This is attractive, especially because there is no totally convincing explanation for the difference between the two types of trust. However, unfortunately, both *Re Keen* (1937) and *Re Bateman* (1970) are clear enough. Fourthly, it can be argued that it is not certain that the communication rule is violated in this case. As *Re Keen* establishes, communication and acceptance must be made before or *simultaneously with* the execution of the will and it is arguable that a process of communication and acceptance that began prior to the execution of the will and which was completed soon after is 'simultaneous' for this purpose. Of course, the matter is not free of doubt, but secret trusts operate under the court's equitable jurisdiction which has always been flexible enough to assist those believed worthy of its protection.

Assuming, then, that the communication and acceptance of the trust were validly made, Lucy faces other problems. It might be thought that the terms of the trust contradict the terms of the will and this is prohibited by *Re Keen* (for example, as I 'have' communicated). However, this point is met if the above argument about the simultaneous nature of the communication and acceptance of the details is adopted. Likewise, although Betty is not given the precise details of the trust, because they are contained within a locked safe, it is clear from *Re Boyes* (1884) that communication of the means of identifying the beneficiaries is acceptable if it is made at the relevant time (the simultaneous argument again) and if it is out of the power of the testator to change those details. Thus, assuming that Thomas has not kept a key to the safe and cannot change the identity of the beneficiary after his will has been executed, Lucy will be able to claim the £10,000.

The next legacy to consider is that to Clive.

Whether the London Dogs' Home can claim the £20,000 depends on a number of factors. The first and crucial issue is whether there is any attempt at all by Thomas to impose a trust on his brother. Only if the instructions to Clive can be construed as the manifestation of an intention to impose a trust is there any possibility that the charity may claim the gift under a fully secret trust (*Re Snowden* (1979)). The issue is not clear cut, but the fact that 'Clive agrees' to Thomas's suggestion is further evidence, along with the words of the will, of the imposition of a trust obligation, readily accepted. At this point, then, we can say that the Dogs' Home may have a claim to the £20,000 on Thomas's death. Yet, as we have seen when discussing the legacy to Arnold, a fully secret trust does not become constituted – in the sense of giving perfect rights to the beneficiaries – until the testator's death. Here, however, it is not the testator who revokes the trust, but the trustee who revokes his acceptance of the obligation. Does this destroy the trust and may Clive claim the £20,000? According to *Re Maddocks* (1902), the beneficiaries will have no claim in these circumstances because the trust has not yet arisen but there are *dicta* in the judgment of Lord Buckmaster in *Blackwell v Blackwell* (1929) that indicate that equity will not let such a trust fail for want of a trustee, as is, indeed, the case with half secret trusts (*Re Smurthwaite* (1871)). Of course, the logic is with the *Re Maddocks* rule, but as a matter of practical justice, perhaps the best view is that, if the testator has had time to amend his will after the trustee's revocation of acceptance but before his own death, the absolute gift on the face of will takes effect – the property would go to Clive. If, however, the testator had had no time to make alternative arrangements after the trustee's action but before his own death, equity may act to prevent fraud or inequitable conduct on the part of the legatee and either provide a new trustee to carry out the terms of the trust or compel the legatee to hold the property on resulting trust for the testator's estate (the trustee's conscience would be bound: *Westdeutsche Landesbank Girozentrale v Islington LBC* (1996)). The latter of these is more consistent with the idea that the trust had not formed until the testator's death. In our case, therefore, the issue turns on whether Thomas had time to make alternative arrangements. If he did, we can presume he was happy with Clive keeping the £20,000; if he did not, we should imply a resulting trust for the estate.

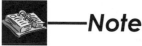 ## Note

The danger with problems of this type is that students are content to remain with the most obvious answer, viz, that the half secret trust fails. A moment's thought will reveal the danger in this since it must always be remembered that equity encompasses a flexible set of principles, not rules written in concrete.

Question 9

Joanne, a rich property developer, made her will in 1998. She leaves her personal affects and shares in Build & Co 'to Smith and Jones equally in the knowledge that you will carry out my hopes'. In 1997, she had told Smith that she wanted both Smith and Jones to hold the personal effects in trust for her illegitimate son, Arnie. Smith had readily agreed, although Jones did not know of this arrangement. Moreover, in 1999, Joanne had asked Smith to hold the shares on trust for her lover, Tim, and he had agreed again. In the same will, Joanne leaves her town house 'in the trust of William and Mary for the purpose with which they are familiar'. When Joanne had told William and Mary of her intentions in 1996, they had readily accepted her plan of allowing them to live in the house providing that they left it by their will to the Homeless Charity.

Joanne died in 2001, and Jones has come to claim his share of the personal effects and shares. However, Smith wishes the personal effects to go to Arnie, and although Tim died in 2000, he (Tim) left all his property to Joe – the son of Joanne and Tim – who now claims the shares, despite being a witness to Joanne's will. In addition to this, the Homeless Charity would like to know whether they can expect to receive the town house when William and Mary die, even though both have now denied that they are bound and wish to leave the house to their own son.

Advise the parties.

Answer plan

- Fully secret or half secret trusts: a matter of construction;
- fully secret trusts and two trustees: whether the agreement of all is required;
- half secret trusts of land;
- the problem of the predeceased beneficiary under the secret trust; and
- secret trusts operate outside the Wills Act; the position of witnesses.

Answer

The questions raised by this problem concern the law of fully secret and half secret trusts. Fully secret trusts arise where property is left to a person absolutely by will but, before her death, the testatrix has asked the legatee to hold the property on trust for a third party and that legatee has agreed (*McCormick v Grogan* (1869)). Half secret trusts are similar, save that the property is left in the will to the legatee expressly on trust and the objects of the trust (the beneficiaries) are not disclosed, their identity being communicated to the trustee and accepted by him prior to, or simultaneously with, the execution of the testatrix's will (*Re Keen* (1937)). In both cases, the secret trustee will then hold the property on trust for the secret beneficiaries who may compel the legatee/trustee to hand it over. In our problem, as well as the difficulty of establishing whether any fully secret or half secret trust exists, there are the added complications of property being left to two or more legatees and the fact that some of the claimants would be disentitled if the Wills Act 1837 was applicable, viz, those who predecease the testatrix and those who are witness to her will.

Let us consider, first, the shares and personal effects left to Smith and Jones.

The first and most difficult question in respect of the bequest to Smith and Jones is to determine the nature of the trust, if any, that is imposed upon either or both of them. It is only if a trust is established that Arnie and Joe (via Tim) may have a claim to the property. The terms of the legacy to Smith and Jones is equivocal. It is true that Joanne has intimated in her will that the property given to Smith and Jones has been earmarked for some special purpose. Indeed, she comments that she is confident they will carry out her hopes. This might seem to suggest that a half secret trust can exist, being a trust openly expressed in the will. However, in order to impose a trust on the legatees, the words used must be sufficient to impose a trust obligation as a matter of law: there must be certainty of intention (*Re Snowden* (1979); *Margulies v Margulies* (2000)). In our case, the words used by Joanne are not such as to impose a trust in all circumstances and they are merely precatory (expressions of hope). According to *Re Conolly* (1909), precatory words will not impose a trust if they may also be taken as evidence of an absolute gift. Although the matter is for debate, the better view is that the will of Joanne imposes no trust in respect of the property given to Smith and Jones, especially since Joanne is prepared to be explicit in respect of other property in the same will (for example, the house 'in trust' to William and Mary). Consequently, Smith and Jones are entitled to the property absolutely, at least on the face of the will.

However, the next question is whether the legatees, being absolutely entitled, are subject to a fully secret trust. Certainly, as the facts make clear, at least one of the trustees has been asked to hold the shares and personal effects on trust for third parties and has accepted. As far as the validity of the fully secret trust *per se* is concerned, it is immaterial that acceptance of the trust of the shares is not given until after the will is executed. Such acceptance may be given at any time up to the testatrix's death (*Re Snowden* (1979)). Note, however, that the property is given absolutely to both Smith and Jones equally and Jones is claiming his portion of both the personal effects and shares. We must determine, therefore, whether Smith's acceptance of the trust obligation (which clearly means he must hold his share for Arnie and Tim) is sufficient to bind Jones as well.

The principles applicable here are set out in *Re Stead* (1900) and, although they are not necessarily logical, they are at least relatively clear. Thus, with a fully secret trust, if the property is given absolutely to the legatees as tenants in common, then only those who accept the trust are bound by it. The reason commonly attributed to this view is that the gift is not tainted with any fraud in procuring the execution of the will, see *Re Stead*. If Smith and Jones are tenants in common of the personal effects and shares, Smith must hold his portion on trust, while Jones may keep his portion absolutely. If, on the other hand, the property is given to Smith and Jones as joint tenants (and this may be the case, given that the property is given 'equally'), then if anyone accepts the trust obligation *before* the will is executed, all are bound, regardless of their own position; but, if acceptance takes place *after* the will, only those who accept are bound. So, assuming Smith and Jones take the property as joint tenants, both will be bound by the fully secret trust in respect of the personal effects, because Smith accepted before the will was executed. Conversely, only Smith will be bound by the trust of the shares as his acceptance came after the will and does not bind Jones. Jones may take the shares absolutely as the will indicates.

The final question in respect of Smith and Jones's legacy is the identity of the beneficiaries of the personal effects and Smith's trust of the shares. Clearly, for the personal effects, Smith and Jones hold the property on trust for Arnie and he may make a successful claim. However, there is a difficulty with Smith's trusteeship of his portion of the shares because Tim, the original beneficiary, has died before the testatrix. The most cogent theory explaining fully secret trusts emphasises that they do not arise (that is, they do not bind the property and give enforceable rights to the beneficiaries) until the testatrix dies (for example, *Blackwell v Blackwell* (1929)) because that is when the trust becomes constituted by the passing of property under the will to the trustee. On this analysis, Tim's estate should not be entitled to the shares, since there is no beneficiary at the time the trust comes into existence. However, there is the direct authority of *Re Gardner (No 2)* (1923) that allows a claim by the successors to a beneficiary who predeceases the testatrix, provided that the trust was communicated and accepted before the beneficiary's death (as here). This may be decisive in favour of Tim's estate and, at least, it makes it clear that Tim is not disentitled by the Wills Act 1837 (which normally voids a gift by will if the legatee dies before the testatrix): this gift is by a trust operating outside the will. Finally, although, under the Wills Act 1837, a person may not be entitled to a legacy if he witnesses the will in which the gift is contained, Joe is not disbarred from claiming the shares via Tim because, first, secret trusts operate outside the will and witnesses may claim (*Re Young* (1951)), and, secondly, Joe can assert that he is not claiming under the secret trust at all, but under the will of Tim, who was the trust's beneficiary.

We must next consider the house left to William and Mary. Although, once again, the terms of the devise to William and Mary is not unequivocal and although use of the word 'trust' does not always impose a trust at law (see, for example, *Tito v Waddell (No 2)* (1977)), it is relatively clear, on the face of the will, that the house has been left to William and Mary expressly as trustees. This is a half secret trust and, at the very least, William and Mary must hold the house eventually for Joanne's estate on resulting trusts (*Re Keen* (1937)). In such circumstances, William and Mary cannot leave the property to their own son, but can it be claimed by the Homeless Charity? The facts make it clear that Joanne had communicated her intentions to William and Mary, who had agreed to her wishes, before she had executed her will, and this, in principle, raises a trust in favour of the named beneficiary (*Re Bateman* (1970)). Moreover, in *Ottaway v Norman* (1972), it was accepted that an obligation imposed on the trustees under a fully secret trust to leave property in their will to another was perfectly acceptable. Of course, our case involves a half secret trust, but there is no reason why the same principle should not be applicable. If it is objected that trustees under a half secret trust are not entitled to be beneficiaries (*Re Rees* (1950)) – as William and Mary appear to be during their lifetimes – we may adopt the judge's reasoning in *Ottaway* that the secret trust comes into existence on the legatee's/trustee's death, and not on that of the testatrix. Hence, William and Mary are not beneficiaries under the half secret trust and the charity may claim the house.

There is, however, one final problem. The declaration/constitution theory of secret trusts assumes that these trusts are normal, express trusts which operate outside the will. However, the trust property in this case is land and, according to s 53(1)(b) of the Law of Property Act (LPA) 1925, express trusts of land must be evidenced in writing if they are to be enforceable. Indeed, according to *Re Baillie* (1886), a half secret trust of land must be evidenced in writing if it is to be valid. The half secret trust of this house is purely oral, and would seem to fail if this reasoning is adopted. Yet the rule in *Re Baillie* (1886) has been subject to much criticism and in *Ottaway*, a fully secret trust of land was upheld on facts similar to these without the need for writing. So, despite the authority of *Baillie*, it might be possible to argue that this half secret trust should be enforced in favour of the charity, perhaps on the ground that 'equity will not allow a statute (s 53(1)(b) of the LPA) to be an instrument of fraud'. The only problem with this is, of course, that the trustees cannot possibly take the house themselves because they are named as trustees and so fraud in this sense is not possible. We would have to adopt a wider definition of fraud, perhaps a desire to prevent fraud of the beneficiaries. Subject to this last issue being resolved in favour of the charity, they may claim the house on William and Mary's death.

Note

Another typical examination problem, this time with the complication of two legatee/ trustees. Note, again, that there is more here than first meets the eye, especially in relation to secret trusts of land.

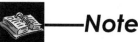

Question 10

Sam has recently died. By his will, he bequeathed his large collection of rare stamps to 'Peter and David absolutely'. In addition, in a separate clause in the will he left his house to William 'on trust for purposes I have communicated to him'.

Before he died, he told Peter that both he and David were to hold the stamps on trust for Becky, his illegitimate daughter. A letter repeating the same instruction to David was found amongst Sam's personal effects after his death. David has informed you that he only became aware of Sam's wishes regarding the stamp collection following his death. Before his death, he orally told William that the house was also to be held on trust for Becky.

William was killed in a car crash a week before Sam died.

Advise Becky as to whether she is entitled to any of the properties.

Answer plan

- Requirements in order to create a fully secret trust
- Communication to one of several intended trustees
- Standard of proof
- Requirements for a half secret trust
- Intended trustee pre-deceasing the testator
- S53(1)(b) of the Law of Property Act 1925

Answer

Sam's will has effected two transfers – the first concerning a large collection of rare stamps to Peter and David, the second is in respect of a house to William. We will deal with the consequences of each of these dispositions in turn.

The stamp collection

The transfer in the will is to Peter and David apparently beneficially on the face of the will. There is no indication that these two individuals take other than for their benefit. However, before Sam died he told Peter that both himself and David were required to hold the collection on trust for Becky, Sam's illegitimate daughter. This arrangement raises the possibility of a fully secret trust being created in favour of Becky. We will now examine how far this is the case.

A fully secret trust is one where the legatee takes the property beneficially on the face of the will but subject to an understanding between the testator and themselves concerning the property during the lifetime of the testator. The *existence* of the trust, as well as its *terms*, are fully concealed by reference to the will. This appears to be evident in the problem. In this context, the court draws a distinction between a mere legacy on the one hand, and a legacy subject to a secret trust. The essence of the distinction is that in a legacy subject to a secret trust, the testator communicates the terms of the trust during his lifetime to the legatees. In this respect, it is immaterial that the communication of the terms is made before or after the execution of the will, provided that it is made before the testator's death. Applying this principle to the facts of the problem Sam, during his lifetime, has communicated the terms of the trust to Peter, namely that both legatees are required to hold on trust for Becky. Thus far, it is clear that Peter has knowledge of the terms of the trust and is subject to an equitable obligation to carry out the testator's wishes. Has Sam, during the relevant time, communicated the terms of the trust to David? We are told that a letter was found among Sam's personal effects repeating the instruction to David. But the issue is whether this letter was received by David during Sam's lifetime? It would appear that this is not the case. The conclusion here is that David was unaware of Sam's wishes. The implications of this finding will be explored below.

The next requirement for the creation of a fully secret trust is that the intended trustees must accept the terms of the communication made to them. Acceptance for these purposes may be expressly declared by the trustees in the sense that they positively acknowledge the existence of an obligation to act as trustees. There is no evidence that this is the case on the facts of the problem. But acceptance may also be inferred by the silence or acquiescence of the trustee, during the testator's lifetime, see *Moss v Cooper* (1861). Of course this can only be the case where the trustee is aware of the terms of the communication. The rationale is that it would be a fraud on the testator (not to mention the intended beneficiary under the trust) for the trustee to deny the agreement made with the testator. Accordingly, Peter, by implication, has agreed to become a trustee for Becky.

Would David be obliged to hold on trust or would he take part of the property beneficially? To put the question another way the issue is when a testator leaves property by will to two persons apparently beneficially, but informs one of the apparent legatees of the terms of the trust, would the person who is unaware of the trust be bound to hold upon trust or not. The solution adopted by the courts, which is far from adequate, depends on the status of the co-owners and the time when the communication was made to those who are aware of the trust. If the informed legatee or devisee was told of the terms of the trust before or at the time of the execution of the will and the multiple owners take as joint tenants, the uninformed legatee is bound by the terms of the trust communicated to the informed legatee. The reason commonly ascribed for this solution is that no one is allowed to claim property under a fraud committed by another. This was stated by Farwell J in *Re Stead* (1900). The assumption that is made is that the informed trustee attempted to defraud the testator, irrespective of the reason for failure to inform the ignorant trustee. On the other hand, if the communication of the terms was made subsequent to the execution of the will only the person aware of the terms of the trust is bound, for in this case there is no fraud. On the facts of the problem, Peter and David take as joint tenants for they are co-owners without any words of severance, but we are not told when Sam communicated the terms of the trust to Peter. If the communication was made before or at the time of the execution of the will this would be sufficient to subject David to a trust in favour of Becky. If the communication was made later, David will take part (half) of the property beneficially, and Peter will hold the other portion on trust, see *Re Stead*.

The final point involves the standard of proof to establish the trust. If there is no fraud the standard of proof is a balance of probabilities, but if there is an allegation of fraud the standard exceeds a balance of probabilities but is not as high as beyond a reasonable doubt, see *Re Snowden* (1979). There is no clear definition of fraud but it has been suggested that where the intended trustee denies the existence of a trust this involves an allegation of fraud. Since David disputes the existence of an obligation on his part (failure to communicate) it is arguable that this imposes a higher standard of proof on Becky.

The house

The terms of the will indicate the existence of a trust but the details of the trust are concealed. This is consistent with an intended half secret trust. In order to create such a trust the testator is required to communicate the terms before or at the time of the execution of the will. If the terms of the trust are communicated after the execution of the will, even during the testator's lifetime, the evidence is not admissible, see *Blackwell v Blackwell* (1929). The reason commonly attributed to this rule involves compliance with the formal requirements under s 9 of the Wills Act 1837 in respect of post-will communications. Commentators have suggested that it is a confusion of probate rules with trusts rules. In any event the courts have not demonstrated a willingness to modify the principle. Applying this principle to the facts of the problem we are told that Sam told William of the terms of the trust before his death. But we are not told specifically at what time the communication was made. If the communication was made before or at the time of the execution of the will Becky would be entitled to prove the terms of the trust, otherwise the intended trust will fail and the property will be held on resulting trust for Sam's estate.

There are additional problems in that William has pre-deceased the testator, would this have an effect on the potentially valid half secret trust? Although there are no decided cases, it is arguable that since the trustee takes as trustee on the face of the will the trust ought not to fail, provided that the terms of the trust could be established. This is in accordance with the maxim, 'equity will not allow a trust to fail for want of a trustee'. The alternative is that the intended half secret trust fails by virtue of the probate doctrine of lapse. This rule, it may be pointed out, is applicable where a person takes beneficially under a will. In half secret trusts this is not the case. An additional issue is whether the terms of the trust could be established in the absence of both William and Sam. If this is not the case a resulting trust will arise in favour of Sam's estate.

Another issue concerns the lack of writing in respect of the terms of the trust. The argument here is that s 53(1)(b) of the Law of Property Act 1925 enacts that a 'declaration of trust in respect of land or any interest therein must be manifested and proved by some writing signed by the person able to declare the trust or by his will'. Clearly, the will does not declare the trust and the subject matter is land, but the issue is whether Sam ought to have manifested the terms of the trust in writing. We are told that he orally told William of the terms. Is s 53(1)(b) applicable to the transaction or does s 53(2) exempt the testator from the requirements of s 53(1)(b)? Section 53(2) enacts that 'This section shall not affect the creation or operation of implied resulting or constructive trusts.' This involves the classification of half secret trusts. If they are treated as intended express trusts s 53(1)(b) may be required to be complied with. In *Re Baillie* (1886) the court decided that half secret trusts are required to comply with the predecessor to s 53(1)(b). Non-compliance with the sub-section makes the trust unenforceable for lack of evidence in writing. Thus Becky may not be able to enforce the trust of land. If, on the other hand, the trust is treated as constructive s 53(2) will exempt Sam from the requirements of s 53(1)(b). An argument in support of this view is that the trust is created to prevent fraud. This was the original basis for such trust and may still be applicable today.

3 The Inherent Attributes of a Trust:

The Three Certainties and the Beneficiary Principle

Introduction

In the previous two chapters we have looked at the formalities needed to create a trust, the necessity for the trustee to be invested with title to the trust property in order that the trust be properly constituted and the curious exception to some of these rules found in the law of secret trusts. We have not yet begun to explore the factors which are elemental in the trust concept. In this chapter, two of the inherent characteristics of the trust will be examined: the requirement of the 'three certainties' and the 'beneficiary principle'.

The 'three certainties' is simply a shorthand description for a set of conditions which, when fulfilled, epitomise the trust. In simple terms, every trust must be established with:

(a) certainty of intention, so as to indicate that the holder of the property is under a trust obligation and must use the property according to the terms of the trust;

(b) certainty of subject matter, so as to ensure that the property which is the subject matter of the trust obligation is clearly defined or definable; and

(c) certainty of objects, so as to ensure that the beneficiaries to whom the trustee owes his onerous duties are clearly ascertainable and in whose favour the court can enforce the trust should the trustee fail in those duties.

As we shall see, the method of determining whether the three certainties exist may vary from trust to trust, especially with certainty of objects. In addition, where charitable trusts are concerned, the certainty of objects rules to be discussed below are not applicable and reference should be made to Chapter 4 for the definition of 'charity'. Finally, there is no statutory guidance as to the nature of the 'three certainties' and there is no substitute for a thorough grounding in case law.

The 'beneficiary principle' is very closely related to the need for certainty of objects for it expresses the idea that every non-charitable trust must have a human beneficiary. In other words, it is generally impossible in English law to establish a trust for a purpose, unless that purpose can be regarded as charitable (see Chapter 4). Thus, nearly every attempt to place a duty on a trustee to achieve non-charitable aims instead of holding the property for ascertainable individuals is doomed to failure. Once again, the beneficiary principle is easy to state, but difficult to apply in concrete cases because of the sometimes confusing precedents which are available.

Question 11

It is a cardinal rule of English law that all trusts must be certain of words, certain of subject matter and certain of objects.

Discuss.

Answer plan

- Three certainties and their purpose;
- certainty of intention: distinguish from powers, terms of art;
- certainty of subject matter: various tests and usefulness in clarifying trust property;
- certainty of objects: reasons for, different tests for;
- trusts which have different requirements: charities and anomalous exceptions.

Answer

It has been said many times, and bears repetition, that the trust imposes one of the most powerful forms of obligation in English law. It is to be expected, therefore, that the imposition of a trust on the recipient or holder of property is not to be achieved lightly. The trustee will have onerous duties to perform and is amenable to the coercive jurisdiction of the court at the suit of the beneficiaries. Moreover, certainty as to the nature and extent of the trust property and the interests of the beneficiaries is no less crucial. How else can a trustee administer the trust property in the manner required by the terms of the trust. The importance of these matters has long been recognised and is now summed up by the principle that a trust cannot exist without the 'three certainties' (*Knight v Knight* (1840)). According to Lord Eldon in *Wright v Atkyns* (1823), the validity of a trust depends on 'first, that the words must be imperative ... secondly, that the subject must be certain ... and thirdly, that the object must be as certain as the subject'. In short, there must be certainty of intention (or words), certainty of subject matter and certainty of objects.

Certainty of intention means that the person who is attempting to establish the trust must make it clear by the words he uses that the holder or transferee of the property is under a mandatory legal obligation to carry out the wishes of the settlor in so far as the law allows. However, as 'equity looks to the intent rather than the form' (*Re Williams* (1897)), no particular form of words or magic formula is required to impose a trust on the holder of property. The word 'trust' is a technical expression imposing an obligation on the trustees. However, the difficulty arises when alternative expressions have been used by the intended settlor. This issue becomes one of construction of the words used and the surrounding circumstances, including the conduct of the settlor, to determine whether a trust was intended or not. What is required is an intent to require the holder of property to carry out the settlor's wishes as opposed to a mere moral or honourable obligation. Consequently, words expressive of a mere hope or desire (precatory words) do not disclose a sufficient intention to create a trust unless, on the whole construction of the gift, this is the intention of the settlor (*Lambe v Eames* (1871); *Re Conolly* (1909)), although a settlor's use of words which have previously been held to establish a trust is good evidence of certainty of intention (*Re Steele* (1948)). Indeed, other factors may count for or against the imposition of a trust, as where the care which the settlor has taken (or not taken) to mark out the trust property or define its objects reflects on his intention to establish a trust in the first place (*Re Kayford Ltd* (1975)). As ever, the matter is one of construction and, in some cases, even use of the word 'trust' will not impose a trust at law, as where the word was intended to denote a political not a legal obligation (*Tito v Waddell (No 2)* (1977)). Necessarily, the circumstances in which a court will accept that there is sufficient certainty of intention to place a legal obligation on the holder of property to carry out the settlor's wishes will vary from case to case. In the recent case, *Duggan v Governor of Full Sutton Prison* [2004] The Times, 13 February, the Court of Appeal decided on policy grounds that a trust was not intended of prisoners' money handed over to the Governor on arrival at the prison. If there is not sufficient certainty of intention, the holder or recipient of property will be absolutely entitled to it and may use it as he or she wishes, either in conformity with, or contrary to, any hope or desire that the settlor may have expressed when transferring the property.

Certainty of subject matter is an equally vital element in the formation of a trust. As noted previously, if the property which is said to be the subject matter of the trust or the interests of the alleged beneficiaries under the trust are not certain, the 'trustee' cannot possibly perform the duties which the settlor has imposed upon him. At the outset, however, it is important to note that the subject matter of a trust may be uncertain in two distinct ways: first, the actual property may not be clearly defined or definable, and, secondly, the interests of the beneficiaries may not be defined or definable. First, *Sprange v Barnard* (1789) illustrates the former point, where a settlor left some shares to X 'and all that is remaining' after X's use in trust for A and B equally. Clearly, the subject matter of the trust for A and B was uncertain, as there was no certainty as to what would be left after X had made his decisions. Likewise, cases where tangible property belonging to several persons has been amalgamated and a trust is alleged over a certain number of those items will not result in a trust at law because the precise property is not identified, as in *Re London Wine Co (Shippers) Ltd* (1976), where alleged trusts over specific cases of wine failed because there had been no separation of the trust property from other stock in the company's warehouse (*quaere* whether the Sale of Goods Act 1995 has changed this). Of course, if the 'trust property' were separated or clearly marked, there would be no problem, nor, possibly, if the subject matter of the trust was expressed as a fixed proportion (say, one fifth) of the total property and not as a certain specific number of items. However, as more recent authority shows (*Hunter v Moss* (1993)), an alleged trust over a specific amount of *intangible* property (such as a number of shares in a company) which, by definition, are indistinguishable from other property of the same type in the hands of the alleged trustee is not void for uncertainty of subject matter because any person calling for the execution of the trust would know, with certainty, whether the trust had been performed. This has been confirmed by *Holland v Newbury* (1997), where the intangible nature of the property (shares) was the clear reason for being able to distinguish *London Wine*. Of course, such a justification (certainty of execution) could apply to tangible property (provided each specimen was identical to the others) and perhaps the 'clear execution' test should be adopted for all forms of trust property, be it tangible or intangible. The rigour of this aspect of the requirement of certainty of subject matter is also mitigated by the principle that the subject matter can be rendered certain by construction of the document or an external determinant. So, in *Re Golay* (1965), a trust of 'reasonable income' was held to be certain as 'reasonableness' was an objective limitation that could be decided by the court. Such a benevolent construction of a trust instrument is typical of a court of equity and is not surprising when it is appreciated that uncertainty of subject matter normally will cause a resulting trust in favour of the donor (assuming that certainty of intention did exist). In special cases, as where the court interprets the disposition as an absolute gift to the donees subject to a specific trust of part of it for some limited object, the failure of the specific trust for uncertainty of subject matter will allow the original donees to keep the property absolutely and not hold on resulting trust (*Hancock v Watson* (1902)).

The second way in which the 'subject matter' of the trust must be certain concerns not the property itself but the extent of the beneficiaries' interests in that property. For example, in *Boyce v Boyce* (1849), a trust of two houses (obviously certain *per se*) failed because one of the two beneficiaries was given power to choose which property she desired and, having failed to do so, the second beneficiary was unable to take any interest under the trust. Admittedly, however, this type of uncertainty is unusual, since it is rare for the extent of the beneficiaries' interests to go undefined or to be undefinable (but see recently *Re Challoner Club Ltd* (1997)) and in many cases the trustees are given power to determine each beneficiary's share under the umbrella of a discretionary trust.

The last of the three certainties, and perhaps the most important, is the need for certainty of objects. This is another way of saying that the beneficiaries under the trust must either be named individually or be described by reference to a class description that is itself certain in scope. An example of the former is where property is given on trust in equal shares 'for my children A and B', and an example of the latter is where property is given on trust 'equally between my children'. In the former case, the objects of the trust are necessarily certain as they are named individuals, and in the latter case, the objects of the trust may be certain provided that it is possible to say with certainty who the children of the settlor actually are. This appears straightforward enough, but it is a crucial feature of the validity of a trust since failure to specify certain objects will mean that the trust fails and the property will be held on resulting trust for the settlor or the testator's estate.

Unfortunately, this simple picture of the certainty of objects rule can become clouded when trying to determine whether certainty of objects exists in practice. In simple terms, problems with certainty of objects arise in relation to three distinct concepts. First, there are 'fixed trusts', being trusts where the trustees have no discretion as to whom benefits under the trust are to be given or in what shares: both the share and the right of the beneficiaries to that share are fixed by the settlor. In cases such as this, the test for certainty of objects, where the objects are defined by a class description (for example, 'to my children in equal shares') is that it must be possible to draw up a complete list of all the objects: viz, the number of all the beneficiaries must be known because otherwise the property cannot be distributed equally (*IRC v Broadway Cottages Trust* (1955)). In the recent decision of *OT Computers v First National Tricity Finance Ltd* [2003] EWHC 1010, the High Court decided that the expression 'urgent suppliers' used by the claimant company in an attempt to protect its suppliers was void. The expression was considered too vague to satisfy the test for certainty of objects. Secondly, there are discretionary trusts (confusingly also known as 'trust powers'), being trusts where the trustees have a duty to distribute the trust property, but a discretion as to whom within a particular class shall actually benefit and in what shares. An example is where property is given on trust 'to such of my children and in such proportions as my trustees shall decide'. For discretionary trusts, the test for certainty of objects is less strict than that for fixed trusts because the trustees do not actually have to know the identity of every beneficiary, as not every person within the class of beneficiaries will benefit from the trust. Consequently, the test for certainty of objects for a discretionary trust is whether it is possible to say with certainty whether any given individual is, or is not, a member of the class. There is no need to compile a complete list (*McPhail v Doulton* (1972)). The third concept where certainty of objects is relevant is not a trust at all: it is a power of appointment. A power of appointment is a power given to a person (who may or may not be a trustee) to distribute property among such persons within a named class as the person exercising the power (donee of the power) chooses, in such shares as he chooses, or not at all. It differs from a discretionary trust in that a donee of a power has no duty to distribute the property at all and may legitimately make no selection. The test for certainty of objects of powers is the same as that for discretionary trusts, despite the fact that one is mandatory and the other voluntary (*McPhail v Doulton* (1972)).

It will be appreciated, then, that, as far as certainty of objects is concerned, it is necessary, first, to identify exactly what the settlor has created (fixed trust, discretionary trust or power), and then to apply the relevant test for certainty of objects to it. However, it is not always easy to make this initial and important distinction and this only complicates the practical application of the certainty rules. Indeed, even for certainty of intention and certainty of subject matter, we have seen that there is considerable flexibility in the court's approach: the former is largely a matter of construction and defects in the latter can be cured by a court taking a sympathetic view of the donor's instructions.

—————— Question 12 ——————

To what extent is it necessary to be able to distinguish between a trust and a power, particularly when considering the need for certainty of objects under a discretionary trust or power of appointment?

Answer plan ———————————

- Trusts and powers in outline: certainty of beneficiaries;
- discretionary trusts;
- powers: types of powers;
- similarities and opportunities for confusion; and
- differences in subsidiary certainty rules: administrative unworkability and capriciousness.

—————— Answer ——————

The essential nature of a private trust is that a trustee will hold property on trust for identifiable beneficiaries. Save in the case of charities and a small number of exceptional situations, it is not possible to have a trust for a pure purpose. The essential duty imposed upon a trustee is to distribute the trust property according to the wishes of the settlor or testator and in conformity with the terms of the trust, and this is a duty which cannot be delegated to an agent or professional adviser: s 11(2) of the Trustee Act 2000. In this, they will be supervised by the court and be subject to suit by any disaffected beneficiaries: the trust is mandatory and must be carried out. For these reasons, it is of paramount importance that the objects of the trust – the beneficiaries – should be readily identifiable. In the language of Lord Langdale in *Knight v Knight* (1840), 'every trust must have certain objects'. In many cases, of course, the beneficiaries of a trust will be named by the settlor and then there is no doubt that the certainty requirement is fulfilled, as where property is left 'on trust for Mr Smith and Mrs Jones'. However, in other cases, the settlor or testator may have decided to identify the beneficiaries by a class description without naming them individually, as where property is given on trust 'for my relatives' or 'for my friends'. Clearly, gifts on trust for classes of persons who are not named must also have certain objects, for how else will the trustees know how to carry out the trust and the court be sure that they have done so properly?

In similar fashion, the creation of a 'power of appointment' will only be valid if the objects of the power can be ascertained with certainty (*Re Gulbenkian* (1970)). A power of appointment is literally a power given to a person (who may or may not be a trustee) to decide the destination of property, often the property of a testator or settlor. It is similar to a trust save only that the donee of the power (the person who exercises the power) is not under a duty to distribute the property but has complete freedom whether to do so or not. The power is said to be voluntary, and if it is not exercised the donee of the power may keep the property himself, or the settlor/testator may have provided for a 'gift over in default of appointment' (that is, a direction as to where the property should go if the power is not exercised). In general terms, powers of appointment fall into three classes: first, general powers of appointment, where the donee has power to appoint the property among the whole world, including himself, and so such powers are akin to absolute ownership of the property (for example, *Re Beatty (decd)* (1990)); secondly, hybrid powers of appointment, where the donee of the power has power to appoint the property among the whole world except a defined class of individuals (for example, *Re Hay* (1981)); and thirdly, special powers of appointment, where the donee has power to appoint the property among a defined class of individuals (for example, *Re Gulbenkian* (1970)). Obviously, for powers of the second and third type, the excluded or included class of objects of the power must be defined with certainty in order that it is possible to decide whether the power has been validly exercised or not. An example is where the donee has power to appoint 'among his friends' or 'to anyone except his brothers'.

There is, then, a fundamental difference in principle between a trust and a power: the former is mandatory and must be carried out, while the latter is voluntary and may go unexecuted. Unfortunately, in practice, it is very easy to confuse trusts and powers, especially since most powers are given to people who are otherwise trustees and who hold the property itself on trust but have a power (not a trust obligation) over it (being so called 'fiduciary powers'). In practice, very real problems arise because special powers given to trustees can be virtually indistinguishable from discretionary trusts. A discretionary trust exists where trustees are under a duty to distribute trust property among a class of beneficiaries (which a court will enforce), but have a choice as to which of those beneficiaries shall actually benefit and in what proportions. However, as we have seen, the donee of the power does not have to make any appointment at all and the court will not compel him to do so. In any given case, deciding whether there is a trust or a power – and consequently a duty to distribute or not – depends on the court's construction of the instrument which establishes the arrangement. On this, views can legitimately differ, as in *McPhail v Doulton* (1971), where the question of construction as a trust or power went all the way to the House of Lords.

It is now clear that there are crucial differences between a discretionary trust and a power and, although some case law has tended to blur the distinction somewhat by suggesting that a court might exercise a fiduciary power (one given to a trustee) where the donee is unable or unwilling to do so (*Mettoy Pension Trustees Ltd v Evans* (1990); *Re William Makin & Sons Ltd* (1993)), it is still important to be able to distinguish between the two concepts. For example, the scope of the duties of a trustee under a discretionary trust are wider than those of a donee of a power, even a fiduciary one. Obviously, discretionary trustees must carry out the trust and distribute the property, but their duty to consider when and to whom to distribute the property is much wider than that of a donee of a power. A donee of a fiduciary power has merely to consider from time to time whether to exercise the power, and his survey of the range of objects of the class need not be as extensive as that undertaken by a discretionary trustee (*McPhail v Doulton*

(1971)). Indeed, the donee of a pure power (that is, a donee not in a fiduciary position) seems to be under minimal duties, perhaps only to protect those entitled in default of appointment by not exercising the power in favour of anyone outside the class (*Mettoy Pension Trustees Ltd*).

In one respect it has been recognised that discretionary trusts and powers of appointment should be subject to the same principles. The House of Lords, in *McPhail v Doulton* (1971), decided that the test for deciding whether the objects of a discretionary trust were sufficiently certain and the test for deciding whether the objects of a power were sufficiently certain, should be the same, not least because the classification of a disposition as a discretionary trust or a fiduciary power usually turns on fine points of construction. It would be inequitable to make their validity (if the tests were different) depend on such subjective issues. Consequently, according to *McPhail*, the test for certainty of objects of a discretionary trust and a power is the *Re Gulbenkian* test, formally applicable only to powers: viz, that it must be possible to say with certainty whether any given individual is, or is not, a member of the class of beneficiaries or objects (the 'given postulant' test). No higher test was needed for discretionary trusts (as was previously the case: *IRC v Broadway Cottages Trust* (1955)) because, even if the court was called on to execute the discretionary trust, it did not have to divide the trust property equally and did not need to know all the members of the class: that, after all, was not what the settlor intended.

The assimilation of the tests for certainty for these two concepts has brought considerable relief to those charged with making the difficult distinction in practice between a discretionary trust and a power. Of course, as we have seen, fundamental differences between the concepts remain and there will always be cases where it is important to make the distinction *per se*. For example, it seems that 'administrative unworkability' cannot invalidate a power in the same way that it can invalidate a discretionary trust, almost certainly because of the less pressing duties of a donee of a power (*R v District Auditor ex p West Yorkshire MC* (1986)). Likewise, if 'capriciousness' has any application to powers (for example, *Re Manisty* (1974)), it is unlikely that it adds anything to the rules concerning discretionary trusts. However, be that as it may, the decision in *McPhail* should be welcomed because, although there are differences between discretionary trusts and powers, those differences are now related primarily to their operation, not to their validity.

Note

These first two questions (Questions 11 and 12) are very general and require a good knowledge of the case law. The answers to both questions could be expanded considerably. For example, for Question 12, a student could go on to examine the analysis of the 'is or is not test' put forward in *Re Baden (No 2)* (1973), particularly the three different approaches of the judges in that case to a practical application of the test. See Question 13 below.

Question 13

Does the 'is or is not test' propounded by the House of Lords in *McPhail v Doulton* provide clarity in relation to the need for certainty of objects in the creation of a discretionary trust or power?

Answer plan

- Explain the 'is or is not test';
- the move to the 'is or is not test';
- three views of the test: *Re Baden* and redefining concepts; and
- other tests of certainty.

Answer

Since the decision of the House of Lords in *McPhail v Doulton* (1972) much ink has been spilt over the meaning of the 'is or is not' test (given postulant test) in relation to the certainty requirements for the creation of discretionary trusts and powers. The central issue arises because both discretionary trusts and powers of appointment give trustees or donees of the power (as the case may be) a discretion to distribute property to specific individuals selected from a class of objects who are themselves defined by reference to a generic term. Thus, property on discretionary trusts 'for my employees' raises the same issue as property to be appointed 'among my friends', for in each case it must be possible to determine who is an 'employee' or who is a 'friend' in order to ensure that the trustees or donees are acting lawfully. Consequently, failure to define the objects of the discretionary trust or power with sufficient certainty will render the trust or power void (*Re Baden (No 2)* (1973) (*sub nom McPhail v Doulton (No 2)* (1973))).

Until the decision in *McPhail v Doulton*, there was a different test for certainty of objects depending on whether the settlor had established a discretionary trust or a power. For a discretionary trust, the test for certainty of objects used to be whether it was possible to draw up a complete list of the class so that, if the trustees made no selection from the class (despite their duty to do so), the court could divide up the property equally between all potential beneficiaries in execution of the trust (*IRC v Broadway Cottages Trust* (1954)). However, in *McPhail*, Lord Wilberforce pointed out that equal distribution among the entire class of potential beneficiaries was probably the last thing the settlor intended (why else give a discretion to the trustees?) and consequently, there was no reason to apply the 'fixed list' test to discretionary trusts. Moreover, given that it was often extremely difficult to distinguish in practice between a discretionary trust and a power, it was not sensible to cause the invalidity of discretionary trusts by insisting on a higher test of certainty when the distinction between a trust and a power could turn on the finest point of construction. Consequently, the House of Lords decided that the test for certainty of objects for discretionary trusts should be the same as that for powers: viz, whether it is possible to say with certainty whether any given individual is, or is not, a member of the class of objects specified by the testator or settlor (*Re Gulbenkian* (1970)).

Unfortunately, this test is easy to state but difficult to apply. After the House of Lords had decided in *McPhail v Doulton* what the appropriate test for discretionary trusts should be, the case was remitted to the High Court for determination whether the trusts in that case conformed to it. From the decision in the High Court, the matter was appealed to the Court of Appeal, where, in three separate judgments, the validity of the *McPhail/Baden* trusts were confirmed, all three judges agreeing, but for different reasons, that the discretionary trusts in favour of various classes of persons, including 'employees' and their 'relatives and dependants', were sufficiently certain as to objects. Essentially, then, the decision of the Court of Appeal in *Re Baden (No 2)* (1973) (*sub nom McPhail v Doulton (No 2)*) provided the opportunity for a thorough explanation of the 'is or is not' test, but what emerged was three individual interpretations of what the test required in practice.

Before examining the judgments in that case in detail, an important distinction needs to be drawn between different kinds of uncertainty of objects, as this may help to explain the issues at the heart of the problem. It will be remembered that the objects of a discretionary trust or power may be defined by reference to a class description: 'employees', 'friends', 'relatives', etc. When deciding if it is possible to say whether any given individual is or is not a member of these classes, it is important to distinguish between 'conceptual' uncertainty and 'evidential' uncertainty. A class description is conceptually uncertain when the words used by the settlor or testator do not have a precise meaning in themselves, irrespective of the factual circumstances surrounding the particular case. For example, if the class of beneficiaries or objects of the power are 'my friends' or 'people with whom I am acquainted', there will be conceptual uncertainty of objects because the concepts used by the settlor are inherently uncertain: the class description is in itself inherently vague and imprecise. Conversely, a class description is evidentially uncertain when it is impossible to determine whether, in fact, a person falls within the class description. The issue is one of evidence, not of the meaning of the words used to define the class. Thus, a trust 'for my employees' may be evidentially uncertain if there is no method of determining who is in fact an employee, even if the concept of an 'employee' is clear enough. As we shall see, it is disputed whether the 'is or is not' test requires conceptual certainty of the class of objects, evidential certainty of the class of objects or both.

Starting first with the judgment of Stamp LJ in *Re Baden (No 2)* (1973), it is clear that he approached the 'is or is not' test literally. In his view, in order for there to be certainty of objects for a discretionary trust or power, it must be possible to say with certainty whether any given individual was or was not a member of the class in fact. In other words, conceptual and evidential certainty of the class was required, for otherwise it would not be possible to say whether anyone *was not* a member of the class. It will be appreciated that this is a rigorous standard as it may mean that a trust or power is declared void even though the settlor has drafted his dispositions very carefully, the fault lying in lack of evidence outside of his or her control. For example, a discretionary trust or power for 'my employees' would be void simply because there was not enough evidence to prove positively or negatively who actually was an employee, even though the concept of 'an employee' was in itself clear and unambiguous. Consequently, there has been much criticism of this view of the *McPhail* test, not least because it requires a degree of certainty barely less than the 'complete list' test so decisively rejected by the House of Lords in that case.

A recognition of these difficulties was at the heart of Sachs LJ's rejection of this literal approach in the second judgment in *Re Baden (No 2)*. In his judgment, the crucial question was whether the class was conceptually certain. If the concept employed by the settlor had a precise and certain meaning, the trust or power would not be defeated by evidential difficulties. In other words, if it could be said whether any person was or was not a member of the class in theory, the *McPhail* test was satisfied. A person who could not prove evidentially that he or she was within the conceptually certain class would be regarded as outside it. For example, the 'is or is not' test would be satisfied by class descriptions, such as 'employees' or 'sons', which were in themselves inherently precise, but not by vague concepts such as 'friends' or 'acquaintances'. This very practical and workable view has much to commend it because it avoids confusing questions about the inherent validity of the trust or power (conceptual certainty) with difficulties surrounding its execution (evidential certainty). It is, perhaps, the most justifiable of the views to emerge from *Re Baden (No 2)*.

The third judge in the case, Megaw LJ, adopted the least stringent interpretation of the 'is or is not' test and one that nearly every class description will satisfy. In his view, the test was satisfied if it could be said of 'a substantial number' of persons that they were within the class conceptually, even if it were not possible to make a clear decision about every potential beneficiary or object. His reasoning was simply that the trustees/donees of the power could effectively administer the trust or power in such circumstances and, therefore, it should not be invalidated. As indicated, this test will be satisfied by most class gifts because there will be few class descriptions that do not have a central meaning and where it is not possible to say of a 'substantial number' (whatever that means) whether they are in the class or not. Indeed, Megaw LJ's analysis does not sit well with the House of Lords' formulation in *McPhail* that it must be possible to say of *any given person* whether they are or are not within the class. Indeed, it is arguable that Megaw LJ's approach is but a variant from the 'one postulant approach' that was overruled by the House of Lords in *Re Gulbenkian*.

This is the state of affairs after *Re Baden (No 2)*: we know, in principle, the test for certainty of objects for discretionary trusts and powers, but we have been given different views about how to apply it in practice. Furthermore, it is clear from *Re Baden (No 2)* that it is possible first to construe the settlor's class description and then apply the 'is or is not' test to the class description so construed. So, in *Baden*, Sachs and Megaw LJJ decided that 'relatives' actually meant 'able to trace descent from a common ancestor' and, therefore, on application of the 'is or is not' test, the class so redefined was certain. Stamp LJ, on the other hand, thought 'relatives' meant 'next of kin' and was both conceptually and evidentially certain for that reason. Clearly, this power of construction will allow a court to render most class gifts certain if it so chooses, simply by redefining the testator's class description in a manner that makes the test easier to be satisfied. Another difficulty is that there is no agreement as to whether questions of conceptual certainty can be delegated by the settlor to a third person, as where the settlor directs that his brother may conclusively determine who is a 'friend'. On the one hand, this removes the question of objective validity of the trust or power from the hands of the court (*Re Wynn* (1952)) but, on the other, it has merit in that it clearly reflects the settlor's wishes (*Dundee General Hospital Board v Walker* (1952)). If we then remind ourselves that absolute gifts to individuals subject to a condition precedent (for example, '£100 to any person who is my friend') are subject to a completely different test of certainty (viz, whether it could be said of just one person that he or she satisfies the condition (*Re Barlow* (1979)) and that class gifts and gifts subject to a condition precedent can be easily confused, it is apparent that the certainty rules for discretionary trusts and powers are not defined with as much clarity as we might like. Again, even if the objects of the trust or power are sufficiently certain, there are the further hurdles of 'administrative unworkability' in discretionary trusts (*R v District Auditor ex p West Yorkshire MC* (1986)) and 'capriciousness' with powers (*Re Manisty* (1974)) to surmount. All in all, a person predicting in advance whether a discretionary trust or power has sufficiently certain objects may make a well informed estimate, but cannot be entirely confident that he or she will be right.

 # Question 14

Assess the validity of the following dispositions in the will of Thomas, who died in December 2005:

(a) £10,000 to my Aunt Agatha, knowing that she will use the money in order to secure the future of my daughters;

(b) my houses in Penzance and St Ives on trust for my daughters, Amanda and Barbara, for their lifetimes and thence in equal shares between such of my other kinsfolk now living as may be resident in the county of Cornwall, save only that no person of the Protestant religion shall be entitled to any portion; and

(c) the residue of my estate to my Executors for such of my colleagues at work as they shall in their discretion think fit.

Thomas worked for the National Health Service at various hospitals throughout his life, but spent the last 10 years of his working life in Penzance General Hospital, which was destroyed by fire just after his retirement in 2003.

Answer plan

- Brief introduction to the concept of the three certainties;
- certainty of intention: construction of the gift;
- certainty of objects: fixed trusts; conditions precedent; and
- certainty of objects: trust or power; test for certainty; construing the gift; evidential difficulties; administrative unworkability.

Answer

It is a cardinal principle of the law of equity that a trust may only be valid – that is, enforceable by the beneficiaries against the trustee – if it has been created with certainty of intention, certainty of subject matter and certainty of objects (*Knight v Knight* (1840)). Along with the beneficiary principle, these three certainties represent the inherent attributes of a trust. The requirement for certainty of intention (or certainty of words) ensures that the potential trustee of property is clearly placed under a duty to use the property in the way intended by the settlor or testator. Such certainty exists where the words used by the settlor or testator reveal the imposition of a trust obligation on the intended trustee as distinct from an intention to transfer the property to that person absolutely. It is what distinguishes a transfer by way of trust from a transfer by way of absolute gift (*Re Conolly* (1909)). The second of the three certainties, certainty of subject matter, requires that both the property which is to be the subject matter of the trust (*Palmer v Simmonds* (1854)) and the extent of the intended equitable owners' beneficial interests (*Boyce v Boyce* (1849); *Re Challoner Club Ltd* (1997); *Margulies v Margulies* (2000)) are certain, or at least capable of being rendered certain. This will ensure that the trustee is aware of the precise scope of his or her duties under the trust. Thirdly, there must be certainty of objects in order that the trustee should know in whose favour he or she must perform the trust, so identifying who may apply to the court should the trustee fail in this duty. The precise requirements of certainty of objects vary for different kinds of trusts and powers but, in all cases, a settlor's or testator's failure to define their objects with sufficient certainty will mean that the property is held on resulting trust for the settlor or residuary legatees (*McPhail v Doulton* (1971)). This particular problem concerns various aspects of the 'three certainties', and each limb of Thomas's testamentary disposition will be considered in turn.

(a) £10,000 to Aunt Agatha

The issue raised by this disposition is whether the gift of £10,000 to Aunt Agatha is by way of trust or as an absolute gift – in other words, whether there is sufficient certainty of intention to create a trust. If a trust is created, then it becomes necessary to consider whether there are any valid objects of the trust and whether they are defined with sufficient certainty.

The imposition of a trust over the money requires Thomas to have imposed a mandatory obligation upon Aunt Agatha to carry out his wishes. This is purely a matter of construction of the words used (*Lambe v Eames* (1871)), although it is clear that precatory words (words of expression, hope or desire) will not of themselves impose a trust on the recipient of property in the absence of corroborative evidence (*Re Conolly* (1909)). In our case, the words used by Thomas are stronger than precatory words: Thomas does not 'hope' or 'wish' that Agatha will carry out his wishes, he 'knows' that she will. However, it is still not certain that this is enough to constitute a trust obligation. For example, in *Re Adams and the Kensington Vestry* (1884), a gift 'in full confidence that …' was held to be absolute and not mandatory in the way of a trust and in *Margulies v Margulies* (2000) some communications from the testator were mandatory and some were precatory and the court decided that this demonstrated an overall lack of intention to create a trust. On balance, it is likely that the bequest to Aunt Agatha will be construed as an absolute gift, essentially because of the absence of any other indication that this is intended to be a trust. Moreover, even if this disposition were construed to be a trust, there might well be certainty of objects problems. While it is obvious that a trust in favour of 'my daughters' is perfectly certain as to objects, the disposition in this case is 'in order to secure the future of my daughters'. A literal reading of this suggests that this is a trust for *purposes* connected with Thomas's daughters, and trusts for purposes are void (*Re Endacott* (1960)). Of course, it might be possible to construe the disposition (if it were a trust in the first place) in favour of the daughters *per se* (compare *Re Osoba* (1979)) or as a trust saved by the *Re Denley* principle. However, these difficulties in defining the objects of the trust precisely only add to the doubts surrounding the lack of certainty of intention (eg, *Re Kayford* (1975)). Consequently, in all probability, this is an absolute gift to Aunt Agatha, who may use the property for the benefit of Thomas's daughters if she chooses, but cannot be compelled to do so (*Lassence v Tierney* (1849)).

(b) The houses in Penzance and St Ives

It is clear from the wording of the second disposition in Thomas's will that a trust is intended. Although use of the word 'trust' does not always impose a trust in law (*Tito v Waddell (No 2)* (1977)), there is nothing here to suggest otherwise. Likewise, the subject matter of the trust is certain, always assuming Thomas did own a house in Penzance and St Ives. The problem is, then, one of certainty of objects. Clearly, there is no difficulty with the life interests given to Thomas's daughters, who are both named. The disposition will operate under the Trusts of Land and Appointment of Trustees Act 1996, with Amanda and Barbara being given the rights to possession, etc, established by that statute. The problem arises with the class of persons entitled to the reversionary interests, being 'my kinsfolk now living as may be resident in the county of Cornwall' and then subject to an exclusion against any person of the Protestant religion.

First, it is necessary to determine the nature of the trust affecting the two houses for this will help determine whether there is certainty of objects of the reversionary class. The houses are given in equal shares to the 'kinsfolk', etc, and thus Thomas has fixed in advanced the share of each person within the class. The trustees have no discretion to apportion the trust property among the class but must divide it up equally. This is a fixed trust and because the court must be able to execute the trust in default of the trustees and divide the property equally, the test of certainty of the objects is the 'complete list' test laid down in *IRC v Broadway Cottages Trust* (1955). It must be possible to draw up a complete list of all Thomas's 'kinsfolk' who currently reside in the county of Cornwall.

This may prove difficult, not because of the residence restriction, for that should be easy enough to determine, but because 'kinsfolk' is an imprecise concept. It will only be possible to draw up a list of kinsfolk if we know what 'kinsfolk' actually means. Such inherent uncertainty in the concept used by Thomas to define his class may prove fatal unless the court is prepared to redefine the concept for the trustees in the same way that the Court of Appeal redefined 'relatives' in *Re Baden (No 2)* (1973). This should not be ruled out since a court of equity will generally prefer validity to invalidity, especially if the trustees' duties are not otherwise difficult to perform evidentially. Finally, even if the court adopts a benevolent attitude to the fixed trust, there is still the requirement that no person may have a share if he or she is 'of the Protestant religion'. Clearly, the point is that 'not being a Protestant' is to be a condition precedent for entry to the class of beneficiaries. Consequently, the scope of the condition precedent must also be certain because, otherwise, it will be impossible to determine who has been excluded. The test of certainty for conditions precedent is that it must be possible to say with certainty whether one person would or would not fulfil the condition (*Re Allen* (1959) and *Re Barlow* (1979)). As is clear from *Re Tuck* (1978), a condition precedent related to religion can be regarded as certain under this test although, in that case, a third person was given the task of deciding who fell within the religious condition. Subject then to it being possible to define what qualifies a person as 'a Protestant', the condition precedent will be valid. If the fixed trust for the class fails for other reasons, the validity or not of the condition precedent is irrelevant.

(c) The residue of Thomas's estate

The gift of residue for 'such of my colleagues at work' raises, once again, the problem of certainty of objects, those objects being defined by reference to a class description. As regards this disposition, it is clear that the executors are given a discretion as to whom from among the class they shall select to receive a portion of the residue, and in what proportions. So, this part of Thomas's will discloses either a discretionary trust for the class or a special power of appointment given to the trustees to appoint among the class. Of course, the difference is crucial so far as the executors are concerned because, if this is a discretionary trust, they are under a mandatory obligation to make a selection from among the class and distribute the property whereas, if this is a power, they may decide not to distribute and cannot be compelled to do so. Whether this disposition discloses a trust or a power is a matter of construction and, as *McPhail v Doulton* (1972) shows, the distinction is not always easy to draw. In our case, it is important that there is no gift over in default of appointment, perhaps suggesting that the executors *must* choose from among the class, although the absence of a gift over does not always foretell a trust, since the testator may be content to allow the property to revert to next of kin if the power is not exercised (*Re Weekes* (1897)). On balance, however, given that the gift to this class is already of the residuary estate and consequently the beneficiaries in default would be difficult to identify, we can legitimately surmise that Thomas intended this to be a discretionary trust.

Since *McPhail v Doulton*, the test for certainty of objects of a discretionary trust and a power have been assimilated and, even if this is a power, the test we must apply is whether it is possible to say with certainty whether any given person is, or is not, a member of the class (*McPhail*). Unfortunately, although this test is easy to state, it is difficult to apply because the leading case on its application (*Re Baden (No 2)* (1973)) gives us three alternative approaches. According to Stamp LJ, the test is satisfied only if it is possible to say in fact whether any given person is, or is not, a member of the class and this requires both the class to be defined with precision and there to be enough evidence available to make positive or negative choices in respect of all potential applicants. This is a strict test and if this is the correct approach, it is unlikely that Thomas's disposition will be valid: for example, in view of the fire at his last place of work, will there be sufficient employment records to indicate with whom he worked, even if it were possible to say who then qualified as a 'colleague'? Secondly, even if we take Sachs LJ's approach, it may not be possible to hold this discretionary trust valid. In his view, the test is satisfied if it is possible to say, in theory, whether any given person is, or is not, a member of the class, irrespective of whether there is enough evidence to make such a decision. The class must be conceptually certain in the sense that the concept used by the settlor must be precise. The corollary is that evidential difficulties will not invalidate a trust because any person who cannot prove that he or she is a member of the class will be deemed to be outside it. However, it is likely that Thomas's disposition cannot satisfy even this less strict version of the 'is or is not' test: that is, the concept of a 'colleague' may be too imprecise to allow us to say who is or is not within its ambit, even in theory. The only hope would be if the court were prepared to re-interpret 'colleague' in some way that made it more certain, perhaps as 'fellow employee' (*Re Baden (No 2)* (1973)). Finally, we come to Megaw LJ who proposed the least strict version of the 'is or is not' test, believing it to be satisfied if it could be said of a substantial number of persons that they were inside the class, even if it could not be said of every potential person whether he or she was or not. It may be that Thomas's dispositions would satisfy this version of the test for it seems possible to say of many people that they were his 'colleagues', even if we could not say definitely of every person who presented themselves whether they were or were not. Unfortunately, however, Megaw LJ's approach does seem at variance with that of the House of Lords in *McPhail*, and it is the view of the 'given postulant' test that is commonly criticised (being vague and imprecise). Most commentators prefer the approach of Sachs LJ.

The conclusion is then that Thomas's third disposition fails for uncertainty of objects. It may be that a court would be prepared to redefine the concept of 'colleague' so as to make it more certain and then apply the 'is or is not' test to the class description so redefined (as in *Re Baden*), but that cannot be guaranteed. Indeed, even then, the executors face one more hurdle, for it may be that the class of the discretionary trust is 'administratively unworkable' and so void for 'secondary uncertainty'. This concept was expounded by Lord Wilberforce in *McPhail* and it is clear from *R v District Auditor ex p West Yorkshire MC* (1986) that if the settlor or testator stipulates a class so large that the trustees cannot effectively fulfil their duties, nor exercise their discretion properly under a discretionary trust, that trust will fail. In our case, Thomas's large number of former places of work may bring the class description within this principle. This will be a matter of judgment, and many people would argue that a trust should not be void for administrative unworkability simply because the class is large, but only when this makes it impossible for the trustees to carry out their duties properly.

Note

This is a typical problem on the three certainties, with concentration on certainty of objects. When considering certainty of objects, it is important to appreciate that the three versions of the *Baden* test may cause different results for the validity of the trust or power. All must be considered and *Baden* should *not* be regarded as having a clear *ratio decidendi*.

Question 15

George, a wealthy banker, comes to you for advice about a number of financial arrangements he wishes to make for his family and others. He has already drawn up a trust deed which appoints Abbott and Hardy as his executors and trustees and charges them with distributing:

(a) a reasonable amount of the money from my account at the Bounty Bank, within three years of my death, between such of my employees as my wife shall determine, the remainder to be divided equally between my children; and

(b) £1,000,000 to the inhabitants of my old village of Stanbrooke in such proportions as my trustees shall in their discretion determine.

During your discussions with George, it transpires that he has several bank accounts at the Bounty Bank and that his employees number over 5,000. Furthermore, your own researches reveal that the village of Stanbrooke now forms part of Greater London and is now officially called the London Borough of Stanbrooke. George also wishes to give his trustees the authority to distribute the residue of his estate among struggling authors and artists resident in the UK, providing that, if the residue is not distributed fully within three years, it should be given absolutely to some charity of his trustees' choosing.

He seeks your advice on all of his proposals.

Answer plan

- The three certainties in outline;
- trust or power: certainty of subject matter; certainty of objects; conditions precedent;
- administrative unworkability; and
- discretionary trust or power: which is preferable when considering the testator's wishes?

Answer

The various proposals put forward by George need to be considered in the light of the three certainties required to establish a valid trust. In particular, this problem raises preliminary questions about certainty of subject matter and calls for a distinction to be drawn between trusts and powers, as this will define the nature of the trustees' duties. Finally, as George intends to make a number of class gifts – that is, gifts to a group of people who are not named individually but defined by reference to a shared characteristic – it is necessary to consider whether the objects of his trusts or powers satisfy the requirement for certainty of objects.

(a) Reasonable amount of money from George's account at the Bounty Bank, etc

It is clear that George intends to transfer the money in his 'account' to his executors and trustees for them to hold at the direction of his wife. The first point must be to advise George that there is a danger that his disposition will be void for uncertainty of subject matter, irrespective of whether it is a trust or a power. There are two problems in this regard. On the one hand, the property held to his wife's direction is said to be 'a reasonable amount' of money standing in a bank account. This is indeterminate and it is unclear over what proportion of the money George's wife may exercise her discretion. There is apparent uncertainty of subject matter. In *Re Golay* (1965), a trust of 'reasonable income' was held to be certain (reasonableness being an objective limitation that could be decided by the court), but the best advice would be to warn George not to rely on the court adopting a similarly generous construction of his will. He should be specific about the amount given to his wife's discretion. Likewise, and in any event, there is manifest uncertainty of subject matter, given that George has not identified from which of his accounts at the Bounty Bank the money is to be drawn (see, by analogy, *Boyes v Boyes*). This should be cured by a more accurate description of the specific source of the subject matter of the proposed trust/power, perhaps by use of an account number.

George should also be advised that this disposition could be construed in two ways, each investing his wife with different responsibilities and having fundamentally different consequences for his employees. First, this could be a non-exhaustive discretionary trust in favour of his employees, with a fixed trust in equal shares for his daughters of that amount of money which remains undistributed. Secondly, this could be a power of appointment given to his wife – probably as a non-fiduciary – with a fixed trust in default of appointment for his daughters in equal shares. The matter is not academic because, if the first construction is adopted, George's wife will be under a duty to distribute at least some money amongst the class of employees, who can then be regarded as beneficiaries under a trust able to compel her to do so. If, on the other hand, the second construction is adopted, George's wife will have a mere power to distribute among the employees, which she may or may not exercise as she chooses. The employees would be merely objects of the power with no enforceable claim to the property, with the daughters being regarded as the beneficiaries in default under the fixed trust.

Clearly, for both George's wife and the employees, resolution of this issue is important. The disposition itself gives little away, although leaving the 'remainder' to his daughters does suggest an intention to benefit at least some of his employees and hence a duty to distribute (a discretionary trust) might be implied. Conversely, it is rare to see the power of discretion under a discretionary trust being given to someone who is not a trustee (the wife), and it might be thought that the reference to George's daughters is intended to be a gift over in default of appointment, thus indicating a power (*Mettoy Pension Trustees Ltd v Evans* (1990)). To avoid this confusion, George should be advised to indicate clearly both the nature of his wife's duties and the rights of his employees. However, in at least one respect, it does not matter whether this is a discretionary trust or power because, since *McPhail v Doulton* (1971), the test for certainty of objects for discretionary trusts and powers has been the same. Moreover, it is likely that it *is* possible to say with certainty whether any given person is, or is not, an 'employee', and thus the class of beneficiaries or objects (as the case may be) is certain. This would be so whether Stamp LJ's, Sachs LJ's or Megaw LJ's analysis of the 'is or is not' test put forward in *Re Baden (No 2)* (1973) is accepted as correct, for there appear to be no evidential problems such as would trouble Stamp LJ. Finally, if this disposition is construed to be a discretionary trust, George should not fear that his disposition will be void for 'administrative unworkability'. There is nothing here to compare with the trust in *R v District Auditor ex p West Yorkshire MC* (1986), as the class of 5,000 does not seem too disparate or large to prevent his wife making a rational selection. Likewise, if this is a power, there is no 'capriciousness' here within the meaning given by Templeman J in *Re Manisty* (1974).

(b) £1,000,000 to the inhabitants of my old village of Stanbrooke, etc

This is clearly an attempt to establish a discretionary trust in favour of a class of beneficiaries defined by reference to a geographical condition. The intention is clear from the words used by George (that is, the trustees *shall* distribute), and the subject matter is certain. Any difficulty that there may be arises from doubts as to the certainty of the objects of the intended discretionary trust. There are three issues here, the first of which may be resolved by construction of George's disposition.

The first potential difficulty arises from the fact that the 'village' of Stanbrooke apparently is no more, having been subsumed by the London Borough of the same name. However, although this appears to raise questions concerning the certainty of the objects of the class, it will not be fatal to the validity of George's discretionary trust. For example, it may be possible to identify the old village and, in any event, there is no reason why, on a benevolent construction of the terms of the trust, the London Borough should not be taken to be the relevant geographical limitation. The matter is really one of ascertainability of the class rather than of certainty proper. However, the second difficulty is more pressing: whether, under the *McPhail* test of certainty of objects for discretionary trusts, it is possible to say with certainty whether any given person is, or is not, an 'inhabitant' of Stanbrooke. Much depends on whether the description 'inhabitant' is conceptually certain (compare Sachs LJ in *Re Baden (No 2)* (1973)), for there is unlikely to be any evidential difficulties once the class is geographically defined. In this sense, Stamp LJ's interpretation in *Baden* will not cause difficulties. Thus, if 'inhabitant' can be said to be certain – perhaps construed to mean 'resident' – George's discretionary trust will be valid. This is the most likely result, given the court's preference for validity rather than invalidity. Note, also, that in *R v District Auditor ex p West Yorkshire MC* (1986), a discretionary trust for 'inhabitants' did not fail the 'is or is not' test of certainty. Finally, there is always the danger that a court would decide that a class defined geographically was 'administratively unworkable' in the same way that the court in *West Yorkshire* went on to hold the discretionary trust void even though it had passed the 'is or is not' test. In that case, there were some 2.5 m potential beneficiaries and it must be a question of degree in each case whether the trustees can exercise their responsibilities under the trust in the light of the size and composition of the class. If there is a danger of this in our case – and to some extent it will depend on the geographical construction given to the trust – George would be best to define his class with greater precision so as not to overburden his trustees.

The final issue raised by George concerns the residue of his estate. George's desire to have his trustees distribute the property among 'struggling' artists and authors, and thence to a charity, might be best achieved by giving his trustees a power of appointment in favour of the artists, subject to an express discretionary trust for charity by way of gift over in default of appointment. There will be no problem with certainty of objects in respect of the discretionary trust for charity because 'charity' is a legal term of art and has, by definition, a certain meaning (see, for example, *Commissioners for Special Purposes of Income Tax v Pemsel* (1891)). A power in favour of 'struggling' artists and authors presents more difficulties, as it may well be that such a description will fail the 'is or is not' test as being conceptually uncertain (*Re Baden (No 2)* (1973)). The likelihood is that 'struggling' will be regarded as too subjective and that the power will fail the test. Indeed, even if George attempts to avoid evidential difficulties by delegating questions of fact to a third party (*Re Coxen* (1948)), it is unclear whether he could also avoid difficulties of conceptual certainty by delegating this issue (*Re Wynn* (1952); *Dundee General Hospital Board v Walker* (1952)). George should rethink this part of his proposed will, perhaps substituting a gift to a charity concerned with authors and artists instead of the power which attempts to benefit them directly.

Question 16

To what extent have the courts withdrawn from the fundamental principle that private purpose trusts are invalid?

Answer plan

- The beneficiary principle and its purpose;
- recognised exceptions and the problem of perpetuity;
- *Re Denley*;
- unincorporated associations: exception to, or application of the beneficiary principle; and
- *Quistclose* trusts.

Answer

When a person accepts the obligation of a trustee, he or she submits both to the jurisdiction of the court of equity and to the onerous duties of trusteeship. It is inherent in the concept of a trust that a court must be able to control and enforce the trusteeship and, if necessary, compel the trustees to carry out their duties. There are several methods by which a court can exercise an effective enforcement jurisdiction, not least by requiring that all trusts have certain objects. Similarly, it is equally important that there must actually be *someone* in whose favour the court can decree performance of the trust and who can apply to the court to enforce its terms. Consequently, with the exception of charitable trusts (which can be enforced by the Attorney General on behalf of the Crown as *parens patriae*), a trust must be made for the benefit of human beneficiaries. There must be a *cestui que trust* in whose favour the court can decree performance (*Morice v Bishop of Durham* (1804); *Re Wood* (1949)). This is the 'beneficiary principle', and it means that, with the exception of charities, nearly all trusts for a purpose are void (*Re Endacott* (1960)).

The beneficiary principle – or the rule against non-charitable purpose trusts as it is sometimes called – is fundamental to the validity of a trust. Many examples abound of trusts for purposes being declared invalid because they are not for the benefit of ascertained or ascertainable individuals. For example, in *Re Astor* (1952), a trust for, *inter alia*, 'the establishment, maintenance and improvement of good understanding, sympathy and co-operation between nations' was held void and in *Re Endacott* itself, a testamentary trust 'for the purpose of providing some good useful memorial to myself' failed for want of a human beneficiary. In fact, as *Re Astor* demonstrates, the worthiness of the settlor's purpose is *prima facie* irrelevant in determining the validity of the trust, for unless the settlor's intended purpose is so beneficial to the community that it amounts to a charity, it cannot be upheld because of the absence of anyone to enforce it and the difficulty in deciding whether its objects have been achieved (see, also, *Southwood v AG* (2000): trust for demilitarisation not a charity and void as a purpose trust). This is the basic principle, but it would be a unique rule of equity that had no exceptions. After all, equity, as a system of law, developed in order to mitigate the harshness of the rigid common law rules. Not surprisingly, therefore, there are a number of exceptional situations where trusts have been held valid despite being apparently or actually for a non-charitable purpose.

The first point to remember is that the meaning of every trust must be determined in the light of the words used by the settlor or testator. It is perfectly possible for a trust which, on its face, appears to be for a purpose to be construed as a trust for an individual or individuals (*Re Sanderson* (1857)). A good example is provided by *Re Osoba* (1979), where a trust 'for the training of my daughter' was construed to be a trust absolutely for the daughter, the testator's expression of purpose (that is, 'for training') having no legal effect. The point here is that these trusts are not purpose trusts at all, and that, as a matter of construction, the indication of a purpose or motive for the absolute gift is of no legal importance. They are trusts for individuals with a non-legal, super-added motive.

In contrast to the above category, it is also clear that special kinds of purpose trusts which actually benefit individuals directly or indirectly may be upheld by the court, providing certain conditions are met. This is known as the *Re Denley* principle, although there may well have been examples of this type of trust before that case (for example, *Re Abbott* (1900)). It is important to realise that these trusts are a true exception to the beneficiary principle. They are trusts for purposes which the court holds valid simply because there are individuals with *locus standi* who can apply to have the purpose carried out. Of course, the individuals directly or indirectly benefited have no equitable interest in the trust property itself: they are not beneficiaries in law. The essence of the matter, as explained in *Re Denley* (1969), is that the beneficiary principle is designed to eliminate purpose trusts of an abstract or impersonal nature, so that any purpose which may be accomplished with certainty and which does thereby confer a benefit directly or indirectly on human beneficiaries should not be declared void. Thus, in *Re Denley*, a trust for the maintenance of a sports ground (a purpose) for use by the employees of a company (the individuals indirectly benefited) was valid on the ground that the employees had *locus standi* to ensure that the trustees put the purpose into effect.

However, because a *Re Denley* type of trust is a true purpose trust, it must not infringe the rule against perpetuities. Under this principle, those non-charitable purpose trusts which, as an exception to the beneficiary principle are regarded as valid, must not last longer than the perpetuity period; that is, for no longer than a certain maximum duration (*Morice v Bishop of Durham* (1804)). The reason is that as a matter of public policy, property should not be tied up indefinitely and so be lost to the general economy. The maximum period for which a *Re Denley* purpose trust may last is 'a life in being' plus 21 years. A 'life in being' is simply a person alive at the time the purpose trust comes into existence (usually named by the settlor or testator or implied from the trust document) and it is the length of that person's life, plus 21 years, that defines the maximum period of duration of the trust. More important, however, is the rule that it must be possible to say at the outset of the trust whether its duration will be confined to the perpetuity period and any possibility – of even the most remote and speculative kind (see, in another context, *Figg v Clarke* (1997)) – that it will not, will render the trust void for perpetuity. Consequently, in order to avoid perpetuity, the purpose trust must be expressly or impliedly limited to operate within the perpetuity period by the terms of the trust. This can be achieved by naming the lives in being and limiting the trust to 21 years from the death of the last survivor, by limiting the trust to 21 years from the testator's death (who will have been the life in being), or by restricting the trust to 'such period as the law allows' (*Leahy v AG for New South Wales* (1959) and s 15(4) of the Perpetuities and Accumulations Act 1964). In *Re Denley* itself, the trust was limited specifically to the perpetuity period and so was upheld by the court.

The *Re Denley* principle is a refinement of the rule against purpose trusts and, in principle, it can operate to validate any purpose trust that meets both the requirements of perpetuity and the need for ascertainable individuals indirectly benefited. In addition there are some purpose trusts for very specific purposes which are regarded as valid as being anomalous exceptions to the beneficiary principle. These are so called 'trusts of imperfect obligation'; 'imperfect' because there is no beneficiary as such to enforce the trust. Although the categories may not now be extended (*Re Endacott* (1960)), they have been held valid because the trustees were prepared to undertake the purpose, because the purpose was certain, because there was no perpetuity and because the court had sympathy with the specific motive of the testator on the occasion the validity of the trust was challenged. However, the exceptional nature of these trusts, usually linked to a testator making provision for certain matters after his death, makes it likely that even these exceptional cases will be void if an attempt is made to establish them by *inter vivos* trust. Again, as noted above, because these are purpose trusts, the rule against perpetuities applies in the same way as it applies to *Re Denley* type trusts. There must be some express or implied limitation to perpetuity when the purpose trust is established (*Morice v Bishop of Durham* (1804)).

The specific purpose trusts which may be valid under these principles are, first, trusts for the erection or maintenance of tombs or monuments, either to the testator or some other person (*Mussett v Bingle* (1876)), it being assumed in the case of trusts to erect monuments that this task will be completed within the perpetuity period, while trusts to maintain monuments must be limited to perpetuity in the usual way (*Re Hooper* (1932)). Secondly, trusts for the upkeep of animals after the testator's death, providing, again, that they are limited to the perpetuity period (*Mitford v Reynolds* (1848)). However, the matter is not entirely clear as, in one case (*Re Dean* (1889)), the judge accepted that a purpose trust for the care of an animal could be valid for the life of the animal, and this is not generally taken to be a sufficient perpetuity period in law. Likewise, in other cases, it is not clear whether the gift was for the animal *per se* or to a person provided he looked after the animal (*Pettingall v Pettingall* (1842)). Thirdly, trusts for the saying of masses for the soul of the testator may be upheld (*Re Gibbons* (1917)), although they may occasionally be charitable (*Re Hetherington* (1990)), again if limited to perpetuity. Fourthly, and very exceptionally, a trust for the promotion of fox hunting was upheld in *Re Thompson* (1934) on a spurious analogy with the animals cases.

Finally, brief mention should be made of two other matters which relate to the beneficiary principle. First, there are many examples of settlors and testators attempting to give property to *unincorporated* associations – such as the local brass band or gardening club – which appear to fall foul of the beneficiary principle. The problem is simply that unincorporated associations have no legal personality and cannot, therefore, be beneficiaries under a trust. The difficulties this poses have been avoided by construing gifts to unincorporated associations not as gifts on trust for their purposes but as gifts to the individual members of the association who will then use the property to carry out the functions of the association (*Re Recher's Trust* (1972) and *Artistic Upholstery Ltd v Art Forma (Ltd)* (1999)). This is so even if the settlor's or testator's gift is expressed to be for a purpose. Once again, what seems to be a purpose trust is not so taken, because of a favourable construction by the court. Likewise, so called *Quistclose* trusts (from *Barclays Bank v Quistclose Investments* (1970)), whereby a person (A) gives money to another (B) for the single purpose of enabling B to pay his debts to a creditor (C) appear to be purpose trusts – the payment of a debt. However, they have been variously analysed as either a form of the *Re Denley* trust (*Re Northern Development Holdings* (1978)) or as a trust for the creditors with a resulting trust for provider of the money (A) should the recipient (B) not use the money to pay his debts (*Carreras Rothmans v Freeman Mathews Treasure* (1985) and *Burton v FX Music* (1999)). Whatever their true basis, such trusts are not easily proven – as in *Box v Barclays Bank* (1998)).

In conclusion, it remains true that English law refuses to admit the validity of non-charitable purpose trusts as a matter of principle. However, the *Re Denley* principle, the anomalous exceptions, the imaginative constructions placed on gifts to unincorporated associations and, above all, the wide meaning given to charity, means that only the purest examples of purpose trusts which have no element of community benefit are likely to be invalid today.

Consider the validity of the following dispositions in the will of Elizabeth, who died in 2000:

(a) £10,000 for the erection and maintenance of a suitable monument to myself in the village of my birth and for an annual memorial service in the parish church;

(b) £15,000 to the vicar of St Mary's Parish Church to be used as she pleases in the knowledge that nothing will be done which diminishes respect for the church; and

(c) £50,000 to my trustees to be spent on the provision of tennis courts for use by the residents of my home village.

Would it make any difference if Elizabeth had stipulated that the projects should be completed within two years of her death or that of her children, whichever was the later?

Answer plan

- Anomalous exceptions to the beneficiary principle: severability of gifts and perpetuity;
- trusts, absolute gifts and purposes; and
- *Re Denley* gifts: the appropriate perpetuity rule.

Answer

In *Re Endacott* (1960), Lord Evershed MR forthrightly stated that 'a trust by English law, not being a charitable trust, in order to be effective, must have ascertained or ascertainable beneficiaries'. This rule against non-charitable purpose trusts is often seen as a fundamental principle which cannot be violated even if the intended purpose trust is clearly capable of achievement, certain in its objectives, does not tend to a perpetuity and does not offend against public policy. Thus, the lack of a legal person – human or corporate – who can enforce the trust and initiate the court's equitable jurisdiction is regarded as fatal (*Re Shaw* (1952)). Of course, there are qualifications and exceptions to this principle, some dependent on the court giving a benign and purposive construction to the recipients of the property (for example, in the case of an unincorporated association (*Re Recher's Trust* (1972)) and some truly outside the scope of the beneficiary principle. This problem raises several of these issues and calls for both the construction of Elizabeth's will and the application of the *Re Endacott* principle. In addition, because there are circumstances in which special types of purpose trust may be valid, consideration must also be given to the rule against perpetuities. This will be done once the inherent validity of each of Elizabeth's dispositions has been considered.

(a) £10,000 for monuments, etc

This is an attempt to establish a purpose trust or, more accurately, a purpose trust with three different aims: the erection of a monument, the maintenance of that monument and the holding of an annual memorial service. The starting place must be *Re Endacott* itself, for not only does this firmly establish the beneficiary principle in English law, it was a case involving an unsuccessful attempt to establish a trust for the provision 'of some useful memorial to myself'. However, *Endacott* also accepted that there were a limited number of specific purpose trusts whose validity had been accepted by the court, albeit for reasons of sentiment or expediency. One of these, as demonstrated by *Mussett v Bingle* (1876) and *Re Hooper* (1932), is trusts for the erection or maintenance of monuments or graves, at least if the executors of the will are prepared to carry out the trust. *Prima facie*, this would seem to be authority for the validity of Elizabeth's trust for the erection and maintenance of a monument to herself, providing questions of perpetuity can be resolved. Indeed, our case is distinguishable from the failed trust of *Re Endacott*, as that involved a 'memorial', although it seems that even 'monuments' must have a funereal character to fall within the limited exception.

Unfortunately, however, apart from perpetuity problems, there is a further difficulty as the trust is also for an annual memorial service for Elizabeth. While it is possible that a trust for the purpose of saying a mass in private for a testator may be a valid purpose trust (*Re Gibbons* (1917)), it seems that Elizabeth's purpose falls outside that limited exception to the beneficiary principle. There is authority from a former colonial court that a private, non-Christian ceremony to perpetuate the memory of a person may be the subject of a valid purpose trust (*Re Khoo Cheng Teow* (1932)), but it is unlikely that such a trust would be accepted today, especially in the light of the clear direction from *Re Endacott* that the categories of valid purpose trusts are not to be extended. Consequently, questions of perpetuity aside, we seem to have one potentially valid purpose trust and one that is certainly void. It then becomes a matter of construction whether the voidness of one part invalidates the whole, for it may be possible to sever the presumptively valid purpose trust, especially if some discrete portion of the £10,000 can be set aside for its completion. The remainder would result to the testator's estate, as would the whole amount if there is no severance or if there were a general perpetuity problem (see below).

(b) £15,000 to the vicar of St Mary's, etc

The validity of this gift depends almost entirely on the construction that is placed upon it. There are four possible alternatives. First, this might be an attempt by Elizabeth to give the vicar of St Mary's a power of appointment over the £15,000, where the object of the power is a purpose. There is no rule in English law that makes it impossible to create a power for a purpose, precisely because exercise of the power is entirely voluntary for the donee of the power (the vicar) and thus enforcement (and lack of people to enforce) is irrelevant. However, there must be an intention to establish a power (an intention to establish a void purpose trust is not sufficient (*IRC v Broadway Cottages* (1955)), the objects of the power must be certain and there must be no perpetuity. In our case, it is not clear that there is an intention to establish a power (for example, there is no gift in default of appointment) and the direction that the vicar may do as she pleases may even indicate an absolute gift. In any event, it is likely that the purpose of the power would be regarded as too uncertain within the test for certainty of objects of powers (the 'is or is not' test) established in *Re Gulbenkian* (1970). The second possibility is that this disposition is regarded as neither a trust nor a power, but as an absolute gift to the vicar of St Mary's *per se*. The point is of some importance as, if this is an absolute gift, the vicar may keep the property for herself and do with it as she pleases. There are several examples of gifts being regarded as absolute despite the fact that the testator has attached some expression of motive or desire to the bequest, including *Re Osoba* (1979) and *Re Andrews* (1905). However, whether we can regard Elizabeth's disposition within this category is unclear, for although it is possible to regard Elizabeth's expressions of hope as without legal effect, imposing no trust at all (that is, the vicar may do 'as she pleases'), it may be important that the vicar of St Mary's is not named, but identified by her office. This does suggest that the money is not intended for that person individually, but in virtue of her official capacity.

A third possibility may be that this is a gift for charitable purposes, being for the advancement of religion (*Re Fowler* (1914)). In some cases, a gift to a clergyman on trust to do as he pleases has been taken to indicate a trust for the advancement of religion (*Re Flinn* (1948)). However, once again, in our case, there is no clear indication that any trust was intended and, even if it were, the general vagueness of the testator's instructions suggests that the gift may be used for other purposes that are not wholly for the advancement of religion: advancement is not the same as non-obstruction. Fourthly, this may be a straightforward, non-charitable, purpose trust which is void under *Re Endacott*. So, depending on the construction of the gift, this disposition discloses either no trust or power at all, being an absolute gift; a power for a purpose, which is probably uncertain and therefore void; a charitable purpose; or a void purpose trust.

(c) £50,000 on tennis courts

This appears to be a simple purpose trust: after all, the trustees will be under a mandatory obligation to erect tennis courts. However, instead of being void for want of a human beneficiary, this purpose trust appears to be valid under the *Re Denley* (1969) principle. According to this case, the rule against purpose trusts is intended to invalidate only those trusts which are abstract and impersonal. If a purpose trust directly or indirectly benefits a class of ascertained or ascertainable individuals, it will be valid as the individuals may be given *locus standi* to apply to the court in the event that the trustees do not carry out the trust. The individuals directly or indirectly benefited have no equitable interest in the trust property itself, although they do provide the means of enforcement. Indeed, with the exception of the perpetuity issue, our case is very similar to that in *Re Denley* itself where the purpose was the provision of a sports ground for employees. Applying that case, this disposition is presumptively valid.

Finally, we come to problems of perpetuity. According to the rule against perpetual trusts, those non-charitable purpose trusts which, as an exception to the beneficiary principle, equity regards as valid, must not last longer than the perpetuity period, being a life in being plus 21 years (*Morice v Bishop of Durham* (1804)). Furthermore, the question of perpetuity must be resolved at the date the disposition comes into effect and, to be valid, there must be no possibility of the purpose lasting longer than the perpetuity period. This usually means that it is necessary for the testatrix to make some express or implied limitation to perpetuity in the trust instrument itself (*Leahy v AG for New South Wales* (1959)). In our cases, although a trust for the erection of a monument will be presumed to be completed within the perpetuity period, a trust for its maintenance must be specifically limited to the period. The same is true for the trust for the annual memorial service, even if it is otherwise valid. Likewise, the *Re Denley* type trust must be limited to perpetuity. There are no such limitations and all these trusts would seem to fail for perpetuity if nothing else. Similarly, any power given to the vicar of St Mary's would fail were it not exercised within the perpetuity period.

Finally, should Elizabeth have stipulated that the projects were to be completed within two years of her death, this would ensure that there is no problem of perpetuity: Elizabeth would have been the life in being and the purposes would be completed within 21 years of her death. Likewise, any children Elizabeth might have must be alive when she (Elizabeth) dies, so a stipulation referring to them will constitute them as lives in being and projects to be completed on their death will also be within the perpetuity period.

Note

As with all questions on purpose trusts, the prospect of the gift being charitable must be borne in mind. Likewise, problems of perpetuity should not be avoided or ignored as even an otherwise valid purpose trust might thereby fail.

Question 18

Lord Rich wishes to give £10,000 to the Redshire branch of the National Association of Landed Gentry for their general purposes. He discovers that each branch's bank account is in the name of the local officers but that there is a 'Memorandum of Agreement' in which each branch agrees to abide by the rules of the National Association. He comes to you for advice as to how best to achieve his wishes, and he is concerned that the money be effectively prevented from falling into the hands of the local officers personally.

Answer plan

- Unincorporated associations: various constructions and respective merits;
- trusts for purposes;
- trusts for individuals as joint tenants or tenants in common (*Neville Estates v Madden* (1962));
- trusts for individuals and contractual relations (*Re Recher's Trust* (1972); *Artistic Upholstery Ltd v Art Forma (Ltd)* (1999));
- trusts for present and future members of the association (*Bacon v Pianta* (1966));
- trusts for purposes, with ascertained individuals (*Re Denley* (1969)); and
- mandates.

Answer

Lord Rich faces something of a problem. As a starting point, it is necessary to consider the nature of the National Association of Landed Gentry in order to discover what action Lord Rich may take to achieve his aims. First, there is no indication here that the National Association of Landed Gentry (or its branches) is a charitable organisation. If it were, the intended donation would cause no difficulties since money given on charitable purpose trusts is perfectly valid and the money would be forever dedicated to the charitable objects (*Commissioners for Special Purposes of Income Tax v Pemsel* (1891)). There is nothing to support this conclusion and it must be discounted. Secondly, although it is not clear, it is doubtful whether this association has legal personality in its own right. For example, it does not appear to be incorporated as a public or private company, a supposition confirmed by the fact that the bank accounts of the local branches are in the names of the local officers and not the association itself. If the association did have legal personality, it could be the object of a simple trust or absolute gift in its favour and Lord Rich would be able to make his donation safe in the knowledge that the money would be used for the purposes of the association as outlined in its articles of incorporation. Thirdly, the association and its local branches could be regarded as unincorporated associations within the outline definition provided by *Leahy v AG for New South Wales* (1959) and discussed in *Conservative & Unionist Central Office v Burrell* (1982). This does seem most likely and, even if it is true that some contractual relationship must exist between the members of the group before it can be regarded as an unincorporated association in law (*Burrell*), such a relationship will be provided by the 'Memorandum of Agreement' which incorporates the national rules into each local branch, including the Redshire branch. The consequences of adopting this view of the association are considered below. Fourthly, it is possible that our association might even lack the necessary formality to be considered an 'unincorporated association'. In that case, its status is *sui generis*, being a collection of individuals combining for a common purpose and Lord Rich will find it difficult to make a donation for the purposes of the association unless a mandate theory is applied (*Conservative & Unionist Central Office v Burrell* (1982)). This will be discussed below.

The most probable hypothesis is that the Redshire branch can be regarded as an unincorporated association. As noted above, unincorporated associations have no legal personality and cannot be the beneficiaries *per se* of either an absolute gift or a gift on trust. Consequently, it could be that a donation to an unincorporated association for its general purposes should be regarded as a gift on trust for those purposes and, of course, non-charitable purpose trusts are void unless one of the very limited exceptions applies (*Re Endacott* (1960)). This is the heart of the dilemma for persons in Lord Rich's position: the unincorporated association cannot itself be the beneficiary of a donation (having no legal personality) and any trust for its purposes *per se* will be void. Fortunately, there are four possible ways to avoid this conclusion, all of which have the effect of making gifts to the association and its members legally possible.

First, a donation to an unincorporated association might be construed as a gift to the present members of the association as joint tenants or tenants in common, see *Cocks v Manners* (1871) LR 12 Eq 574 (compare *Leahy v AG for New South Wales* (1959)). In other words, there is no purpose trust, but a donation to the members of the association as individuals who, of course, can be the object of a gift or trust. While this would make the donation perfectly valid – it is like any other trust or gift for an individual – it suffers from the drawback that any of the individual members may use *their* shares of the donation for personal purposes and take their shares with them on leaving the association. The very reason that allows the donation to be valid creates the chance that the donor's motive in making the gift will be ignored. This construction would not, in our case, prevent the officers or anyone else from taking a share of the money and using it as they wish.

Secondly, a donation to an unincorporated association might be construed, as before, as a gift to the present members of the association individually, but this time on the basis that the subject matter of the donation (the money) is to be dealt with according to the contract which binds the members of the association together. Again, this is a gift or trust for individuals (and therefore perfectly valid) but the rules of the association form a contract between the members which prevent them taking shares for their own use (*Re Recher's Trust* (1972)). The matter is one of contract, not of trust (see *Artistic Upholstery Ltd v Art Forma (Ltd)* (1999). So, if the contract (the rules) provide for the fulfilment of the purposes of the association, the donor can take comfort that his money will be used for the association's purposes, otherwise breach of contract will occur in respect of which a member can sue: *Artistic Upholstery*. Moreover, providing the members' contract (that is, the association's rules) allows the individuals to distribute the property amongst themselves should they so choose, or even allow the present rules to be changed to allow them to do so, there will be no perpetuity problems. Such are the advantages of this 'contract holding theory' that, if at all possible, all gifts to unincorporated associations will be construed in this manner (*News Group Newspapers Ltd v SOGAT 82* (1986); *Artistic Upholstery*). It allows such gifts to be valid, effectively prevents individuals from gaining a share of the donation unless the association comes to an end, and ensures, so far as the rules (contract) allow, that the donor's money is used for the association's general purposes.

A third solution is really an alternative version of the two constructions just considered: namely, that the donation is construed as a donation on trust or gift for individuals (either as joint tenants, as tenants in common, or as bound by their contract), but this time for the present and future members of the association (*Bacon v Pianta* (1966)).

Unfortunately, this construction suffers from a danger of perpetuity in that the future members of the association may become entitled to the property (that is, they become members of the association) too far in the future, outside the perpetuity period. This would invalidate the gift because 'future interests' (that is, interests of persons not yet members of the class of beneficiaries) must vest within a life in being plus 21 years of the date of the gift. There are ways of remedying the situation (for example, 'wait and see', and class closing rules under the Perpetuities and Accumulations Act 1964), but this construction should be avoided where possible.

Fourthly, there is a possibility that, even if the donation to the unincorporated association is construed as a gift on trust for its purposes, it may be saved from voidness in certain situations by the *Re Denley* (1969) principle. According to this principle, if a purpose trust directly or indirectly confers a benefit on a group of individuals, it may be valid if it is limited to the period of perpetuity (*Re Lipinski* (1976)). The *Denley* principle may apply to any kind of purpose trust in appropriate circumstances, but its application to unincorporated associations is controversial. According to Oliver J in *Re Lipinski*, the *Denley* principle might apply if the association was 'inward looking'; that is, confers a benefit on its members and not on the public at large. That might be the case with our association. However, Vinelott J, in *Re Grant* (1980), doubted whether *Re Denley* could ever save a gift to an unincorporated association, even if *Denley* did validate some other types of purpose trusts. In fact, in our case, even if *Re Denley* was followed, there would be problems of perpetuity.

Finally, if the Redshire branch cannot be regarded as an unincorporated association at all (with a preference for the contract holding theory), there is the possibility that Lord Rich may make a valid donation via a mandate (*Conservative & Unionist Central Office v Burrell* (1982)). The mandate theory is not fully developed but, essentially, it involves the donor giving a mandate to the treasurer of the group to use the donation in a particular way on behalf of the donor which mandate becomes irrevocable when the money is so used. However, doubts about who owns the money before it is spent and how the mandate can be enforced, mean that this solution should not be adopted unless no other construction of Lord Rich's donation can be adopted.

To conclude, we can give some concrete advice to Lord Rich, encouraging him to ensure that his donation is treated as a gift or trust for the individual members of the association (through clear drafting) and on the understanding that the contract holding theory applies. This last construction will be presumed by the court if possible and Lord Rich should ensure that there is nothing in the rules of the association which prevents it from being adopted.

4 The Law of Charities

Introduction

Charitable trusts are valid purpose trusts. This means simply that it is perfectly possible to establish a trust for the achievement of a purpose, provided that the purpose in law is regarded as charitable. As far as charities are concerned, it is not important that there is no human beneficiary capable of enforcing the trust because the Attorney General may take action in respect of all charitable trusts on behalf of the Crown. Moreover, valid charitable trusts are not subject to certain aspects of the perpetuity rule and may be of unlimited duration. Furthermore, when compared to valid private trusts (that is, trusts for human objects), charitable trusts have other advantages; they enjoy considerable fiscal privileges including exemption from many taxes. Hence, many of the decided cases involve the Inland Revenue seeking to deny charitable status. Likewise, there are special rules applicable to the failure of charitable trusts (the principles of *cy-près*) which may oust the normal rules of resulting trusts, and there is a separate body of rules dealing with the administration of charities and the conduct of business by charitable trustees.

Obviously it is of singular importance to be able to distinguish between charitable purposes and non-charitable purposes. The former will be valid and enforceable, as well as having other advantages over private trusts, and the latter will be void unless they fall within one of the exceptions to the beneficiary principle considered in the previous chapter. Yet, despite the unquestionable importance of charitable trusts, there is little by way of statute law that provides a definition of charitable status. The Charities Bill 2004 marked the first attempt by Parliament to adopt a statutory definition of charities. However, the Bill was abandoned at its final stages owing to lack of Parliamentary time due to the general elections. The Bill introduced a statutory definition by reference to a two-step approach – the listing of a variety of charitable purposes and the public benefit test. The Bill contained a list of 12 charitable purposes. This was intended to be a comprehensive list of charitable activities. Most of the purposes, in any event, were charitable before the Bill was introduced. The meaning of 'charity' is to be found principally in previous case law and the opinions of the Charity Commissioners.

Question 19

The advantages of charitable status are a persuasive argument in favour of a statutory definition of the meaning 'charity' for English law.

Do you agree?

Answer plan

- Charities and the beneficiary principle: advantages of validity, practical advantages and relationship to purpose trusts;

- definition of charity (*Pemsel's* case);
- flexibility versus idiosyncrasies and inconsistencies; and
- whether the 'advantages' of charitable status should be considered when deciding whether a trust is charitable.

Answer

It is a fundamental principle of equity that a trust must be capable of enforcement if it is to be valid. For private trusts, this means that a court will not recognise their validity unless there is a human beneficiary, defined with sufficient certainty, capable of coming to court and triggering the equitable jurisdiction. Consequently, with some limited exceptions, private purpose trusts are void (*Re Endacott* (1960)). However, it is also apparent that some purpose trusts may serve a public purpose and could, in effect, provide funds for the achievements of aims and goals that would benefit the community at large. The recognition of this public function of certain kinds of purpose trust finds concrete form in the law of charities. A charitable trust is a trust for a purpose, but where the purpose is regarded as sufficiently beneficial to the community at large to warrant acceptance of its validity. It should not be thought that this means that charitable trusts may be established for uncertain or uncontrollable purposes or that charitable trustees may go unsupervised in the execution of their duties. On the question of enforcement, it matters not that there is no human beneficiary capable of enforcing the trust because the Crown acts as *parens patriae* through the Attorney General in order to ensure that the charitable trustees carry out the terms of the trust. In this task, the Attorney General is supported by a number of legislative provisions regulating the administration of charities (for example, the Charities Act 1960, the Charities Act 1993 and specific parts of the Trustee Act 2000 (for example, s 30) and by the extensive supervisory functions of the Charity Commissioners. Moreover, although it is true that charitable trusts are trusts for a purpose, the common law provides a definition of charitable status which is designed to ensure that there is some measure of certainty of objects. Consequently, not every apparently 'beneficial' purpose is accorded charitable status. Before a purpose trust can be regarded as charitable it too must fulfil a test of certainty of objects, although now the test is supplied by the common law definition of 'charity' (*Blair v Duncan* (1902)).

As well as the two differences between private trusts and charitable trusts just considered, there are other ways in which charities are distinct from other valid trusts. First, charitable trusts may last in perpetuity because it is not contrary to public policy for money to be permanently dedicated to charitable purposes beneficial to the community. Likewise, a gift over from one charity to another, which could be triggered if the original charity should fail to observe some limitation placed on the use of the property by the donor, will not fail if it takes effect outside the perpetuity period (*Christ's Hospital v Grainger* (1849)). This is simply because 'charity' is regarded in law as indivisible, irrespective of the actual group or body carrying out the purpose. Secondly, and in a similar vein, should a charitable trust fail – perhaps because it has achieved its objects or because the body administering the funds becomes defunct – the normal rules of resulting trusts may be displaced. Instead, the money can be used for purposes as near as possible to the original (now defunct) purposes under the rules of *cy-près* (*Re Prison Charities* (1873)). Thirdly, there are some differences in the way charitable trustees may administer a charitable trust and some difference in the scope of their powers and duties. For example, the 'delegable functions' of a trustee of a charitable trust under the Trustee Act 2000 are different from those of a trustee of a private trust (ss 11, 12). Again, the number of charitable trustees who may be vested with title to land is not limited to four if the land is to be used for charitable purposes (s 34(3) of the Trustee Act 1925) and there are different rules concerning remuneration (payment) of trustees of charitable trusts (s 30 of the Trustee Act 2000). Similarly, the public nature of charities means that charitable trustees may have a more extensive duty to safeguard the trust property than private trustees, although as ever this will depend on the precise facts of each case (see, for example, Sched 1 to the Trustee Act 2000).

These matters are of profound importance for the validity of an alleged charitable trust and its day to day administration. Much time has been spent in court trying to decide whether a disputed purpose trust is charitable and valid, or merely purposive and void. However, in addition to these inherent and practical differences between charitable and private trusts, there is a further advantage enjoyed by charities which makes the acquisition of charitable status a considerable benefit. Charitable trusts enjoy important fiscal advantages, in that they are exempt from certain forms of taxation, and donations made to them attract tax advantages for the donor and the charity. The amount of money in taxes forgone in the UK is in the region of £1 bn each year and it is obvious that the granting of charitable status is a prize of some worth. In concrete terms, charities are exempt from income tax, capital gains tax, stamp duty, corporation tax and some (though not all) forms of value added tax. Likewise, premises used wholly or mainly for charitable purposes – be they offices or charity shops – are entitled to between 80% and 100% relief from business rates. Moreover, as an incentive for charitable giving, donations to charity may attract tax relief for the donor as well as permitting the charity to claim back from the Treasury the tax paid by the donor on the donation.

With these advantages in mind, it should come as no surprise that many of the cases involving disputed charitable status involve the Inland Revenue, as with *Commissioners for Special Purposes of Income Tax v Pemsel* (1891). What is surprising, however, is that there is no statutory definition of what amounts to 'charitable' status. In fact, the definition of a 'charity' – if that is the correct description for such an amorphous body of law – is based on a general statement of the meaning of charitable purposes contained in the Preamble to the Statute of Charitable Uses 1601 and developed thereafter through a mass of case law when new and more diverse trusts claimed charitable status.

Traditionally, charitable trusts are said to fall within four broad categories, being those identified by Lord Macnaughten in *Pemsel's* case: viz, trusts for the relief of poverty; trusts for the advancement of education; trusts for the advancement of religion; and trusts for other purposes beneficial to the community. However, tempting though it is to treat this dictum as akin to a statutory definition of charity, it should not be so regarded. In reality, this fourfold classification represents a useful descriptive tool rather than a precise analysis of the meaning of charity (*Scottish Burial Reform and Cremation Society Ltd v Glasgow City Corporation* (1968)). The most crucial point seems to be that, for a trust to be charitable, it must fall within 'the spirit and intendment' of the Preamble of 1601 and it is not enough simply that a purpose is beneficial to the community: it must be one which is beneficial and which the law regards as charitable (*Scottish Burial Reform*). This is particularly important when considering the fourth category of charity referred to in *Pemsel* because not every purpose trust which confers a benefit on the community will be charitable (*Barralet v Attorney General* (1980), *Peggs v Lamb* (1994) and *Southwood v AG* (2000)), despite some suggestions to the contrary (*Incorporated Council for Law Reporting for England and Wales v Attorney General* (1971)).

In truth, such is the wealth of accumulated material available to a court that the granting of charitable status can often lie principally in the discretion of the court, especially since both precedents and analogies can be found to support a claim of charitable status for most trusts that are not obviously non-charitable. At one time, the scale of fiscal and other advantages enjoyed by charities caused some judges to wonder whether the motives of the settlor or testator in seeking to establish a charitable trust, particularly if he or she were primarily concerned with fiscal advantages, should be relevant in deciding whether charitable status existed (*Scottish Burial Reform* (1968) and *Dingle v Turner* (1972)). Now, however, it seems that an attempt to establish a charitable trust must be viewed benignly (*IRC v Guild* (1992) and *IRC v Oldham Training and Enterprise Council* (1996)) and that fiscal considerations should not be used to deny the existence of a charitable trust otherwise validly created (*IRC v McMullen* (1981)). The definition of charity should now be regarded as one of law and operating independently of the advantages which charitable trusts enjoy. Of course, it is unrealistic to expect decisions concerning charitable status to be taken in a vacuum and, no doubt, prevailing social and economic trends, the perceived advantages of a purpose to the community and, perhaps, the judge's own view of public policy will play a part. Such flexibility is easy to maintain when the case law is so diverse. There are relevant legal principles, but these represent the parameters for decisions rather than specific rules requiring specific solutions. The 1601 Preamble itself, the *Pemsel* categories, the need for all charities to display a public benefit and the exclusion from the class of charity of any purpose that excludes the poor (*Re Macduff* (1896)) or which are political (*Southwood v AG*) are just some examples.

There is, then, a flexibility here and with it comes a necessary measure of uncertainty. On the other hand, if we were to replace this with a statutory definition of charitable status, would it allow the courts to mould the definition of charity to take account of present needs, or would it rather reflect past experiences? Likewise, if the statutory definition were flexible enough to allow for the slow evolution of the law, would the definition be of any real use, or be more useful than the common law? In practice, much of the actual decisions about charitable status are taken by the Charity Commissioners who receive many hundreds of applications from trusts each year to be registered as charities. Although the Commissioners may apply only the principles established by the courts and, of course, reference may be made to the court in cases of doubt or dispute, this body of accumulated material contains a wealth of expertise for determining charitable status. This should be borne in mind in any discussion of the definition of charity for the Charity Commissioners are specialists and professionals and it is they who administer this body of law on a day to day basis. As so many of the reports of the Charity Commissioners demonstrate, it is not the definition of charity that is the real problem, for it poses only marginal difficulties when novel cases or contentious purposes are put forward. Of more concern was the lack of statutory intervention to control existing charities, a matter now addressed by the Charities Act 1993.

The Charities Bill 2004 introduced an intended statutory definition of a charity. Although the Bill was lost owing to a lack of Parliamentary time, it had the distinction of laying down a statutory definition of charity for the first time. It adopted a definition by reference to a two-step approach - the listing of a variety of charitable purposes and the public benefit test. Clause 2(2) contained a list of 12 charitable purposes. This was intended to be a comprehensive list of charitable activities. Most of these purposes, in any event, were charitable before the Bill was introduced. These purposes were:

(a) the prevention or relief of poverty;

(b) the advancement of education;

(c) the advancement of religion;

(d) the advancement of health [including the prevention or relief of sickness, disease or human suffering];

(e) the advancement of citizenship or community development;

(f) the advancement of the arts, heritage or science;

(g) the advancement of amateur sport [involving physical skill and exertion];

(h) the advancement of human rights, conflict resolution or reconciliation;

(i) the advancement of environmental protection or improvement;

(j) the relief of those in need, by reason of youth, age, ill-health, disability, financial hardship or other disadvantage [including the provision of accommodation and care to the beneficiaries mentioned within this clause];

(k) the advancement of animal welfare;

(l) any other purpose within sub-clause (4).

With the exception of amateur sport, all of these purposes were charitable under the current law.

Clause 2(4) endorsed the common law approach to charitable objects by reference to the purposes declared in paragraphs (a) to (l) above. This involved considering the 'spirit and intendment' of the preamble and reasoning by analogy by reference to decided cases.

Clause 3 laid down the second part of the definition of a charity namely the 'public benefit' test. Clause 3(1) stipulated that each of the listed purposes indicated above is required to satisfy the public benefit test. Clause 3(2) declared that *no presumption* will be made to the effect that a purpose satisfies the public element test. Thus, if there is a dispute as to the validity of a charitable purpose, the trustees of the organisation is required positively to establish that the purpose has a real and substantial benefit to society.

Clause 3(3) consolidated the case law meaning of public benefit. This involved a two step test of demonstrating a benefit to society and that those eligible to receive benefits must comprise a large enough group to be considered as the public and without a personal or private relationship being used to limit those who may benefit.

In summary, the intended legal re-definition of a charity in terms of classifying the objects into 12 purposes coupled with the statutory test of public benefit, had done little more than to consolidate the law. The courts will continue to adapt the law to keep abreast with the changing needs of society.

Note

This is a very general question, susceptible to many different answers. However, an unprofitable approach would be to concentrate solely on the *Pemsel* definition of charity. That is tempting, but does not address the issue. The question asks about the advantages of charitable status and how this reflects on the definition of charity: it does not ask for a discussion of that definition in detail.

Question 20

Consider the validity of the following gifts in the will of Daphne, who died in 2005:

(a) £100,000 to my trustees for the establishment and maintenance of a walled garden within the precincts of St Luke's church, for the quiet reflection of the parishioners;

(b) £10,000 to my trustees to be distributed to such organisations involved in the protection of the environment and related causes as they shall in their absolute discretion select; and

(c) £50,000 to my trustees for the promotion of tennis in the public schools of Derbyshire.

Answer plan

- Brief introductory points about the definition of charity;
- trusts for the *promotion* of religion: activities within a religious context *per se* might not be enough;
- trusts for other purposes beneficial to the community and questions of exclusivity of charitable purpose; and
- trusts for education: issue of public benefit.

Answer

In this problem, Daphne has attempted to establish trusts for the achievement of certain purposes. It is trite law that a trust cannot exist for a purpose, save in the most exceptional circumstances or unless that purpose be in law charitable (*Re Endacott* (1960)). As far as Daphne's three distinct dispositions are concerned, it is highly unlikely that any of them falls into the category of valid private purpose trusts. There is nothing here that would fall within the exceptional categories identified in *Re Endacott* and any possibility of the trust for the establishment of a walled garden falling within *Re Denley* (1969) is negated by the fact that this trust (as with the others) is clearly a perpetuity. Fortunately, however, charitable trusts do not require human objects and are not void even if of perpetual duration. The crucial question then becomes whether any of these three dispositions falls within the common law definition of charitable status. Before considering this in detail, brief mention should be made of some basic points. First, a charitable trust will not exist unless the trust property is devoted exclusively to the charitable purpose (*Attorney General of the Bahamas v Royal Trust Co* (1986)). Secondly, all charitable trusts (with the exception of trusts for the relief of poverty) must be for the 'public benefit', although this will be satisfied in different ways by different types of charity (*Oppenheim v Tobacco Securities Trust Co Ltd* (1951)). Thirdly, the definition of charity is a matter of law, independent of the testator's intentions (*National Anti-Vivisection Society v IRC* (1948)). Fourthly, although charities may be conveniently divided into trusts for the relief of poverty, trusts for the advancement of education, trusts for the advancement of religion and trusts for other purposes beneficial to the community (*Commissioners for Special Purposes of Income Tax v Pemsel* (1891)). These categories are not written in stone (*Scottish Burial Reform and Cremation Society Ltd v Glasgow City Corporation* (1968)). Finally, every charitable trust must fall within the 'spirit and intendment' of the Statute of Charitable Uses 1601, bearing in mind that this has been developed by precedent and analogy and is now represented by a wealth of case law and decisions of the Charity Commissioners.

(a) '£100,000 to my Trustees for the establishment and maintenance of a walled garden within the precincts of St Luke's church, for the quiet reflection of the parishioners'

This particular trust does have the potential to fall within the *Denley* exception to the rule against purpose trusts, although this is unlikely in practice because of the donor's intention to establish a trust in perpetuity. However, it may be that this trust is within the scope of trusts for the advancement of religion and is thereby charitable. There is no doubt here that the proposed trust is connected with a religious establishment and questions concerning the disputed status of some faiths and beliefs are not relevant (see, for example, *Funnell v Stewart* (1996)). Yet, it is unclear whether trusts for religious purposes *per se* can be charitable if they are not otherwise for the advancement of religion

(*Oxford Group v IRC* (1949)). Furthermore, in our case, the actual purpose seems to be the establishment of a walled garden 'for quiet reflection' and it might be argued that this is not even a religious purpose, as believers are not the only persons able and willing to engage in contemplation (*Re Macaulay's Estate* (1943)). On the other hand, gifts for the maintenance and enhancement of buildings within a church are routinely held to be charitable (*Re Raine* (1956)), as are some matters connected with the church even though they appear far removed from the promotion of the religion itself (*Re Royce* (1940): benefit of church choir). In fact, the maintenance of churches is expressly within the Preamble to the 1601 Statute. The matter here is one of construction of the trust instrument in the light of existing case law. The fact that the walled garden must be erected within the fabric of a church is powerful evidence in favour of a charity for the advancement of religion, as is the fact that the anticipated benefit will fall on parishioners (*Re Norton's Will Trusts* (1948)). The only other tenable view is that the reference to 'quiet reflection' may introduce a non-charitable element into the equation and may make the gift void as not being exclusively devoted to charity. Finally, should it be held that this purpose falls within the definition of charity *per se*, it is clear that there is a sufficient element of public benefit. The walled garden would be open to all parishioners and we can legitimately assume that these are neither numerically negligible nor 'a class within a class' (*Williams Trustees v IRC* (1947)). This case is not on a par with *Gilmour v Coats* (1949). In that case, the contemplative nature of the purpose was held to confer no public benefit because the value of prayer could not be proven and because the nuns were cloistered and did not participate in community life. Our case, however, is similar to *Neville Estates v Madden* (1962), where there was a sufficient element of public benefit because the persons enriched by the advancement of religion continued to be members of the community.

(b) '£10,000 to my trustees to be distributed to such organisations involved in the protection of the environment and related causes as they shall in their absolute discretion select'

It is perfectly in order for a charitable trust to allow the trustees some discretion in the selection of charitable objects provided, of course, that the trustees are required by the trust to exercise that discretion in favour of objects that are exclusively charitable (*Houston v Burns* (1918)). In this particular case, there are two issues: first, whether the 'protection of the environment' is itself charitable; and secondly, whether the trustees' ability to use the money for 'related causes' has any bearing on the matter.

As far as the protection of the environment is concerned, this is likely to be a purpose that falls within the category of 'other purposes beneficial to the community', the so called fourth category identified in *Pemsel*. This is despite the fact that there is some doubt as to how we are to determine whether any given purpose is charitable within this fourth class. According to Russell LJ in *Incorporated Council for Law Reporting for England and Wales v Attorney General* (1971), a court is entitled to assume that if a purpose is in itself beneficial to the community, it is also charitable in law. On the other hand, the more traditional approach requires that there must be some precedent or analogy with the 1601 Preamble or previous case law before a new purpose which is beneficial in itself can also be regarded as charitable (*Williams Trustees v IRC* (1947); *Peggs v Lamb* (1994)).

Fortunately for our case, there is considerable authority that a trust for the protection of the environment is charitable. Certainly, the preservation of historic buildings and gardens is charitable (*Re Verrall* (1916)), as are trusts for natural amenities (*Re Corelli* (1943)). In addition, although not formally binding, the Charity Commissioners regard trusts for the promotion and protection of the environment as charitable and this must be persuasive evidence of the strongest kind. What, then, of the trustees' ability to use the money for 'related causes'? This, again, is a matter of construction. If 'related causes' can be interpreted to mean exclusively environmental purposes, then there should be no problem with the validity of this charitable gift and it is suggested that this is the most sensible view of Daphne's disposition. If, on the other hand, 'related causes' may encompass worthwhile but non-charitable purposes, then the gift may fail as not being exclusively devoted to charity (*Blair v Duncan* (1902)), at least unless the non-charitable purpose is merely subsidiary to the performance of the charitable object (*Re Coxen* (1948)) or can be severed from it (*Lambert v Thwaites* (1866)). Finally, we should note that there is little doubt that this charitable purpose fulfils the essential requirement of public benefit. There is no stipulation limiting use of the property to any specific class or type of person and nothing that suggests that the benefits of the charity *per se* are private and intangible. Subject, then, to resolving the 'related causes' issue, this is a charitable gift.

(c) '£50,000 to my trustees for the promotion of tennis in the public schools of Derbyshire'

This is the most straightforward of Daphne's dispositions. The Preamble to the Statute of 1601 itself talks of 'schools of learning', and there is no doubt that the endowment and maintenance of independent (that is, 'public') schools is a charitable purpose, even if some charge is made to parents for tuition fees, providing that the school is non-profit making. More importantly, it was recognised by the House of Lords in *IRC v McMullen* (1981) that a trust to provide sporting facilities for schools was itself charitable as furthering the education of pupils. This would seem to cover our case. Moreover, if it should be objected that the scope of Daphne's charitable purpose is limited to a particular area and might fail the test of public benefit (whereas in *McMullen* it was any school within the UK), the trust in *Re Mariette* (1915) was charitable and this concerned the provision of sporting facilities at just one school (and that was an independent one). *A fortiori*, a trust for the promotion of sport in several schools must be charitable.

Question 21

What is the meaning of 'public benefit' in the law of charity and how do the courts determine whether it exists?

Answer plan

- The need for a public element in charitable purposes in order to justify their exceptional status and their advantages;
- two meanings of public benefit: type of benefit and range of benefit;
- varying nature of public benefit according to each purpose; and
- various decisions.

Answer

It is a fundamental principle of the law of charities 'that a trust is not charitable unless it is directed to the public benefit'. So spoke Lord Simmonds in *Oppenheim v Tobacco Securities Trust Co Ltd* (1951), confirming a principle that is at the heart of the definition of charity. There is no surprise in this, for not only do charitable trusts have to satisfy less stringent rules for their creation and operation, they also enjoy the protection of the

Attorney General and, most importantly, they benefit from extensive fiscal advantages. If the community at large is to subsidise charities financially, it is apparent that the charity itself must be for the benefit of the public. However, while few would argue that charitable trusts must satisfy a requirement of public benefit, there is disagreement as to how this can be both tested and proved. Clearly, as we shall see, 'public benefit' may mean different things in different circumstances and there is no doubt that the degree to which this requirement is applied can vary from charity to charity. Consequently, much turns on the type of charity being considered and on the precise limitations (if any) which the donor has placed on the gift.

As a starting point, it must be realised that 'public benefit' has two distinct meanings, although this is not always made clear in the reported cases. First, all charitable purposes must be for the public benefit: that is, it must be inherent in the purpose that it is beneficial to the community. Nothing that is harmful to the community at large or to the public interest can ever be charitable and perhaps this is why no valid charitable trust can exclude the poor (*Re Macduff* (1896)) and why certain allegedly harmful religious sects can be denied charitable status. In other words, the purpose itself must be beneficial, otherwise the advantages of charitable status will be denied. Secondly, most potential charitable purposes must have a sufficient element of public benefit in order to attain charitable status. That is, the purpose which is regarded as beneficial must not normally be confined to such a small section of the population, or be so limited by the stipulations of the testator, as to deny an element of public participation in the purpose. As noted, these two different elements of the 'public benefit' requirement are often equated, but lack of either, when required, can invalidate what appears otherwise to be a perfectly valid charitable trust.

First, then, what does it mean to say that a charity must be beneficial to the public – that is, of such worth that it requires recognition by the law? As is well known, charitable trusts are often divided into four categories (*Commissioners for Special Purposes of Income Tax v Pemsel* (1891)) and this has consequences for the first aspect of the public benefit requirement. If a purpose can be shown to be for the relief of poverty, for the advancement of education or for the advancement of religion, it will be presumed to be inherently beneficial (*National Anti-Vivisection Society v IRC* (1948)). What is important is that the purpose falls within the meaning of relief of poverty, advancement of education or advancement of religion as elucidated in the accumulated case law and, if it does, this is enough to demonstrate its beneficial effect. Of course, it is possible to demonstrate that, say, a trust for the advancement of religion is harmful to the community or lacks tangible benefits (compare *Gilmour v Coats* (1949)) and that would be enough to deny charitable status. Yet the burden of proof is with the person seeking to demonstrate lack of public benefit, rather than requiring the charity to prove benefit. It is enough if the purpose is within one of the first three *Pemsel* categories.

Conversely, however, when one is considering the fourth category of charity – trusts for other purposes beneficial to the community – it is clear that the beneficial nature of the purpose needs to be positively established before its charitable status can be admitted. How is this to be done? Traditionally, when determining whether any purpose was charitable within the fourth category, the courts would look to the Preamble of the Statute of Charitable Uses 1601 and previous cases, and then decide whether there was either a precedent or an analogy for the charitable status of the new purpose (*Williams Trustees v IRC* (1947); *Scottish Burial Reform and Cremation Society Ltd v Glasgow City Corporation* (1968); *Peggs v Lamb* (1994)). The point is that not all purposes which are beneficial to the community may be charitable: rather, we are concerned with purposes which are beneficial in a charitable sense as divined from the spirit and intendment of the 1601 Preamble. Obviously, this could mean that a perfectly useful and worthy purpose might fail to be recognised as a charity simply because of a lack of existing precedent, although in practice this is highly unlikely given the wealth of material and the extensive discretion which judges enjoy. Nevertheless, it has been suggested in some cases (for example, in *Incorporated Council for Law Reporting for England and Wales v Attorney General* (1971)) that if a purpose is shown to be beneficial to the community *per se*, this should be enough to guarantee charitable status unless some positive harm or unwanted effect can be proven. This approach, which does not appear to have been taken up generally (see the criticism in *Barralet v Attorney General* (1980)) apparently makes it more likely that the meaning of charity will be able to evolve rapidly and in tune with changing patterns of social and economic behaviour. However, we must ask whether, in fact, the 'novel' approach really does offer more chance of charitable status than the old 'precedent and analogy' doctrine. In one sense, the new approach merely reverses the burden of proof when it comes to the beneficial and charitable nature of purposes within the fourth category and it is highly unlikely that a judge well versed in the law of charities could fail to find a suitable precedent or analogy for a novel purpose that clearly deserved charitable status. Consequently, despite this rather theoretical argument about how one establishes whether a purpose falls within the fourth category of charity, it is clear that the courts are more concerned to establish positively the public benefit of this class than with the other, more obviously beneficial purposes.

This leads us to consider the second sense in which 'public benefit' is used within charity law: that is, to convey the idea that the public itself, or a sufficient section of it, must benefit from the charitable purpose. Put another way, the law admits the special status and privileges of charitable trusts and requires in return that the benefits thereby granted are not confined to a select few, especially those with some special status or those with an affinity with the person establishing the charitable trust. Once again, however, this general statement of principle must be qualified for it is clear that charities for the relief of poverty are not subject to as stringent a test of public benefit as other types of charity (*Isaac v Defriez* (1754)). For example, trusts for the relief of poverty of employees of one company or the members of one club (*Re Young* (1951) and see *Re Segelman* (1996)) may be charitable despite the fact that this would probably fail the normal tests of public benefit (see below). Likewise, trusts for 'poor relations' are perfectly valid (*Re Scarisbrick* (1951)), and now this exception from the public benefit requirement has been confirmed by the House of Lords in *Dingle v Turner* (1972).

With the special status of trusts for the relief of poverty firmly in mind, how is it possible to determine whether a trust is for the public benefit in the sense of casting its benefits sufficiently widely? There are a number of different points to consider. First, it is obvious that the benefits of a charitable trust must not be restricted to a group of people that are numerically negligible (*Oppenheim v Tobacco Securities Trust Co Ltd* (1951)). The point is that the class of persons who may benefit from the charitable purpose must not be narrowly restricted by definition: it matters not that only a small group of people actually enjoy the benefits of the charitable purpose so long as those benefits are available to the public should they come forward (*IRC v Baddeley* (1955)). In *Baddeley*, Lord Simonds drew a distinction between a form of relief accorded to the whole community yet, by its nature, advantageous only to a few. This type of relief will satisfy the public benefit test. On the other hand a form of relief accorded to a select few members of the community out of a large number willing to take advantage of it runs a risk of not satisfying the test. Of course, what is 'numerically negligible' depends on the facts of each case and may vary for different types of charity.

Secondly, and in a similar vein, although the benefits derived from the charity may be limited to a class of persons (not being numerically negligible; for example, the inhabitants of Whiteshire), they may not be confined to 'a class within a class'

(*Williams Trustees v IRC* (1947)). Although this can only be a 'rule of thumb', the idea is that one limitation on the class of persons who may derive a benefit from the charity does not destroy the 'public' character of the trust, but a second or third limitation may well make it so difficult for the public at large to qualify for the charitable benefit that there is no real public benefit at all (*IRC v Baddeley* (1955)). However, one must be careful not to rely overmuch on a rigid application of this principle for there are many class limitations (such as age, location or gender) which will not deprive a class of its public character even if combined with another restriction.

Thirdly, and most controversially, it is possible that a trust will not be regarded as charitable, as lacking the essential element of public benefit, if the potential class of persons likely to benefit are united by a common personal bond. This is known as the '*Compton* test' (from *Re Compton* (1945)), and it was confirmed by the House of Lords in *Oppenheim v Tobacco Securities Trust Co Ltd* (1951). Essentially, the point is that if the class intended to benefit from the charity shares a common personal relationship – perhaps they are all employees of one company or relatives of one person – they may not be capable of being regarded as a section of 'the public', even if numerically very great, as in *Oppenheim* itself. However, there are difficulties here and there are doubts whether this 'personal nexus' test is suitable to determine questions of public benefit. As much was stated in *Dingle v Turner* (1972), although that case was concerned with the relief of poverty which is outside the test and therefore renders its criticisms of *Oppenheim* strictly *obiter*. One important criticism is that it is unclear exactly what the personal nexus test is designed to prevent. For example, does the test invalidate trusts where there is a personal connection between the members of the class and the donor of the money or creator of the trust, or does the test invalidate trusts where there is a personal nexus existing the members of the class *inter se*, irrespective of their relationship to the donor? To put the question another way, is an employer prevented from establishing an educational trust for her employees? – or is an employer prevented from establishing an educational trust for any group of persons who share a personal connection (such as descendants of the first Mayor of London) even though that personal connection is not with the employer? If the personal nexus test prevents the second type of trust, then it seems rigid and unnecessary and simply replaces judgment with arbitrariness. The objection that not every member of the public has the potential to join this class – because the tie that binds is 'personal' – is not persuasive. Every charity that utilises a class description may exclude certain persons. For example, a trust for 'women in Wales' forever excludes men. Conversely, if it is the former, then at least it can be justified on the ground that it prevents a donor from using the charitable status of a trust to obtain a private benefit for himself (tax relief and employee fringe benefits) and for persons in whom she has a direct interest (relations, employees, etc).

In short, then, to require a charitable trust to be for the 'public benefit' encompasses a whole range of different policy considerations about the nature of charity. At the very least, being aware of the two distinct meanings of 'public benefit' should enable a more thorough analysis of the essence of 'charity'. Yet, even within these two broad umbrellas there are shades of meaning and different approaches, not least because the range of charitable purposes is diverse, extensive and expanding.

Question 22

Ivor Evans, managing director of Chem Inc, the former State owned chemical industry, wishes to establish certain trusts with his own money and with that of the company (which he is empowered to do). He desires to take advantage of the generous fiscal arrangements involving charities, both for his own benefit and for the sake of those who will benefit from the charity. He has four objects in view, viz: first, with his own money, to set up a trust to provide scholarships for study in the field of chemistry at a UK university for disadvantaged children living in Cardiff of Welsh speaking parents; secondly, with his own money, to provide cut price food and drink for the Miners' Welfare Club where his aged father is a member; thirdly, with the company's money, to establish a conference centre for the fostering of understanding between the UK and the Far East in order to promote trade in agrochemicals; and fourthly, with the company's money to establish a nursery school for the children of employees.

Advise Ivor Evans of the extent to which these goals can be achieved within the law of charity.

Answer plan

- The extent to which a court should consider the motives of a settlor in establishing charitable trusts;
- trusts for education: public benefit, class within a class;
- trusts for a purpose, or for poverty or within the Recreational Charities Act: also charitable trust for a relative;
- trust for international co-operation or for education: self-interest; and
- trust for education: personal nexus test.

Answer

This question raises difficult issues about the meaning of charitable status, the meaning of public benefit as a test of that status and the extent to which statutory intervention has enabled the achievement of specific kinds of charitable purpose. In general, reference must be made to the case law on the meaning of charity, especially *Commissioners for Special Purposes of Income Tax v Pemsel* (1891) and cases which follow it, to the various ways in which a court will determine whether an apparently charitable purpose has a sufficient element of public benefit, to the Recreational Charities Act 1958 and the extent to which the fiscal advantages enjoyed by charities should influence a court in deciding whether to declare a trust charitable in the first place.

Clearly, the donor in this case has specific purposes in view, and it is important to advise him at the outset that each purpose should be allocated a specific and certain sum of money, distinct from that set aside for the other purposes. The reason for this is twofold: first, to ensure that if any one of the four purposes is declared void as a non-charitable purpose trust, that it will not then taint any other disposition; and secondly, in recognition of the fact that different charitable purposes have different tests for whether there is a 'public benefit' and should, therefore, be kept discrete if possible (*IRC v Baddeley* (1955)). In addition, it would be prudent to inform the donor that while his motives in establishing the trusts are usually irrelevant in deciding whether a purpose is charitable – charitable status being a matter of law, not intention (*National Anti-Vivisection Society v IRC* (1948)) – some case law suggests that the donor's desire to achieve fiscal advantages for himself can be relevant in denying charitable status in marginal cases (*Dingle v Turner* (1972); *Scottish Burial Reform and Cremation Society Ltd v Glasgow City Corporation* (1968)). In more recent cases, however, it has been stated that fiscal considerations should not be used to deny the existence of a charity otherwise validly created and that a benign construction of a charitable purpose should be adopted wherever possible (*IRC v McMullen* (1981); *IRC v Guild* (1992)). Consequently, we need only warn Ivor Evans that the trusts should be so constructed as to conform to the conditions required for charitable status, particularly that of public benefit, and that any hint that these were merely tax reduction schemes should be avoided. What is required is a clear charitable purpose and a clear benefit to the community: if fiscal advantages are thereby given, all well and good.

Turning then to the first alleged charitable purpose – the establishment with his own money of a trust to provide scholarships for study in the field of chemistry at a UK university for disadvantaged children living in Cardiff of Welsh speaking parents – it is immediately apparent that there are two possible ways in which this purpose might be regarded as charitable. First, this could be regarded as an educational charity for, clearly, the primary motive is to establish scholarships for academic study (*McGovern v Attorney General* (1982); *IRC v Educational Grants Association Ltd* (1967)). If this is so, the donor may well have difficulties in establishing that it is for the benefit of the public or a section thereof. The class of persons entitled to such scholarships is quite restricted, needing to fulfil three conditions (being disadvantaged, living in Cardiff, and of Welsh speaking parents). While the reference to 'disadvantaged' does not negate public benefit (after all, that is the essence of charity), overall this may well be regarded as a 'class within a class' and so too narrowly drawn to confer a benefit on the public, as in *Williams Trustees v IRC* (1947), itself a case concerning persons from Wales. On the other hand, in this case, the donor is not attempting to benefit persons with whom he is personally connected (as in *Educational Grants Association Ltd*). In the end, it will be a matter for judgment, although if the donor wishes to avoid these problems he could amend the class limiting factors. Secondly, it is possible that this might be regarded as a trust for the relief of poverty, in that it is for 'disadvantaged' persons. However, although this construction would avoid the 'public benefit' difficulties just discussed (*Dingle v Turner* (1972)), the better view is that the purpose of the trust is educational and that the disadvantaged nature of the persons who might benefit is a subsidiary factor. In summary, there is a good argument that this will be an educational charity, provided difficulties over the 'public' nature of the benefits thereby conferred can be overcome.

The second intended charity also poses some problems. First, it is unclear whether there is any charitable purpose. On one level, this might be regarded as a trust for the relief of poverty, making the assumption that members of Miners' Welfare Clubs were persons in need of assistance (*Re Coulthurst* (1951)). However, this is not a strong argument as there is precedent to suggest that trusts for the 'working classes' *per se* are not charitable (*Re Sanders* (1954)), although it is immaterial that the intended recipients may have to contribute something in order to obtain the benefit (*Joseph Rowntree Memorial Trust Housing Association Ltd v Attorney General* (1983)). Fortunately, the doubts surrounding the charitable nature of Miners' Welfare Trusts have been removed by s 2 of the Recreational Charities Act 1958, as in *Wynn v Skegness UDC* (1966), provided that the requirement of public benefit is satisfied. Thus, in our case, providing that Ivor Evans's donation can be regarded as for the Miners' Welfare Club *per se* – and not just for the provision of cut price food and drink to a group who happen to be defined as members of the Miners' Club – we need only ask whether they constitute a sufficient section of the public. Generally, it is clear that members of a club or other institution can qualify as a section of the public, providing that membership is not limited to such a small group as to make it self-selecting, and even this might be overcome if the members then go out into the community as better citizens (*Neville Estates v Madden* (1962)). Likewise, although a personal link or nexus between a donor and the class to benefit from a charity will normally negate any public benefit (*Oppenheim v Tobacco Securities Trust Co Ltd* (1951)),

Re Koettgen (1954) suggests that there is no objection if merely a proportion of the intended class are linked to the donor. *A fortiori*, the fact that just one person – the donor's father – is a member of the club does not destroy the public nature of its purpose. This will almost certainly be construed as a charitable gift.

Under the third intended trust, Ivor Evans wishes to use the company's money to establish a conference centre for the fostering of understanding between the UK and the Far East in order to promote trade in agrochemicals. This will be difficult to justify as a charitable trust. In general terms, a trust for the promotion of international harmony and understanding is not charitable (*Re Astor* (1952); *Re Strakosch* (1949)), although it seems that some trusts for the promotion of a trade or occupation may be if they are in some way educational (*Construction Industry Training Board v Attorney General* (1973)). However, following *Re Koeppler* (1984), the establishment of a centre simply as a forum for fostering international relations cannot be charitable unless there is a substantial educational element. There is no evidence of that here, and, indeed, there seems to be a personal motive behind the company's offer to provide these funds.

Finally, there is the aim of establishing a nursery school for the children of employees. The purpose itself seems charitable, being for the advancement of education, at least if the school is non-profit making (*Abbey, Malvern Wells Ltd v Minister of Local Government and Housing* (1951)). Unfortunately, however, there is a very real possibility that this trust will fail because it violates the 'personal nexus test' and therefore fails to be for the benefit of the public (*Re Compton* (1945); *Oppenheim v Tobacco Securities Trust Co Ltd* (1951)). The test put forward in these cases apparently makes it impossible for the persons intended to benefit from the charitable purpose to share a personal link with each other and with the donor of the charitable funds. In our case, a personal link exists because all the children are of employees of the company and the donor is the employer. The case is on a par with *Oppenheim*. Needless to say, the efficacy of this test has been challenged (for example, in *Dingle v Turner* (1972)), but it is designed to ensure that a donor does not derive a private benefit, with fiscal advantages, from what is supposed to be a public purpose. Consequently, even though the motives of Chem Inc may be of the purest kind, the fact that this trust would confer benefits on their own employees, making employment at the company more attractive and the workforce more content, is enough to deprive the intended trust of charitable status.

 —Note

This is a fairly standard question on the law of charity, and it calls for a good knowledge of case law and of the meaning of public benefit. Note, also, that the question does not raise one of the other examinable issues, that of the political nature of charities. Generally, a purpose cannot be charitable if it is political, and this includes those organisations which campaign for a change in the law because it is not appropriate for a court to judge whether a change in the law is of public benefit (see *McGovern v Attorney General* (1982); *Bowman v Secular Society* (1917); *Southwood v Attorney General* (2000)).

 ——— Question 23 ———

Consider the validity of the following dispositions in the will of Freddie, who died this year:

(a) £10,000 on trust for the preservation of the habitat of the colony of badgers that is threatened by the work on the Manchester ring road;

(b) £10,000 to the inhabitants of Littleham for the provision of a new swimming pool to be used solely by the residents thereof for such a period as the law allows;

(c) £10,000 to provide scholarships for entry to Cavendish College, my old school, providing that at least 75% of the money be allocated to the sons of old boys; and

(d) £10,000 to my trustees, the income to be used for 30 years by the Lifeboat Association for the provision of rescue crafts, thence on trust for the purposes of the Society for the Promotion of Tiddlywinks.

Answer plan

- A brief note that this question covers both charitable and non-charitable purpose trusts;
- protection of the countryside, possible political objectives, trusts beneficial to the community;
- recreational charities, restricted classes, *Re Denley* purpose trust;
- educational trust: limited beneficiaries, personal nexus; and
- gift to charity, followed by a gift to a purpose trust, perpetuity problems.

——— Answer ———

Freddie, the testator, has included a number of dispositions in his will, all of which involve consideration of purpose trusts or related concepts. At the outset, it is important to bear in mind two general principles, reliance on which will help determine the validity of Freddie's proposed gifts. First, it is not possible to create a trust for a non-charitable purpose, save in the most exceptional cases (*Re Endacott* (1960) and *Re Denley* (1969)). Such trusts are void and the property will result to the estate of the testator. Secondly, and in contrast, should a purpose fall within the legal definition of charity, there may be a perfectly valid purpose trust which may last in perpetuity and which will enjoy considerable legal and fiscal advantages. In fact, the dispositions in this problem concern both charitable and non-charitable purpose trusts.

(a) '10,000 on trust for the preservation of the habitat of the colony of badgers that is threatened by the work on the Manchester ring road'

Although there is little mention of animals in the Preamble to the Statute of Charitable Uses 1601, it is now reasonably clear that a trust for animal welfare may be charitable within the fourth category of charity identified by Lord Macnaughten in *Commissioners for Special Purposes of Income Tax v Pemsel* (1891): viz, purposes beneficial to the community. For example, in *Re Wedgewood* (1915), a trust for the protection of animals was held charitable, as was a trust in favour of a dogs' home in *Re Douglas* (1887). The point is, however, that these trusts are charitable because they benefit mankind – being displays of generosity and human kindness, or as protecting animals useful to man – and not because they benefit the animals *per se* (*Re Grove-Grady* (1929)). Consequently, Freddie's trust must demonstrate some benefit to the public from the protection of these animals and whilst the display of human kindness in this purpose is evident, it might not be enough. Moreover, there is a risk that this purpose will be denied charitable status because of its actual or potential political overtones. It is a clear principle that charities may not engage in political activities and may not attempt to cloak political objectives with more benign purposes (*Bowman v Secular Society* (1917); *McGovern v Attorney General* (1982);

Southwood v Attorney General (2000)). In our case, this might be seen as an attempt to protect the countryside from transport policies approved by Parliament and this can too easily be regarded as political, especially if it involves a campaigning or propaganda element. So, even if this purpose does manifest a sufficient public benefit, the desire to protect animals may be so bound up with political objectives that its charitable status should be denied.

(b) '£10,000 to the inhabitants of Littleham for the provision of a new swimming pool to be used solely by the residents thereof for such a period as the law allows'

This is clearly an attempt to establish a trust for a recreational purpose. In general a trust for recreation or sport *per se* is not charitable (*Re Nottage* (1895)), although the matter would be different if the recreation was tied to an educational purpose (*IRC v McMullen* (1981)) or some other charitable object. Conversely, trusts for the provision of land for recreation can be charitable, even if limited to persons from a particular locality (*Re Hadden* (1932)), although this was not extended to an indoor swimming pool in *Valuation Commissioner for Northern Ireland v Lurgan BC* (1968). In the light of this rather clear authority, it seems unlikely that Freddie's trust will be charitable under the general law. Fortunately, that is not the end of the matter. First, it could be that this trust can be charitable under the Recreational Charities Act 1958 if the recreational facilities are provided in the interests of social welfare (s 1(1) of the Act), this being where the facilities are provided with the object of improving the conditions of life of the people of Littleham, being persons in need of such facilities by reason of age, infirmity or social and economic considerations (s 1(2) of the Act). Moreover, since *IRC v Guild* (1992), it is clear that the persons benefiting from the recreational purpose do not need to be 'deprived' in order to have their conditions of life improved. It is enough if the general conditions of life for members of the public are improved. In our case, providing that the people of Littleham constitute a section of the public (as they are almost bound to do, *Re Hadden* (1932)), this purpose may fall within the Act and be charitable, as was a trust for a similar leisure facility in *Guild*.

Secondly, even if this purpose is deemed non-charitable, it might still be valid as being within the *Re Denley* (1969) exception to the rule against purpose trusts. Indeed, this does seem to be a trust which indirectly benefits ascertainable individuals and it is limited to the perpetuity period by the reference to 'such a period as the law allows'. In fact, the case is very similar to *Denley* itself and Freddie's estate can be content that, at the very least, he has established a valid non-charitable purpose trust.

(c) '£10,000 to provide scholarships for entry to Cavendish College, my old school, providing that at least 75% of the money be allocated to the sons of old boys'

In essence, this aspect of Freddie's will encompasses an attempt to establish an educational charitable trust. There is, of course, no doubt that the provision of scholarships is for the advancement of education (*Christ's College Cambridge* case (1757)). Unfortunately, there is some doubt as to whether this particular trust is for the 'public benefit', this being an essential requirement of charitable status (*Oppenheim v Tobacco Securities Trust Co Ltd* (1951)). Clearly there is a common characteristic shared by most of the persons intended to receive scholarships and this may fall foul of the personal nexus test put forward in *Oppenheim* although, in our case, it is not clear whether being the son of an old boy is 'personal' in this sense. In fact, our doubts about the applicability of the *Oppenheim* test may go further, for there is no common link between the donor of the money and the intended class, merely between most of the class *inter se*. Likewise, there are cases where educational trusts and scholarships for limited classes of persons have been held charitable (*Attorney General v Sidney Sussex College* (1869)). Perhaps the most helpful authority is *Re Koettgen* (1954) where there was a valid educational trust even though the trustees were directed to exercise a preference for employees of a single company in respect of 75% of the total donation. Using that as a reference point, Freddie's trustees may well be successful in establishing the charitable nature of this part of his testamentary dispositions. It ought to be pointed out that *Re Koettgen* was severely criticised by Lord Radcliffe in the Privy Council decision *Caffoor v Commissioners of Income Tax* [1961] AC 584, as essentially an 'employee trust' and comes close to being inconsistent with the *Oppenheim* case. In *IRC v Educational Grants Association* (1967) the Court of Appeal refused to follow the reasoning in *Re Koettgen*.

(d) '£10,000 to my trustees, the income to be used for 30 years by the Lifeboat Association for the provision of rescue crafts, thence on trust for the purposes of the Society for the Promotion of Tiddlywinks'

There is clear authority that trusts for rescue services are charitable, being for purposes beneficial to the community (*Re Wokingham Fire Brigade Trusts* (1951)). The Royal National Lifeboat Institution is a charitable organisation and, by analogy, so should be a gift to this Lifeboat Association for the provision of rescue craft. However, problems arise because, after 30 years, the £10,000 capital sum is to be given to the Society for the Promotion of Tiddlywinks which is most unlikely to be regarded as charitable, being recreational and unlikely to fall within the Recreational Charities Act 1958 (*Re Nottage* (1895) and ss 1(1) and 1(2) of the Act). This is, then, a gift to charity, followed by a gift over for a non-charitable purpose. In these circumstances, there may well be problems with the rule against perpetuities. The gift over to the Tiddlywinks Society takes place 30 years after Freddie's death and since the testator has not named any lives in being, he will be taken to be that life. The perpetuity period expires 21 years after Freddie's death and the trust in favour of the Tiddlywinks Society takes effect outside it. This is fatal to the effectiveness of the gift over (in addition to it being a gift to a non-charitable purpose) because a gift over from a charity to a non-charitable purpose is subject to the normal perpetuity rule (*Re Cooper* (1956)). Consequently, the property would either remain absolutely with the charity if s 12 of the Perpetuities and Accumulations Act 1964 applies (determinable charitable gift becomes absolute) or it will revert to the donor at the end of the perpetuity period if it does not.

Note

This is a difficult problem as it combines the law of charities, non-charitable purpose trusts and perpetuities. It demonstrates the wisdom of a thorough treatment of *all* purpose trusts and an understanding of the close relationship between the charitable and non-charitable variety.

Question 24

In what circumstances may a charitable gift be applied *cy-près*?

Answer plan

- Purpose of *cy-près*;
- difference between initial and subsequent impossibility;
- construing the nature of the failure: hence role for *cy-près*; and
- statutory modifications to *cy-près*: Charities Act 1993.

Answer

In the normal course of events, when a trust fails, the trust property will revert to the settlor or to the testator's estate under a resulting trust. This will be so whether the trust fails because of some initial defect, so that all the original trust property is held on resulting trust (*Sprange v Barnard* (1789)), or because the beneficiaries have received all they are entitled to under the trust and some unexpended trust property remains (*Re Abbott* (1900)). However, charitable trusts are different. There is a public interest in ensuring that once money has been effectively dedicated to charity – and all the advantages of charitable status have accrued – it should thereafter remain in the public domain and be used so far as is possible in fulfilment of the original charitable purposes. Consequently, when a charitable trust fails, the trust property may be applied by the court or Charity Commissioners for charitable purposes as near as possible (*cy-près*) to those originally laid down by the settlor or testator (*Re Prison Charities* (1873)).

The principles governing *cy-près* are to be found in the common law as supplemented by what is now s 13 of the Charities Act 1993 (formerly s 13 of the Charities Act 1960). In essence, property which is subject to a trust for a charitable purpose (and this must be determined before all else) may be applied *cy-près* when the charitable purpose is either impossible or impractical to achieve, or if one of the events specified in s 13(1) of the Charities Act 1993 has occurred. Of course, there are conditions to be satisfied before charitable property can be applied *cy-près* and, if they are not met, the property will then result to the settlor or testator's estate in the normal way, *Re Rymer* (1895). The basic position is that *cy-près* will operate when: (a) a charitable trust fails; and (b) this is a result of either initial impossibility/impracticality or subsequent impossibility/impracticality, itself to be determined under the common law as supplemented by s 13 of the Act.

In order for the court or Charity Commissioners to apply a gift *cy-près*, it is essential that the now failed trust must have been charitable in the first place. This is obvious, but nonetheless crucial, for if the trust was not originally charitable, the property will immediately result to the donor (*Re Endacott* (1960)). Likewise, it must be clear that the charitable trust has actually failed and this is not always readily apparent. For example, in those situations where the donor has intended to make a gift on trust to an avowedly charitable organisation, but that organisation does not exist at the time the gift takes effect, it may be that a successor organisation has taken over the original charity and is entitled to receive the donation. The point in cases such as this is that the gift itself has never actually failed, merely that the organisation administering the gift has changed. Indeed, this approach – which is really about successors in title – can be adopted when the 'new' organisation is carrying on the same purposes as the original organisation (*Re Roberts* (1963)) or when it is not (*Re Faraker* (1912)). In fact, it matters not that the 'new' charity has a different name or operates in a different geographical area. Thus, although some cases look like an application of the trust property *cy-près*, they may be in fact quite distinct and the only way to determine whether there is a successor in title to the original charity (and, therefore, no *cy-près*) is to construe the original gift and decide whether there is any organisation which can legitimately be viewed as a successor.

Assuming, then, that both the donor's original gift was charitable in law and that there is no legal successor to the now defunct original donee, the property of the charitable trust may be applied *cy-près* if there is initial impossibility/impracticality or subsequent impossibility/impracticality in the performance of the trust. As noted below, it is very important to be able to distinguish between *initial* failure and *subsequent* failure, because different conditions for *cy-près* apply to each case.

Cases of initial impossibility or impracticality of the donor's original charitable purpose can arise in an infinite number of situations. Typical examples are where property has been given to a specific charity which no longer exists and has no successor in title (*Re Rymer* (1895)); where a named charitable organisation never existed (*Re Harwood* (1936)); where external factors make achievement of the original purpose impossible (*Biscoe v Jackson* (1887): no land available); and where the intended donees cannot use the gift due to the donor's limitations on its use (*Re Dominion Students Hall Trust* (1947); *Re Woodhams* (1981)). Moreover, although the court has always taken a generous view of what was 'impossible' or 'impractical', since the enactment of s 13 of the Charities Act 1960 (now s 13 of the Charities Act 1993) 'the circumstances in which the original purposes of a charitable gift can be altered to allow the property or part of it to be applied *cy-près*' have been considerably extended. In essence, those circumstances now include cases where although possible to carry out the donor's wishes, it is simply absurd, uneconomical, or pointless to do so. Again, typical examples of *cy-près* under the Act are where a charity's income is either too small or too large for the donor's original purposes or where amalgamation with another charity would achieve more effectively those charitable purposes. In short, the court now has a *cy-près* jurisdiction where the 'original purposes' (see *Oldham Metropolitan BC v Attorney General* (1993)) are possible but not practical or feasible and if this is apparent at the time the gift takes effect there is initial 'impracticality'.

Whatever the reason a charitable trust is deemed initially impossible or impractical (with or without the intervention of s 13), there can be no application of the property *cy-près* unless the terms of the trust disclose a 'paramount intention' to give to charity, otherwise known as a 'general charitable intention'. This was the position before the Act (*Re Wilson* (1913)) and remains so afterwards (s 13(2)). The essence of the matter is that, with initial impossibility or impracticality, the trust property has not yet vested in a charitable purpose because the donor's desired mode of application of it has failed. Consequently, before the court will sanction a different mode of application of that property which will, nevertheless, achieve a similar purpose to that specified by the donor, it must be clear that the donor was more concerned with achieving the charitable purpose *per se* than making a gift to the specific charity that is now defunct. Hence the need for a general charitable intention. Not surprisingly, whether such an intention exists is a matter of construction of each charitable gift, although without the existence of such an intention, the property will result to the donor. For example, in *Re Harwood* (1936), where a named charitable organisation never existed, the courts were very willing to find a general charitable intention, but not so in *Re Rymer* (1895) where there was a gift to a specific charitable organisation which once existed but which no longer existed when the charitable gift was to take effect. In one circumstance, however, a general charitable intention will be deemed to exist by force of statute. Under s 14 of the Charities Act 1993 (formerly s 14 of the Charities Act 1960), property given by anonymous donors shall be deemed to be given for general charitable purposes after suitable advertisements have been made and property raised through collection boxes and raffles, etc shall be deemed from the start to be made with such an intention. This is an entirely practical solution that will prevent large sums of money from being held indefinitely on resulting trust for donors who might never appear.

Turning now to cases of subsequent impossibility or impracticality, once again the circumstances in which a charitable trust may fail on these grounds are innumerable. The heart of the matter is that the trust property has been given effectively to the original charitable purpose or organisation, but subsequently it has become impossible or impractical to fulfil that purpose, as where there is a surplus of funds after the charitable purpose has been fulfilled (*Re Wokingham Fire Brigade Trusts* (1951)). Importantly, in cases of subsequent failure, the trust property already has been dedicated to charity and so there is no need to find a general charitable intention before *cy-près* application can occur. *Cy-près* may take effect upon the subsequent failure, without more, and this is why it is crucial in practice to be able to distinguish it from cases of initial failure. So, in *Re Slevin* (1891), where a gift was made to a charitable institution which existed at the date of the testator's death but which ceased to exist before the money was actually paid over, there was no need to find a general charitable intention in order to apply the money *cy-près*: the property became vested in the charity at the testator's death (which did then exist) and so this was a case of subsequent impossibility.

Cases of such obvious subsequent failure are rare for, normally, the achievement of a charitable purpose has simply become outdated or uneconomic, rather than impossible. As such, under the common law, *cy-près* would not be available and the trust property could not be used effectively. Consequently, in order to allow *cy-près* application to take place in these circumstances, s 13 of the Charities Act 1993 extends considerably the situations in which the court may regard subsequent failure to have occurred. This will now include cases where the charitable purpose has become subsequently impractical or lacks feasibility or is simply uneconomic. Of course, such an extension of the court's powers may well cut across the donor's original intention and for that reason much of the court's jurisdiction under s 13 may be exercised only with regard to 'the spirit of the gift'. While this does not introduce a requirement of a general charitable intention in cases of subsequent failure under the Act, clearly the court cannot proceed immediately to *cy-près* under s 13 without having some regard to the donor's original motives (*Re Lepton's Charity* (1972); *Forrest v Attorney General* (1986): an Australian case construing a similar statutory provision). In fact, s 13 lists five sets of circumstances in which a court may now act in *cy-près* to supplement the position at common law. These include, but are not limited to, cases where the original purposes have been fulfilled (s 13(1)(a)(i)), for example, *Re Lepton* (1972); where the property may be more effectively used in conjunction with other property (s 13(1)(c)); where the original purposes made reference to an area or class of persons who have ceased to be suitable (s 13(1)(d), see, for example, *Peggs v Lamb* (1994)); and where the original purposes have been provided for by other means (s 13(1)(e)). Obviously, these provisions, along with the other situations listed in s 13, give the court considerable power to deal with charitable trust property. This is only to be welcomed given that charities are perpetual, while charitable need changes over time.

To conclude then, it is apparent that the power of a court to apply property *cy-près* both for initial and subsequent impossibility or impracticality depends on a number of factors. Among these, determining whether there has actually been a failure of the original charity can be quite difficult, although s 13 of the Charities Act has helped considerably. Likewise, the search for a general charitable intention in cases of initial failure requires careful thought, as does the meaning of 'spirit of the gift' in s 13. All in all, however, the perpetual nature of charities, the vast number of charitable trusts and the rapidly changing nature of modern society demand an effective *cy-près* doctrine. By and large, this exists.

Note

Cases on the meaning of 'spirit of the gift' in s 13 are rare and rather inconclusive. The best authority is the Australian case referred to above. It is also important to distinguish *cy-près* from cases where one charity succeeds another and takes over its assets. See the problem below.

Question 25

Arnold made his will in 2000, in which he left four gifts of £50,000 each to:

(a) the National Association for the Homeless, an incorporated charity;

(b) the Whale Protection League, a voluntary association;

(c) the Cook Home for the Disabled; and

(d) the Norfolk Bird and Rescue Centre.

When Arnold died this year, it transpired that the National Association for the Homeless had become defunct two years previously and its premises purchased by the UK League Against Homelessness. Likewise, the Whale Protection League had disbanded after disagreements between its members, to be replaced by two organisations, the Whale and Dolphin Sanctuary and the Society for the Humane Harvesting of Whales. It also transpires that there never was a 'Cook Home for the Disabled' and that the Norfolk Bird and Rescue Centre was taken over by the RSPCA and relocated in Cornwall.

Advise as to the proper distribution of Arnold's estate.

Answer plan

- *Cy-près*: general purpose;
- initial or subsequent impossibility;
- gifts to institutions, purposes or named funds; and
- successor organisations.

Answer

Arnold has attempted to distribute his property among several named organisations, none of which exists at the date of his death, at least in their original form. At the outset, it is necessary to determine whether all or any of these gifts are for charitable purposes. If any is not, then the property allocated to that organisation will return to Arnold's estate under a simple resulting trust consequent upon a void purpose trust (*Re Endacott* (1960)). Fortunately, all of the original purposes selected by Arnold appear to be charitable. We are told that the National Association for the Homeless is 'an incorporated charity'; the Cook Home for the Disabled falls squarely within the first category of charity identified in *Commissioners for Special Purposes of Income Tax v Pemsel* (1891), being for the relief of the sick; the Norfolk Bird and Rescue Centre will be charitable (*Re Wedgewood* (1915)), as will the Whale Protection League, providing that it does not engage in political activities.

The importance of deciding that these four purposes are charitable is that it may help determine the distribution of Arnold's estate now that none of the original organisations remain in existence. Simply put, the failure of a charitable trust does not always result in the property being returned to the donor or his estate but may, if certain conditions are fulfilled, be applied by the court or Charity Commissioners *cy-près* – that is, for purposes as near as possible to those originally stipulated (*Re Wilson* (1913)). Broadly speaking, if a charity has failed for 'initial impossibility or impracticality', it may be applied *cy-près* if there is evidence that the donor had a general intention to benefit charity (*Re Wilson*). However, if the charity has failed for subsequent impossibility or impracticality, the property may be applied *cy-près* without the need for such an intention, since it has already been dedicated to charity in perpetuity (*Re Peel* (1921)). In our cases, it will be necessary to determine, first, whether the charitable trust has failed; secondly, whether such failure is initial or subsequent; and thirdly, if there is initial failure, whether there is a general charitable intention. Each of the four purposes identified by Arnold will be considered in turn.

(a) '£50,000 to the National Association for the Homeless', an incorporated charity

It is clear that Arnold has attempted to give his donation to a charity which, although once in existence, does not exist at the date the gift is to take effect, being on the testator's death. If anything, this may be a case of initial impossibility. However, we are told that the premises of the National Association for the Homeless have been purchased by the UK League Against Homelessness and it is arguable that this institution is in fact the successor in title to the National Association. If that is the case, the correct solution may well be that there has been no failure of Arnold's gift at all but, rather, a continuity between his named charity and its lawful successor, which may then receive the donation.

Whether this is a case of initial failure or a case of a successor charity depends on the construction of Arnold's gift in the circumstances of the case. There are three possibilities. First, it may be construed that Arnold's gift is a gift specifically to the institution named in his will (*Re Rymer* (1895)). If this is the case, then there is initial impossibility and a general charitable intention needs to be found if the property is to be applied *cy-près*. Unfortunately, *Re Rymer* also decides that it is difficult to find a general charitable intention when a specific donee that once existed has been identified with such clarity although, as *Re Finger* (1972) demonstrates, this is not entirely impossible. Secondly, the original donation can be construed as a gift to the particular purposes undertaken by the original institution, so that if another institution has taken over those purposes, the property will pass to it automatically as the successor in title (*Re Roberts* (1963)). Thirdly, the original donation can be construed as a gift to the charitable fund administered by the original institution, so that if there is another body now administering that fund, the property will pass to it automatically as the successor in title (*Re Faraker* (1912)). In our case, it is unclear which construction to adopt. According to *Re Vernon* (1972) and *Re Finger* (1972), if the charity is incorporated – as here – then the gift should be construed as a gift to the specific institution *per se* (the first possibility above), while if it is unincorporated the gift should be construed as a gift for the purposes of the original institution. On the other hand, this guidance takes no account of the *Re Faraker* construction. If we follow *Re Vernon*, the donation to the National Association for the Homeless will fail for initial impossibility (being a gift to a specific institution) and will be applicable *cy-près* only if a general charitable intention can be found – something which *Re Rymer*, but not *Re Finger*, says is difficult. Failing such an intention, the property will result back to Arnold's estate. Again, on the basis of *Vernon*, a construction of the gift for purposes does not seem possible. This would mean that the UK League Against Homelessness could not claim the property as of right unless the *Faraker* construction is adopted and the League is now administering the National Association's funds. This we do not know. All in all, a resulting trust seems likely, or *cy-près* if a general charitable intention can be found.

(b) '£50,000 to the Whale Protection League', now dissolved and replaced by the Whale & Dolphin Sanctuary and the Society for the Humane Harvesting of Whales

Once again, assuming this gift to be charitable, we must ask first what is the proper construction to be placed on Arnold's original disposition. This is particularly important in this case as there are two organisations who may claim to be the lawful successors in title to the Whale Protection League. We are told that the Whale Protection League was a 'voluntary association' and, therefore, it may be possible (should we wish – see below) to avoid construing this as a gift to a specific institution which has failed (that is, not

Re Rymer) and so not a case of initial impossibility allowing for *cy-près* only if a general charitable intention can be found. However, it is not easy to choose between the *Re Roberts* construction (a gift for the particular charitable purpose) and the *Re Faraker* construction (a gift to a particular charitable fund). Again, following *Re Vernon* (1962), the unincorporated nature of the original charity might lead us to choose the 'purpose construction', but then we have the dilemma of deciding exactly what the original purpose was. Was it the protection of whales, etc in all circumstances, so that the Whale and Dolphin Sanctuary may claim the gift as carrying on those original purposes? – or was it a gift for the protection of whales from unnecessary hunting, in which case the Society for the Humane Harvesting of Whales may be the lawful successor to the original purpose? Indeed, precisely the same problem arises if we decide to adopt the *Faraker* construction (gift to a fund) instead of the purpose approach. It is not at all clear which of the rival organisations now administers the funds of the defunct society. Consequently, in the absence of further evidence, we might actually prefer a pragmatic solution and decide that this was, after all, a gift specifically to the Whale Protection League, which failed initially at Arnold's death, but where we can infer a general charitable intention so allowing the property to be applied *cy-près*. If the property is applied *cy-près* (as opposed to going to a successor in title), each rival organisation can receive a share, or none at all, as the court decides.

(c) '£50,000 to the Cook Home for the Disabled'

The Cook Home for the Disabled has never existed and therefore there is no doubt that this is a case of initial impossibility. Furthermore, there can be no successors in title to an organisation that never was. The property will result to Arnold's estate unless a general charitable intention can be found, in which case it will be applicable *cy-près*. In this regard, *Re Harwood* (1936) decides that, where a gift has been given to an institution which has never existed, a general charitable intention should be presumed unless there is convincing evidence to the contrary. Although somewhat arbitrary, this guidance has been followed in *Re Satterthwaite's Wills Trust* (1966) and in our case affords good authority for a *cy-près* application of the property.

(d) '£50,000 to the Norfolk Bird and Rescue Centre'

Once again, this donation calls for a decision about the nature of Arnold's gift to the Norfolk Bird Sanctuary. If there is an initial failure of the gift – because it was a gift to that sanctuary and nothing else – the gift may go *cy-près* on the finding of a general charitable intention, or it will result to Arnold's estate. We are told, however, that the Norfolk charity was 'taken over' by the RSPCA and we can infer from this that the RSPCA is to be regarded as the lawful successors in title to the original donees. In other words, there has not been an initial failure of the gift. In view of the fact that the RSPCA operates in protection of all animals – not just birds – it is likely that we can construe the original donation as a gift to the general fund of the Norfolk charity, which fund is now being administered by the RSPCA, as per *Re Faraker*. There is, then, no *cy-près* and no resulting trust, merely a continuation of Arnold's gift in a different form and the £50,000 may be distributed to the RSPCA as successors in title to the Norfolk Bird and Rescue Centre.

Note

There is a crucial difference in law between application of charitable property *cy-près* and distribution of property to a 'new' charity which can be regarded as the successor in title to the original donee. In the second case, there is no failure of the original gift. Of course, if *cy-près* is called for, the property can be distributed to an organisation with similar objects to the original donee – even one which claimed but failed to be a successor in title (as with (b) above).

5 Resulting Trusts

Introduction

Resulting trusts are an essential doctrine in the law of trusts. Apart from relatively rare occasions when the subject matter of a trust will pass to the Crown as ownerless property (*bona vacantia*), resulting trusts provide the last practical means of disposing of trust property should the original scheme of a trust fail. In fact, a resulting trust can arise in such a variety of circumstances that there is only marginal merit in considering it on an undergraduate course as a topic in its own right. For example, resulting trusts need to be considered in relation to secret trusts, the three certainties, the beneficiary principle, charities, formalities and constructive trusts. This is not an exhaustive list, and the use of the resulting trust in these and other cases is best considered alongside the substantive law which it services. Moreover, there is now much academic discussion about the proper theoretical basis of resulting trusts: for example, do they arise by reason of the intention of the parties, by operation of law, out of the implied or express acceptance by the resulting trustee of an obligation affecting conscience, or for different reasons in different circumstances. This has practical consequences, as illustrated by the House of Lords' refusal to impose a resulting trust on the defendant in *Westdeutsche Landesbank Girozentrale v Islington* LBC (1996). As indicated above, much of this debate is outside the scope of an undergraduate course, but there are issues here which need consideration. In this chapter, brief attention will be paid to the attributes of the resulting trust *per se* (assuming that 'resulting trusts' share some common attributes), to issues touching on the rationale for the imposition of resulting trusts and to a typical problem type examination question.

In very general terms, a resulting trust arises when the original arrangement envisaged by the testator or settlor has failed, has not been properly established or has been fully achieved without exhausting the trust's assets. To this extent, it arises out of a disappointed, failed or satisfied purpose of the testator/settlor. Although this is a simplistic picture – see, for example, resulting trusts in the context of co-owned property – it explains why, under a resulting trust, the property returns or 'results' to the person originally entitled to it. To put it another way, resulting trusts may be seen as the consequence of the application of the old maxim that 'equity abhors a beneficial vacuum'. How, and in what cases, this is related to the intention of the person originally entitled to the property or to the state of mind (conscience) of the original trustee are difficult and complex issues.

Question 26

To what extent can it be said that resulting trusts operate to support the equitable maxim that 'equity abhors a beneficial vacuum'?

Answer plan

- General nature of resulting trusts and the maxim that equity abhors a beneficial vacuum;
- types of resulting trust;
- differences between resulting trusts arising out of the failure of an express trust and other resulting trusts;
- possible distinction between 'automatic' and 'presumed' resulting trusts; and
- rejection of such a distinction in *Westdeutsche Landesbank Girozentrale v Islington LBC* (1996).

— **Answer** —

In the usual case, when an express trust is established, the donor will transfer trust property to trustees (or declare himself trustee of it) and at the same time indicate clearly who is to benefit from the trust: in other words, the beneficiaries are identified with some precision and the trustees know for whom they are holding the trust property. In such situations, there is, of course, a perfectly valid trust for the beneficiaries, enforceable by them in court. However, there are many other situations where, for some reason, the main purposes of the donor cannot be achieved, either because the trust is void for lack of compliance with some rule of equity or statute, because of difficulties with the potential beneficiaries or because the original scheme of the trust is unworkable. In these cases, the property is held on trust (because an express trust has been declared), but there may be no beneficiaries lawfully entitled to the trust property. The question therefore arises as to who owns the trust property or, more accurately, who is entitled to the beneficial interest under the trust. Obviously (at least in the great majority of cases), the trustee *qua* trustee cannot keep the property because a trustee is merely the formal owner of the property holding it for the 'real' or equitable owners. The solution to this problem (sometimes known as cases involving failure of an express trust) is provided by the principles of resulting trusts. In *Vandervell v IRC* (1967), Lord Reid said, in respect of a trust, that 'the beneficial interest must belong to or be held for somebody: so, if it was not to belong to the donee or to be held by him in trust for somebody, it must remain with the donor'. This statement epitomises one substantial use of resulting trusts and encapsulates what is meant by the equitable maxim that 'equity abhors a beneficial vacuum'. In short, if there are no beneficiaries entitled to the property, the trustee will hold the property on trust for the donor (or his estate): it will 'result back' to the person who provided it in the first place.

It is important to realise, then, that 'resulting trusts' are a very versatile concept. They represent the solution of last resort when determining the ownership of trust property, failing which the property will fall to the Crown as *'bona vacantia'* (ownerless property), as happened with part of the gift in *Re West Sussex Constabulary Widows Fund* (1971). The circumstances in which a resulting trust may arise are numerous and varied and most cases are unique on their own facts, although this does not necessarily mean that the *concept* of resulting trusts cannot be explained by a general theory. It does mean, however, that it can be difficult, and sometimes misleading, to draw rigid lines around different categories of resulting trust. Of course, the identification of similar sets of circumstances in which resulting trusts can arise is possible, but it should be remembered that the types of resulting trust discussed below do not necessarily differ in nature.

First, one of the most common forms of resulting trust – and one which illustrates the equitable maxim of the question very well – is that which arises when there has been an initial failure of the trust which the donor had intended to establish, either in respect of the whole or part of the trust property. In such cases, the donor will have attempted to create an express trust but it will have failed in whole or in part due to lack of compliance with some rule relating to the validity of trusts, or absence of beneficiaries, or failure to dispose entirely of the beneficial interest. For example, in *Vandervell v IRC* (1967) itself, the donor had attempted to dispose of his interest under the complicated Vandervell family trusts but had failed to divest himself fully of one portion of his property. Hence, that portion resulted to him and he was liable to tax upon it, being its true owner. Likewise, if there is complete failure of the trust for uncertainty of objects, or lack of a human beneficiary (a purpose trust: *Re Endacott* (1960)), or where a charitable gift fails initially and cannot be applied *cy-près* (*Re Rymer* (1895)), the property will result back to the settlor. In all of these cases, the resulting trust arises in consequence of the failure of an express trust and, on one view, is said to operate 'automatically' upon that failure by operation of law (*per* Megarry J in *Re Vandervell's Trusts* (1974)). Whether such trusts are correctly described as 'automatic', suggesting, as it does, that they operate independently of the intention of the person originally making the gift, is open to doubt following *Westdeutsche Landesbank Girozentrale v Islington LBC* (1996). In that case, Lord Browne-Wilkinson said that resulting trusts operate because of an intention on the part of the donor to recover the property should the primary purpose fail. Hence, even in cases where there is failure of an express trust in the sense just discussed, a resulting trust will not arise if there is clear evidence of the donor's intention 'to part out and out' with his property. Such an intention, which would negate the existence of a resulting trust, means that the money is ownerless and will pass to the Crown as *bona vacantia* (*Re West Sussex*). It remains to be seen whether this general approach to resulting trusts (that is, grounding them in the intention of the donor) is accepted. If it is, then the equitable maxim raised in the question is supported only to the extent that the parties' intention does not dictate otherwise. Importantly, not only does such a view strike a discordant note when measured against the once accepted dichotomy of *Re Vandervell*, it also runs counter to a powerful argument that resulting trusts are restitutionary in character and are 'simply' a non-intention based device used to reverse unjust enrichment.

A second example of the use of resulting trusts arises where the primary trust established by the settlor has been completed, yet a surplus of undisposed trust property remains. Again, the traditional view is that the surplus is returned to the donor or his estate under a resulting trust because 'equity abhors a beneficial vacuum'. So, in *Re Abbott* (1900), a gift on trust for the maintenance of two elderly ladies came to an end on the death of the survivor. The initial trust was thus completed and the surplus was held on resulting trust for the subscribers to the sisters' fund. Again, in *Re Gillingham Bus Disaster Fund* (1958), money was raised by subscription for the victims of an accident and it was held that such funds as were not applied for this purpose should result back to the donors because the other purposes intended for the money were void for uncertainty. Again, however, if it is true that intention is an essential element in the use of resulting trusts, evidence of the donor's desire to part forever with his money means that any surplus will not result (*Westdeutsche*). It is also important to realise that in this type of case, there first must have been a *trust* which has been completed (or completed as far as the law allows). It is not sufficient that there was an absolute gift to an individual bound up with a non-binding motive to use the money for some specific purpose which then fails. So, in *Re Osoba* (1979), a gift to provide the donor's daughter with income for her education was construed as an absolute gift to her with merely a non-binding direction to use the money for educational purposes. So, when the daughter's education was complete, the surplus money belonged to her: the original gift was an absolute gift, not a gift on trust for educational purposes and the doctrine of resulting trusts was irrelevant.

This leads us on to another area where resulting trusts may be important. It often happens that money is given in various ways to an unincorporated association for its members or general purposes, as where a local wildlife group raises money from donors and jumble sales. If this association then comes to an end, the surplus assets must be disposed of: equity abhors a beneficial vacuum. At one time, it was thought that these surplus assets should revert to the donors under a resulting trust (for example, *Re West Sussex*) and this solution may still be adopted where special circumstances require it, as with the distribution of the surplus assets of a pension fund (*Air Jamacia Ltd v Charlton* (1999)). If a resulting trust is adopted, equity is filling the beneficial vacuum created by the failure of the initial gift (subject, as before, to questions concerning the relevance of intention). However, in a majority of recent cases, it is evident that the more favoured solution is to distribute the assets of a defunct unincorporated association among the surviving members of the association (that is, not necessarily among those people who provided the money in the first place). This is because a donation to the association need not be construed as a gift on a trust (which subsequently fails) but as an absolute gift to the members of the association subject to their contractual obligations *inter se*, as created by the rules of the association (*Re Recher's Trust* (1972); *Re Bucks Constabulary Fund Friendly Society (No 2)* (1979)). This construction, which ousts the resulting trust because it denies the existence of a primary trust, is more convenient as it does not require an extensive search for the original donors who may be very numerous and elusive. In this sense, it is perhaps significant that the resulting trust solution has been adopted primarily in those cases where the 'donors' are readily ascertainable, as in the surplus funds of pensions case (*Air Jamaica*: resulting trust of employers' and employees' contributions; *Davis v Richards and Wallington Industries Ltd* (1990): resulting trust for employers, employees having already received all they bargained for out of the pension scheme).

Fourthly, we come to a type of resulting trust that has come to the fore in recent years, especially in commercial transactions. Thus, if A (the donor) gives money to B (the trustee) solely in order that B may pay his debts to C, if those debts are not paid, the money will result to A under a resulting trust (*Barclays Bank v Quistclose Investments Ltd* (1970)). This may appear quite straightforward, but there are a number of difficulties with this arrangement. For example, if B pays the money to C, A has no claim, so the operation of the resulting trust in favour of A is dependent upon B carrying out the specific purpose of paying its debts. Does this mean that the trust imposed on B is a purpose trust that is valid under *Re Denley* (1969) (see *Re Northern Developments (Holdings) Ltd* (1978))? Or that the equitable interest in the money is in suspense (*Carreras Rothmans Ltd v Freeman Mathews Treasure* (1985))? Or that A is the beneficiary under an express trust with a power to direct that the money be paid to C, hence excluding resulting trusts altogether? Furthermore, once the trust imposed on B is carried out (that is, he pays his debts), A will have a simple action in debt to recover the money from B: hence A has lost his proprietary right in the property under the resulting trust, to see it replaced by a personal right against B in debt, and all this by B's own actions. In other words, this example of a resulting trust is used in a deliberate way to enable a donor to provide funds for another person (usually a company with which the donor is connected) and to restrict the use of those funds for a specific purpose, failing which the resulting trust comes into operation. The resulting trust is filling the beneficial vacuum, but only for the advantage of the donor and the solution cannot be adopted where no primary trust existed (*Box v Barclays Bank* (1998)). Furthermore, it is an intended consequence of the parties' actions, in the nature of a deliberate 'failsafe'. It is very different from the 'automatic' resulting trusts considered above which might be thought to arise by operation of law because of an unintentional failure of the original arrangements. This type of resulting trust does seem consistent with the 'intention approach' put forward in *Westdeutsche*, and there is little doubt that the principle may now be applied in other circumstances. For example, in *R v CPE Board ex p Mealing-McCleod*, money paid for a specific purpose by a bank (security for the costs of litigation) and held on trust for that purpose, was repaid to the bank when the money was not needed for the purpose.

Finally, brief mention must be made of a different kind of resulting trust. This is the so called 'presumed' resulting trust. A presumed resulting trust does not arise automatically in order to fill a beneficial vacuum (assuming, post-*Westdeutsche*, that this is an acceptable analysis), but exists because of a presumed intention of the parties to create a trust over property. For example, a person who provides part of the purchase money of a house will be presumed to have intended thereby to acquire part ownership of that house under a presumed resulting trust (*Dyer v Dyer* (1788)), and a person who pays for a lottery ticket may claim the winnings by resulting trust even if, as a matter of form, the ticket is 'owned' by another (*Abrahams v Trustee in Bankruptcy of Abrahams* (1999)). As such, this presumption can be rebutted by evidence that the payment of money was as a gift or loan (*Cowcher v Cowcher* (1972)) or by the circumstances of the payment (*Mumford v Ashe* (2000): money provided in a scheme designed to defraud creditors did not generate a resulting trust for the payer). Of course, in one sense, the resulting trust is filling the beneficial vacuum created by the payer's lack of express intention as to why he is paying the money at all but, in effect, this form of resulting trust is not used to determine ownership of apparently ownerless property, but to give effect to the unexpressed intentions of the parties. It is similar in many respects to the constructive trust approach to acquisition of co-ownership as explained in *Lloyds Bank v Rosset* (1991). As will be obvious, this type of resulting trust is fully consistent with the intention approach to resulting trusts adopted in *Westdeutsche*. There is, however, a problem here. Such 'co-ownership' resulting trusts are now more frequently seen as constructive trusts pure and simple, being examples of a trust imposed to remedy unconscionable conduct on the part of the 'paper owner' of property, as in *Midland Bank v Cooke* (1996). Whether they survive as a category of resulting trusts at all is open to question.

In conclusion, it is apparent that equity will go to great lengths to avoid a beneficial vacuum and that the resulting trust is one device used to prevent this. However, given that the categorisation of some resulting trusts as 'automatic' may now be incorrect – as all resulting trusts might spring from intention and a resulting obligation of conscience on the trustee – it could be the case that resulting trusts should not be seen primarily as serving this aim. Moreover, although it is convenient and traditional to categorise resulting trusts according to the factual situations in which they arise, this should not blind us to the common characteristics shared by all resulting trusts: viz, that they identify the person who is to share in the beneficial interest despite not being expressly declared to be a beneficiary of the trust. How this can be explained, and the relationship of certain types of resulting trusts to constructive trusts and also to the law of unjust enrichment (restitution), is a large question, not yet fully resolved.

Question 27

The Over Village Association, a non-charitable, unincorporated body, existed to safeguard the amenities in the village of Over. It derived its funds from members' subscriptions, gifts by will and otherwise, the proceeds of local events such as jumble sales and raffles, money in collection boxes and one large anonymous donation. The village has now been granted Protected Status under European Union Regional Funds and its future is secure. The Village Association is about to be disbanded, but there is disagreement as to what to do with the considerable surplus funds that remain. The treasurer comes to you for advice.

Answer plan

- The link between distribution of funds and validity of gifts;
- the need to consider each 'source' of finance separately;
- resulting trusts, absolute gifts or *bona vacantia*; and
- rules to be adopted by the association, especially the establishment of a winding up mechanism.

Answer

The dissolution of an unincorporated, non-charitable association presents peculiar difficulties in English law. The absence of incorporation often means that there is no established procedure for winding up the association and its non-charitable status deprives the court of the possibility of *cy-près* application of any property held on trust consequent upon failure (or completion) of the original purposes. Consequently, when advising the treasurer of this particular association as to the proper distribution of its surplus assets, recourse must be made to the law of resulting trusts and related principles. In addition, as we shall see, the ultimate destination of the surplus assets may well depend on both the source of each donation and the explanation of how it was given validly.

When an unincorporated association ceases to exist there are three possible destinations for any surplus assets. First, the surplus may be returned to the original donors under a resulting trust. This assumes that the money was given to the association on trust in the first place (that trust having been completed or failed: *Re Gillingham Bus Disaster Fund* (1958)) and that the donor had not intended to part forever with his money (*Westdeutsche Landesbank Girozentrale v Islington LBC* (1996)).

Secondly, the surplus assets might be divided up among those members of the association in existence at the date of its demise. This, in turn, depends on recognising that the original donors transferred ownership of their donations absolutely to the members, so that the property could be dealt with according to the members' wishes as expressed and modified by the rules of the association (*Re Recher's Trust* (1972); *Re Bucks Constabulary Fund Friendly Society (No 2)* (1979); *Artistic Upholstery Ltd v Art Forma (Ltd)* (1999)). Thirdly, it is possible that both the original donors of the property have no interest in the surplus assets (no resulting trust) and that the existing members have no claim either (for example, because the rules prevent them taking a share). In such cases, the surplus assets may fall to the Crown as *bona vacantia* (ownerless property) (*Re West Sussex Constabulary's Benevolent Fund* (1971)).

In determining which of these three possibilities is the most appropriate in any given case, it is important to identify precisely the source of the surplus assets and to examine the reason why each original source of funds could be construed as valid in law when it was given. This is particularly important given that an unincorporated association (as here) has no legal personality of its own. The following analysis of each of the ways in which the Over Village Association received money assumes that it is possible to prove that an identifiable part of the surplus assets was derived from each of these methods of donation.

(a) The surplus derived from members' subscriptions

It might be thought that money derived from members' subscriptions is most appropriately returned to those members under a resulting trust, on the basis that the primary purpose of their subscriptions has failed. Indeed, in some cases, this solution has been adopted and each subscriber (whether still a member at the date of dissolution or not) has received a share proportionate to his or her original contributions (*Re Printers and Transferrers Amalgamated Trades Protection Society* (1899), and see *Air Jamaica v Charlton* in the context of surplus funds of pensions). However, this solution presupposes that the members' subscriptions were given 'on trust' in the first place, which trust has now failed or not exhausted the trust property. If true, this must have been a trust for the purposes of the association even though such trusts for purposes are void under the beneficiary principle (*Re Endacott* (1960)). Consequently, it is now more likely that income derived members' subscriptions will be treated as having been given to the association not by way of trust, but as an absolute gift to the members individually, albeit on the basis that the money is to be used in accordance with the rules of the association, this forming a binding contract between them (*Re Recher's Trust* (1972); *Re Bucks Constabulary Fund Friendly Society (No 2)* (1979); *Artistic Upholstery*). This would mean that any surplus derived from subscriptions belongs to the members absolutely (that is, those at the date of dissolution) and may be distributed among them according to their contract (the rules). If the rules prevent the members taking any surplus assets personally when the association dissolves, then either the rules must be changed prior to dissolution (if permitted by the rules themselves) or the property will pass to the Crown as *bona vacantia*. In our case, therefore, the presumption will be that the members at the date of dissolution of the association may share in the surplus assets derived from subscriptions, provided this is permitted by their contract *inter se* under the rules.

(b) The surplus derived from gifts by will and otherwise

This presents a similar problem to members' subscriptions, although now there is a real choice to be made between the resulting trust option and distribution of the surplus assets among the members. With gifts from identifiable persons, there is a distinct possibility that the money will be treated as having been given expressly for the purposes of the association and for nothing else. In other words, a primary trust for the association's purposes was intended which, having failed, the surplus assets attributable to that source result back to the donors unless there is evidence of a clear intention forever to have parted with the money (*Westdeutsche v Islington LBC* (1996)). Of course, there are problems with this interpretation, not least that trusts for purposes are void (*Re Endacott* (1960)) unless they fall within the *Re Denley* (1969) exception. So, unless this is a *Re Denley* trust, in theory the donors should be able to recover the whole of their original gifts – not merely the surplus after the void purpose had been undertaken and failed. However, although the pure logic of this is compelling, the case law suggests that only the *surplus* assets will result to the original donors and this would probably be the case if the resulting trust option were followed with our association (*Re West Sussex Constabulary Widows Fund* (1971)). Similarly, if gifts to the Over Village Association could indeed be construed on a *Re Denley* basis, the donors would be *entitled* only to the surplus funds under the resulting trust (*Re Abbott* (1900)), the primary purpose trust having been valid, but then failed. Finally, we should not discount the possibility that the *Re Bucks* construction could be adopted and that specific donations could be construed as gifts to the individual members of the association under contract, in which case the same considerations are relevant as those considered above when discussing members' subscriptions.

(c) The surplus derived from a large anonymous donation

The surplus attributable to this gift presumptively is to be dealt with in the same way as that arising from specific individual donations (as above). Of course, should the resulting trust option be followed, the anonymity of this donor creates a difficulty, although the court may well direct that the surplus assets be held in court until claimed by the donor on production of satisfactory evidence, as in *Re Gillingham Bus Disaster Fund* (1958). However, the fact that the donor wished for anonymity might lead to the conclusion either: that he or she had intended to disclaim any future interest in the gift and that it should be taken to be an absolute gift to the members of the association to be used according to their contractual rights *inter se* (*Re Bucks*); or, that a trust for purposes existed but with a resulting trust excluded by intention, with the surplus going to the Crown (*Re West Sussex; Westdeutsche v Islington LBC; Davis v Richards and Wallington Industries*). So, with surpluses arising from this source of funds it seems that all possible interpretations are available.

(d) The surplus arising from the proceeds of local events such as jumble sales and raffles

This source of the association's funds presents the least difficulty. In fact, as made clear in *Re Bucks* (1979), there are two reasons why the resulting trust option should be excluded. First, the people paying for jumble and raffle tickets, etc, are entering into a purchase contract with the association for items of jumble or raffle tickets and they obtain all they are entitled to when that contract is carried out. The 'donors' have no claim on any surplus assets, having received their full contractual entitlement. Secondly, and in any event, it is not the donor's money which goes to the association but the profit from the jumble sale or raffle after deduction of expenses. Thus, the donors do not give a sum to the association at all. Consequently, any surpluses derived from these activities cannot go by way of resulting trust and normally will be treated as an accretion to the general funds of the association to be used by the members individually, subject to their contract *inter se* (*Re Recher's Trust* (1972)). The surplus may be distributed according to the rules of the association as before.

(e) The surplus deriving from money placed in collection boxes

Once again, there is a difficulty here because the identity of the donors may be impossible to establish and, indeed, they are likely to have given in such small amounts that no claim to surplus will be made. Thus, the resulting trust option seems impractical and absurd. However, as Harman J recognised in *Re Gillingham Bus Disaster Fund* (1958), this could be the logical solution, as the donor might well have intended that the money be used for the purposes of the association alone. Why else would he put money in a collection box? In other words, the donor may have intended a gift on trust, whose failure should mean a resulting trust in his or her favour. However, in *Re West Sussex Constabulary Widows Fund* (1971), Goff J was of the opinion that money derived from street collections was given 'out and out' by the donors, thus depriving them of any future claim to it. In that case, Goff J went further and held that even the members of the Benevolent Fund had no claim to the property because the association was not designed for their benefit, being 'outward looking'. Thus, the surplus fell to the Crown as *bona vacantia*. Further, although this is a rather unattractive solution, and something of a last resort, *Westdeutsche v Islington LBC* confirmed that the existence of a resulting trust depended on the donor having an intention to recover his property. Consequently, where there is no such intention, there can be no possibility of a resulting trust. So, in our case, the Over Village Association may also be described as 'outward looking' and it is possible that both the resulting trust (lack of intention) and gift to members (not consistent with the purpose of the original donation) will be excluded.

This is the picture on the eve of the dissolution of the Over Village Association. Obviously, much depends on the reason why the various donations to the association were valid in the first place and the nature of the contract between the members (that is, the rules of the association). The treasurer should ensure that he or she is acquainted with those rules and the fact that it is possible for the appropriate surplus assets to be distributed to those members in existence at the date of dissolution. Failing that, the property may fall to the Crown as *bona vacantia*. Finally, any surplus derived from property which was subject to a primary trust will result to the donors.

Question 28

Is it possible to identify a unifying underlying theory concerning resulting trusts?

Answer plan

- Automatic and presumed resulting trusts;
- Professor Birks's theory;
- Swadling's theory;
- Lord Browne-Wilkinson's theory in Westdeutsche;
- Lord Wilberforce's theory in *Barclays Bank v Quistclose*;
- Lord Millett's theory in *Twinsectra v Yardley*; *Air Jamaica v Charlton*;
- Peter Gibson's J theory in *Carreras Rothmans*;
- Dillon's J theory in *Re EVTR*;

Answer

A resulting trust is created by the court in favour of the settlor or transferor. This trust arises whenever the location of the equitable interest in property is so unclear, that no other person is capable of making out a successful claim to the property. In *Re Vandervell's Trusts (No. 2)*, Megarry J classified resulting trusts into two categories, namely, 'automatic' and 'presumed' (although his decision was reversed by the Court of Appeal). Automatic resulting trusts arise where the beneficial interest under an express trust remains undisposed of. Such trusts arise in order to fill a gap of ownership. The notion here is that such trusts arise by operation of law irrespective of the intention of the transferor or settlor. Indeed, in *Vandervell v IRC*, the transferor, Mr Vandervell was held to have retained an equitable interest in the shares even though this did not accord with his intention. The equitable or beneficial interest cannot exist in a vacuum and as a last resort the court implies a trust in favour of the settlor/transferor. The policy which underpins this type of resulting trust involves the destination of the beneficial interest when the instrument creating the intended trust or gift is silent as to the application of the equitable interest. The automatic resulting trust arises in a variety of situations, such as the failure of an express trust, or the transfer of property to trustees without specifying the terms of the trust, or the transfer of property is made subject to a condition precedent which is incapable of being fulfilled, or where the trust exhausts only some of the trust property. Indeed, it may be possible to classify the occasions which give rise to an automatic resulting trust into two categories, namely:

(a) transfers of property subject to conditions precedent that have failed to occur; and

(b) uncertainty concerning the destination of a surplus of trust funds.

In *Vandervell v IRC* the House of Lords decided that the destination of the equitable interest in the option to repurchase shares was held on a resulting trust for the settlor in order to fill a gap in ownership. Similarly, in *Re Ames* a trust of a marriage settlement that failed was held on resulting trust for the settlor as a last resort. In *Barclays Bank v Quistclose* the House of Lords decided that a transfer of funds on a conditional loan arrangement was held on resulting trust for the lender when the relevant condition was not satisfied. In this case Lord Wilberforce decided that two successive trusts were created. A 'primary' trust for the shareholders (the purpose of the specific loan) and a 'secondary' trust for the lender arising on the failure of the primary trust. Likewise, in *R v Common Professional Examination Board ex p Mealing-McCleod* (2000) the Court of Appeal decided that a Quistclose trust was created where a specific loan from Lloyds Bank was made to the borrower for the purpose of security of costs and subject thereto, to be held on trust for the lender.

However, Peter Millett in an article argued that the 'primary' trust idea was fundamentally flawed on the ground that as an intended express trust there was no beneficiary with a *locus standi* capable of enforcing the trust. Such a trust, if there was one, would be inconsistent with the beneficiary principle. In *Twinsectra v Yardley* (2002) Lord Millett described the Quistclose trust as a simple commercial arrangement akin to a retention of title clause. This arrangement enables the borrower to have recourse to the lender's money for a particular purpose without entrenching on the lender's property rights more than necessary to enable the purpose to be achieved. The money remains the property of the lender unless and until it is applied in accordance with his directions, and insofar as it is not so applied it must be returned to him (the lender). The significance of this analysis of the Quistclose resulting trust is that the lender retains an equitable interest in the sum loaned until the fund is applied to the specified purpose. Whereas, the view of Lord Wilberforce is that the resulting trust springs back to the lender when the specified purpose is not carried out.

Surplus funds are held on resulting trust for the settlor or transferor on the ground that he had parted with the funds for a specific purpose and by implication had retained an interest in the remainder where the specific purpose remained unfulfilled, see *Re Abbott* (1900). The same principle was adopted in *Re Gillingham Bus Disaster Fund* (1958) with regard to anonymous donors although this extension was doubted in *West Sussex Constabulary Fund* (1971).

On the winding up of an unincorporated association with surplus assets available for distribution the resulting trust was the original remedy adopted by the courts. This institution represents, in theory, a solution to the problem, although the more recent cases have considered this basis of distribution with disfavour. This approach was adopted in *Re Printers and Transferrers Society* (1899) and *Re Houbourn Air Raid Distress Fund* (1946). The courts have repeatedly stressed that the resulting trust is unsuitable in this context for the members paid their subscriptions on a contractual basis. The distribution of assets ought to be *effected on a contractual basis*. Accordingly, a second solution adopted by the courts is that the members of a society who make their contributions have received, or are receiving, or expect to receive benefits from the funds of the society during its continuance. On the date of liquidation, such members do not expect the return of their subscriptions or assets of the society, for the members had parted 'out and out' with their subscriptions. Accordingly, the assets of the society may be taken by the Crown as *bona vacantia*. This doctrine means that where property has no apparent owner it will pass to the Crown. This solution is adopted only as a last resort when the settlor, beneficiary and no one else is entitled to claim the property. The property being ownerless, the Crown will step in to fill the gap, see *Cunnack v Edwards* (1896), *Re West Sussex Constabulary Fund* (1971). However, in *Re Bucks Constabulary Fund* (1979) the court decided that a resulting trust for the members of the association was created.

The 'presumed' resulting trust arises, in the absence of evidence to the contrary, when property is purchased in the name of another, or property is voluntarily transferred to another, for example A purchases property and has the legal title conveyed in the name of B, or A transfers the legal title to property to B. In both cases the destination of the equitable title has not been specified. In these circumstances, B *prima facie* holds the property on trust for A, see *Dyer v Dyer, Re Vinogradoff*. This type of resulting trust is created in order to fulfil the presumed intentions of the parties. The presumption will, of course, be rebutted by the transferor's contrary intention wherever, on the evidence, that contrary intention is expressed.

Professor Birks's thesis on resulting trusts is that both types of resulting trusts, automatic and presumed, are based on the intention of the settlor/transferor and to prevent unjust enrichment. If the settlor/transferor does not intend to transfer a beneficial interest to the legal owner the court will create a resulting trust in order to prevent the unjust enrichment of the transferee. The same principle applies where the transferor disposes of his interest to the transferee by virtue of a mistake or on a total failure of consideration. The transferee does not acquire a proprietary interest in the subject matter of the transfer, but is under an obligation to hold the property on trust for the transferor. The view that the resulting trust is created in order to prevent unjust enrichment appears to be circular. Where the transferee appears to have been 'enriched' by the transfer it only makes sense to describe the enrichment as 'unjust' if it has already been acknowledged that the transferee holds the benefit under a resulting trust for the transferor. It is the trust which arises as an automatic incident of the transferor's ongoing beneficial interest that renders 'unjust' the apparent beneficial ownership of the transferee. On the other hand, William Swadling has argued that the resulting trust is displaced by evidence of intention which is contrary to the intention to create a trust. If the transferor intended the transferee to have the equitable interest, the existence of a mistake on the part of the transferor does not change things and does not give rise to a resulting trust. The transferor will be able to recover the mistaken payment at common law on a total failure of consideration. Swadling's theory was endorsed by Lord Browne-Wilkinson in the *Westdeutsche* case.

Megarry J's twofold classification of resulting trusts in *Re Vandervell's Trust* has been the subject of some refinement. Lord Browne-Wilkinson in *Westdeutsche Landesbank Girozentrale v Islington BC*, did not fully agree with Megarry VC's classification and declared that resulting trusts arise on two occasions namely, where there is a purchase in the name of another and where there is a surplus of trust funds. He added that both types of trusts are examples of trusts giving rise to the common intentions of the parties. The automatic resulting trust that Megarry J referred to may not arise because the settlor expressly or by implication may abandon any beneficial interest in the equitable interest, see *Re West Sussex Constabulary Fund*. In this case the court decided that the surplus funds were taken by the Crown on a *bona vacantia*.

The comparison of Lord Browne-Wilkinson's classification of resulting trust with Megarry J's categorisation lie with the 'automatic' resulting trust and whether the basis of imposition of the trust is the common intention of the parties (as Lord Browne-Wilkinson suggested). However, Lord Browne-Wilkinson's classification appears to be incomplete for there is no acknowledgment of a resulting trust that arises to fill a gap in ownership (see *Vandervell v IRC*) or an occasion where a transfer to a fiduciary fails *ab initio* (see *Re Ames*). In addition, Lord Browne-Wilkinson opines that both types of resulting trusts arise by reference to the common intention of the parties.

This notion of a common intention resulting trust was also expressed by Peter Gibson J in *Carreras Rothmans Ltd v Freeman*. The difficulty with this rationale for the creation of a resulting trust is that the boundaries between resulting and constructive trusts become blurred. It is true that in both cases the courts create the trust. In the case of constructive trusts the courts have deliberately left open the boundaries for the imposition of such trusts. The objective here is to prevent the trustee abusing his position. The court retains the power to monitor the transaction and to impose an order that will redress the imbalance. It is unnecessary for the resulting trust to perform the same task but with the added restriction of restoring the property to the settlor or transferor.

In *Re EVTR*, the court decided that a loan made for a specific purpose imposes a constructive trust on the borrower. But if only part of the sum borrowed was used for the stated purpose, the remaining part of the fund, not so applied, was required to be held on resulting trust for the lender. In other words, both a constructive and resulting trust will arise in respect of the use of part of the funds under a conditional loan arrangement.

In *Air Jamaica v Charlton*, Lord Millett emphasised the relevance of intention in the context of a resulting trust. He also added that the resulting trust will arise whether or not the settlor/transferor intended to retain a beneficial interest. In this case a surplus of pension funds was held on resulting trust for the company and its members.

Essentially, a resulting trust arises as a default mechanism that returns the property to the transferor, in accordance with his presumed (or implied) intention, as determined by the courts. Very often the transferor may not have contemplated the possibility of a return of the property (see *Vandervell v IRC*) but this may be regarded as immaterial if, in the discretion of the court, the circumstances trigger a return of the property to the transferor.

Note

These two questions are typical examples of examination material on resulting trusts. They require a knowledge of recent case law and a firm grasp of the distinction between a gift on trust and an absolute gift outright to a donee. The answer is now complicated by the *dictum* that a resulting trust can exist only where supported by the original donor's intention (*Westdeutsche v Islington LBC*). It remains to be seen whether this goes unchallenged. If it becomes the accepted orthodoxy, the distinction between automatic and presumed resulting trusts will have been exploded.

6 Constructive Trusts 1:

The Duty Not to Make a Profit from the Trust and Co-ownership Trusts

Introduction

In the following two chapters we will turn our attention to one of the most versatile of all the forms of the trust concept: the constructive trust. Indeed, so versatile is this concept in the modern law that there really are several types of constructive trusts, all of which bear the same name, but which do not necessarily share the same characteristics or serve the same purposes, save only that they all arise by operation of law consequent upon some defect of conscience on the part of the constructive trustee. In this particular chapter, we will consider two specific kinds of constructive trusts. First, there is the constructive trust that is imposed on a trustee or other fiduciary as a consequence of that person using his or her position to make a personal profit or gain. In essence, this constructive trust requires the trustee or fiduciary to hold to account any such profits on trust for the beneficiaries or persons to whom the fiduciary duties are owed see *Crown Dilmun Ltd v Sutton* [2004] EWHC 52. It is in the nature both of a remedy against the trustee/fiduciary for unauthorised activities and a safeguard that ensures that she acts for the benefit of the trust and not for herself. Secondly, we shall consider the particular principles applicable to the acquisition of interests in land where a person claims a share in a matrimonial or quasi-matrimonial home belonging in law to another. This species of constructive trust is in the nature of a remedy against the legal owner of property, against whom the constructive trust is deployed, in order to achieve equity between the parties.

At the outset, it should be noted that it is notoriously difficult to define with precision the exact circumstances in which a constructive trust may arise. Yet, perhaps that is just as it should be. If there is a common thread that links all types of constructive trusts (and that is debatable), it is that they are used to prevent and rectify inequitable conduct. Consequently, some of the material considered in this chapter may well overlap with material considered elsewhere.

——— Question 29 ———

A trustee must not place herself in a position where her interest and duty conflict.

Discuss.

Answer plan

- Constructive trusts imposed on persons already in a fiduciary position in order to ensure that any profit made by virtue of that position is not retained;
- there is a duty to the trust but a self-interest to keep the profit: thus, merits of trustee's action are not determinative of their right to keep a profit; and
- examples of various circumstances in which this liability can arise.

Answer

According to Lord Herschel in *Bray v Ford* (1896), a trustee or other fiduciary must not place herself in a position where her interest and duty conflict. Similarly, a trustee or fiduciary is not permitted to profit from her fiduciary position. Consequently, any personal gain attributable to the trusteeship or fiduciary position must be held on constructive trust for the beneficiaries of the trust or the persons to whom the fiduciary relationship is owed (*Aberdeen Town Council v Aberdeen University* (1877)). The essence of the matter is that a trustee (or other fiduciary) owes clear and strict duties to administer the trust property or other assets for the benefit of those entitled in equity to that property or assets. In order to ensure that these duties are honoured in full, there is a virtually absolute bar against the trustee using her position for any personal gain. Such is the strictness of this rule that a constructive trust will be imposed on a trustee or other fiduciary irrespective of any intentional deceit, recklessness or negligence on her part (*Regal (Hastings) Ltd v Gulliver* (1942)). It is enough if the trustee or fiduciary has simply placed herself in a position where her duty to the trust has conflicted with her own interest. In *Crown Dilmun Ltd v Sutton* [2004] EWHC 52, the court decided that a fiduciary, who concealed information from his employer concerning the opportunity to redevelop property in order to benefit himself, was accountable to the claimant for the profits received.

This overriding principle of equity is of general application, but it is now recognised that there are a number of identifiable situations where the court will intervene to impose a constructive trust on a trustee or fiduciary. These situations represent accepted occasions when a conflict of interest and duty – irrespective of fault – will result in the imposition of a constructive trust and the holding of any gain or profit for the beneficiaries or persons entitled.

First, as a matter of principle, trustees are under a duty to act without remuneration: trusteeship is essentially gratuitous. The trustee's obligation is to ensure the most efficient running of the trust, without the self-interest of creating unwarranted work for which they could be paid (*Robinson v Pett* (1734)). However, even though the rule is strictly applied, it must be emphasised that there is nothing illegal in a trustee receiving remuneration for her work. Rather, any remuneration so received will presumptively be held by way of constructive trust unless there is some applicable rule of law or statute or specific provision in the trust instrument which allows the fiduciary to retain the payment. Consequently, most professionally drafted trusts will contain a remuneration clause authorising the trustees to be paid, and the court retains an inherent jurisdiction to order remuneration if this would be for the better administration of the trust (*Re Duke of Norfolk's Settlement Trusts* (1981)). More importantly, the Trustee Act 2000 contains general provisions authorising the payment of remuneration or stipulating the circumstances in which remuneration can be paid (ss 28–30). They will provide remuneration for nearly all professional trustees, subject to any express terms of the trust instrument. Other means by which the trustee may properly claim to keep any remuneration arise from the existence of a contract to that effect with the beneficiary (although a promise to fulfil existing duties is not good consideration), under certain statutory provisions (for example, s 42 of the Trustee Act 1942; Judicial Trustee Act 1896), under the special rules relating to solicitor trustees (*Cradock v Piper* (1850)) and where the payment is earned during administration of assets abroad (*Re Northcote* (1949)).

Secondly, there is a rule that a trustee may not purchase for herself certain types of property, in particular rights in property which should properly be purchased for the beneficiaries. So, where a trustee holds a lease for the beneficiaries, if she subsequently obtains a renewal of that lease for herself, the renewed lease will be held on constructive trust for the beneficiaries (*Keech v Sandford* (1726)). This will be so even if it is clear that the landlord would not have renewed the lease in favour of the beneficiaries. The trustee's duty is to act in the best interests of the beneficiaries, not in her own and there is an irrebuttable presumption of law that a trustee cannot take the benefit of the lease for herself (*Re Biss* (1903)). In similar fashion, it has been held in *Protheroe v Protheroe* (1968), that a constructive trust will be imposed on a trustee who purchases the reversion expectant on a lease which is trust property, once again because the trustee should have been concerned to acquire that reversion for the beneficiary, not for herself. This decision has been subject to considerable criticism, especially as earlier authority (*Griffith v Owen* (1907)) seemed to limit the principle to cases where the lease itself was renewable by custom and hence was already approaching freehold ownership. Nevertheless, the case has been followed without demur and may now represent as firm a rule as that of *Keech* itself (*Re Thompson* (1934) and *Popat v Shonchhatra* (1995)).

Thirdly, as explained in *Tito v Waddell (No 2)* (1977), a trustee is unable to purchase the trust property itself. Simply put, the trustee cannot be both vendor (as trustee) and purchaser of property which she is holding for the benefit of another (*Ex p Lacey* (1802)). This is known as the 'self-dealing' rule, although it should be emphasised that, in some circumstances, a trustee will be permitted to retain her purchase if the reasons for the self-dealing rule are not present. Thus, in *Holder v Holder* (1966) an executor (that is, a fiduciary) who had little to do with the administration of the estate was permitted to retain property which he had purchased openly and at market value, despite the fact that, technically, the self-dealing rule had been violated. However, such cases must be examined closely for the overriding principle is that a trustee or fiduciary must not put herself in a position where her interest and duty conflict: it is usually immaterial once that position is reached whether there was any actual conflict of duty and interest.

Fourthly, and in similar vein, the 'fair dealing' rule makes it clear that a trustee may only purchase the interest of the beneficiary if the transaction was at full market value and the trustee disclosed all material facts (*Dougan v Macpherson* (1902)). Again, the trustee must not use her position to gain an advantage when she should be acting for the beneficiaries and so the sale will be disallowed if the trustee had made use of her position to achieve the purchase. Likewise, a trustee cannot sell her own property to the beneficiary without making full disclosure of all material facts (*Re Cape Breton Co* (1885)).

Fifthly, there are a number of cases, involving different factual backgrounds, where the court has imposed a constructive trust on a fiduciary because of a conflict of interest and duty in a business context. For example, it has been held that any fees paid to company directors who hold those directorships because of their legal ownership of trust shares must be held on trust for the beneficiaries (*Re Francis* (1905); *Re Macadam* (1946)). Again, the essence of the matter is that such directors will have received fees only because they were trustees, although if their appointments were not due to their holding trust shares, the fees may be retained (*Re Dover Coalfield Extension* (1908)). Again, in *Williams v Barton* (1927), a trustee who persuaded the trust to employ a firm of stockbrokers from whom he received a commission was held to hold that commission on constructive trust for the beneficiaries and in *Boardman v Phipps* (1966), a solicitor who made a profit from the purchase of shares, having gained important information while acting as a fiduciary, was required to hold that profit on trust. A further example is provided by *Reading v Attorney General* (1951), where an army sergeant was held to be a constructive trustee of monies received for escorting vehicles unsearched through army checkpoints, although in *Regal (Hastings) Ltd v Gulliver* (1942) it was emphasised that neither fraud nor absence of *bona fides* was necessary to trigger the imposition of the constructive trust in these circumstances (see, also, *LSE v Pearson* (2000)). The presence of a good motive may mean, as in *Boardman*, that a fiduciary is entitled to receive equitable remuneration for her skill in achieving a profit, even though the profit itself must be held on trust for the beneficiaries. Obviously, however, this jurisdiction will not be exercised in favour of a fiduciary who is *mala fides* or whose fiduciary duties positively prohibit personal gain (*Guinness plc v Saunders* (1990)).

Clearly the equitable principle that a trustee must not place herself in a position where her interest and duty conflict has many applications. However, it must not be thought that the types of liability discussed above are exhaustive, or that every case of a conflict of interest and duty can be neatly pigeon-holed in to one of these categories. By way of example, in *Attorney General for Hong Kong v Reid* (1992), the Privy Council has held that a bribe accepted by a person in a fiduciary position will be held on constructive trust for the person(s) to whom the fiduciary duty is owed, so disapproving of *Lister & Co v Stubbs* (1890) which for many years had decided that no constructive trust could exist in these circumstances. Consequently, following *Reid*, the person to whom the fiduciary duties are owed will be able to call for the bribe, receive any increase in value in the bribe, and trace the bribe as proprietary owner into whatever property is purchased with it. For example, in *LSE v Pearson* (2000), Pearson owed fiduciary duties to the LSE and had accepted secret payments from a supplier. He was to hold such payments on trust for LSE, irrespective of any corrupt motive. A similar decision was reached in *Daraydan Holdings v Solland Interiors* [2004] EWHC 622, where the court affirmed the principle laid down by the Privy Council in *Reid* and refused to follow *Lister*. The cases illustrate not only is the court's ability to impose a constructive trust always under review, but the principle that a trustee must not place herself in a position where her interest and duty conflict places powerful remedies in the hands of the beneficiaries.

 # Question 30

The Trustee Act 2000 contains widely drawn statutory authority permitting professional trustees to charge for their services. This is a very desirable reform of the pre-existing law.

Discuss.

 ## Answer plan

- Discuss inadequacies in the old law; and
- outline Trustee Act 2000 provisions on trustee remuneration.

The office of trusteeship is inherently gratuitous, springing from the fundamental principle that a trustee must not place himself in a position where his interest and duty conflict (*Bray v Ford* (1896)). Consequently, before the Trustee Act 2000, it was clear both in principle and practice that a trustee should act without remuneration (that is, payment for services rendered), unless there was some specific rule of law or equity under which the trustee could charge. The overriding fear was that the trustee might be tempted to generate income for himself by creating work, thus unnecessarily overloading the trust and acting in his own interest instead of that of the beneficiaries (*Robinson v Pett* (1734)). Of course, it was also true that the gratuitous nature of trusteeship could itself cause problems. For complicated trusts, it is essential that the beneficiaries are able to rely on experienced and professional advisers, but these are unlikely to be willing to act without payment. Even in smaller trusts, the amount of time and effort devoted to the trust's administration may reflect lack of payment and, instead of preventing the overloading of the trust, the absence of payment might result in too little attention being paid to its affairs, a balance needs to be struck.

Prior to the Act, the balance was attempted by acceptance of the principle that there was nothing unlawful in a trustee receiving payment for fulfilling his duties, provided that this could be justified by reference to some specific provision in the trust instrument or a general rule of law. Unfortunately, as discussed below, it is clear that these pre-Trustee Act 2000 principles indicating when a trustee could receive remuneration were haphazard, complicated and altogether unsatisfactory.

By far the most common method by which trustees could have established – and still can establish – a right to receive remuneration is by relying on an express clause in the trust instrument authorising the trustees to be paid (*Willis v Kibble* (1839)). This method will continue to be common for professionally drafted trusts, especially for trusts that employ professional trustees such as banks and investment managers. Such a charging clause can be drafted widely so as to give appropriate recompense to trustees acting in a professional capacity. In addition, under s 28 of the Trustee Act 2000, where such a clause exists and the trustee is a trust corporation or is a trustee acting in a professional capacity, the trustee is entitled to receive such remuneration even if the services rendered could have been provided by a lay (that is, non-professional trustee). This effectively reverses the old law with respect to 'charging clauses' which were always construed strictly against a trustee and prevented charging for work that could be regarded as not within the professional ambit of the trustee. In this sense, the Trustee Act 2000 supports and enhances the efficacy of charging clauses in trusts (see, also, s 28(4)(a): signature of witness to will does not invalidate charging clause in will in favour of that witness). It is a welcome change to the law and releases trust law from the scope of rules developed at a time when trusts were largely private matters undertaken for private tasks.

In the absence of a charging clause in a trust, the law prior to the Trustee Act 2000 made it difficult for a trustee to claim remuneration. So, although the court had (and probably still has) an inherent jurisdiction to order the payment of remuneration, including authorising payment for the first time or varying an existing charging clause (*Re Duke of Norfolk's Settlement Trusts* (1981); *Foster v Spence* (1996)), the power was limited. The court would not authorise remuneration simply for the benefit of the trustee, but only if the payment of remuneration would be for the better administration of the trust. When deciding whether to exercise its discretion, the court would consider every aspect of the case, including how the administration of the trust would be improved, the need to protect beneficiaries from unscrupulous trustees and the essentially gratuitous nature of trusteeship, and only if there was a demonstrable need for professional trustees or if the trustees could not undertake the proper administration of the trust without devoting more of their own time, would remuneration be awarded.

Secondly, although it was possible for a trustee to establish a right to remuneration through the conclusion of a contract to that effect with the beneficiaries, the courts looked with scepticism at such arrangements. For example, the trustee might have been forced into an unfavourable contract (or any contract) by a threat from the trustee to abandon his duties under the trust. Consequently, such contracts were rare (*Ayliffe v Murray* (1740)) and, in any event, the trustee must have offered consideration for the beneficiaries' promise to pay which could not be the promise to carry out the duties under the trust which the trustee is already obliged to perform.

Thirdly, there remain several (relatively limited) statutory provisions that authorise the payment of remuneration to certain types of trustee. It must be emphasised, however, that these provisions do not authorise the payment of trustees generally, but rather are designed to ensure that specific trustees appointed for specific purposes can be paid (for example, under s 42 of the Trustee Act 1925). A trust corporation appointed by the court may be authorised to charge the trust for administering it, and similar provisions exist in respect of the judicial trustee, the public trustee and persons appointed as custodian trustees (s 1(5) of the Judicial Trustee Act 1896; s 9 of the Public Trustee Act 1906; s 4(3) of the Public Trustee Act 1906).

Fourthly, it remains the case that a trustee may be entitled to retain any remuneration received as a result of administering assets abroad, provided that these are received involuntarily (*Re Northcote's Will Trusts* (1949)). This exception is of limited importance and is born more of convenience than of principle. The essence of the matter seems to be that the court regards the payment of remuneration from outside its jurisdiction as presumptively outside its control, unless it is in the nature of a bribe or is otherwise inequitable. Finally, a solicitor trustee has a unique right to receive remuneration for work undertaken on behalf of the trust, provided that these 'profit costs' relate to work undertaken on behalf of the trust generally (and not in respect of his trusteeship alone) and are no greater than those that 'could have been incurred if the solicitor had not been a trustee (*Cradock v Piper* (1850)). Again, this is a limited exception to the general pre-Trustee Act 2000 principles and is akin to the solicitor trustee being paid for work which is in addition to his normal duties as trustee.

Obviously, apart from the use of the charging clause, which is now made more efficacious by the 2000 Act, there was limited scope for a trustee to claim remuneration. The absence of such a clause meant that a trustee had little hope of claiming remuneration unless one of the limited exceptions applied. It was in order to meet this deficiency that the Trustee Act 2000 now provides, in s 29, methods by which different types of trustees may claim remuneration. First, under s 29(1), a trustee who is a trust corporation (not being a trustee of a charity) 'is entitled to receive reasonable remuneration out of the trust funds for any services that the trust corporation provides' provided that no such remuneration is provided for in the trust instrument or by any other statutory provision. Secondly, under s 29(2) a trustee who acts in a professional capacity (not being a trust corporation, sole trustee or trustee of a charity) is entitled to receive reasonable remuneration if every other trustee has agreed in writing to such payment, again provided that no such remuneration is provided for in the trust instrument or by any other statutory provision. In addition, under s 30 of the Trustee Act 2000, regulations may be made concerning the provision of remuneration to trustees of charities who are trust corporations or who act in a professional capacity.

These are wide powers, with ss 29 and 30 providing, for the first time, a general right for trust corporations, trustees acting in a professional capacity (not being sole trustees) and trustees of charitable trusts to be paid for work done on behalf of the trust. It seems now that it is only sole trustees (not being a trust corporation or charitable trustee) that have no general statutory right to remuneration. This is entirely appropriate in an age where the trust has developed beyond the 'family' trust so common in many of the earlier cases.

Note ——————————————————————————

Question 28 addresses the wider issue of when a trustee must avoid a situation where his interest and duty conflict and this raises some issues about remuneration. Question 29 requires an outline knowledge of the 'old' law, much of which is still applicable but of limited practical value, and of the provisions of the Trustee Act 2000.

—————— Question 31 ——————

Barnaby and Alan are trustees of a fund set up in 1990 in favour of Henry and Oliver. The trust property consists of shares in numerous companies, cash on deposit and various property investments. Barnaby is appointed a director of one of the companies in which the trust has a shareholding because the combined total of the trust's shareholding and his own shareholding (which he purchased at the same time the trust invested in the company) makes him a major investor. He is paid £1,000 per annum for this and has received dividends of some £2,000 in respect of his own shares. Getahead plc is a financial services company and attempts to bribe Alan to transfer to them some of the trust's business. Alan is reluctant, but after checking the history of Getahead plc, he persuades Barnaby that they should transfer some £50,000 worth of assets to the company for investment. In return, he receives some shares in Getahead which double in value due to the spectacular success of the company over the next six months. The trust's investment has also doubled. Other trust property includes a leasehold of an office complex in London and, as trustees, Barnaby and Alan are offered the chance to purchase the reversion for £30,000. They refuse, in good faith, on the advice of Getahead, which is predicting a recession. The reversion is, however, placed on the open market, and Alan purchases it for £20,000 at auction. Alan has arranged a sale in six months to a property developer for £35,000.

Discuss.

Answer plan ——————————————————

- Brief introduction to profits by trustees;
- directors' fees;
- share purchase because of information received while in a fiduciary position;
- bribes; and
- interests in property.

—————————— Answer ——————————

This problem raises a number of issues related to the use of constructive trusts as a means of ensuring that trustees behave in all respects in the best interests of the trust which they administer. In the well known case of *Bray v Ford* (1896), Lord Herschel made it clear that there is a paramount responsibility on trustees to ensure that they do not place themselves in a position where their self-interest conflicts with their duty to the beneficiaries. In order to give effect to this principle, the courts are prepared to impose a constructive trust on a person who makes a personal profit or gain by virtue of his fiduciary position. The effect of this is that the profit or gain is then also held for the benefit of the beneficiaries, on the same or similar terms as those governing the subject matter of the trust or fiduciary relationship proper. Indeed, such is the nature of this jurisdiction that the imposition of a constructive trust does not depend on the trustee or fiduciary being *mala fides* but can be imposed if he is entirely honest and acting for what he perceives to be the best of motives (*Regal (Hastings) Ltd v Gulliver* (1942); *LSE v Pearson* (2000)). It is within this framework that the actions of Barnaby and Alan must be judged.

(a)   The actions of Barnaby in respect of the company shares

It has been made clear in a line of cases that if a trustee is appointed a director of a company by reason of the fact that he is the legal owner of shares (that is, he holds the shares on trust for others), any fees thereby received by way of remuneration must be held on the same trusts for the beneficiaries (*Re Francis* (1905); *Re Macadam* (1946)). The point is simply that a trustee is under an obligation to account as constructive trustee for any profits received by virtue of the trusteeship (*Aberdeen Town Council v Aberdeen University* (1877)). Our case is not, however, quite straightforward. As was pointed out in *Re Dover Coalfield Extension* (1908), a director trustee is not bound automatically to hold any personal profits on trust for the beneficiaries, but only after proper enquiry as to the facts of the particular case. Thus, if Barnaby became a director without reliance on the trust shares, he may retain his £1,000 per annum, even if the shares thereafter help him maintain his position (*Re Dover*). Whether this is so in Barnaby's case is not clear from the facts of the problem. In addition, there is a hint of another difficulty, in that Barnaby acquired his shareholding at the same time as the trust invested in the company. If this private purchase was made possible because of Barnaby's position as trustee, there is every possibility that he will be deemed to be a constructive trustee of the shares themselves, in similar fashion to the result in *Boardman v Phipps* (1966). In that case, a solicitor was held to be a constructive trustee of profits made in certain share transactions because he had acquired the knowledge and opportunity to buy the shares by virtue of his fiduciary position. If this is the case with Barnaby, not only will he hold his director's fees and shares on trust for Henry and Oliver (the trust, of course, having reimbursed Barnaby for the cost of the shares), but the £2,000 of dividends will pass to the beneficiaries also, being income from trust property. Note, however, that if there is a provision in the trust instrument authorising Barnaby to receive remuneration for the performance of his duties as trustee, he may be able to retain some of the fees (*Re Gee* (1948)), and if Barnaby is acting 'in a professional capacity' he may be able to claim 'reasonable remuneration' under s 29(2) of the Trustee Act 2000, if the other trustee agrees in writing. Likewise, if he has behaved honestly and fairly throughout, the court might exercise its inherent jurisdiction to award him a sum by way of equitable compensation (*Boardman*).

(b)   Alan and Getahead plc

It is a serious matter for a trustee to accept a bribe as an inducement to breach his obligations to the beneficiaries and it may well involve him in criminal liability. Furthermore, as well as the various civil remedies open to the beneficiaries, it is now clear that the bribe itself will be held on constructive trust for the beneficiaries (*Attorney General for Hong Kong v Reid* (1992), disapproving *Lister & Co v Stubbs* (1890) and applied in *LSE v Pearson* (2000)) and *Daraydan Holdings v Solland*. Consequently, any increase in value of the bribe (or in the property that now represents it) in the hands of the recipient will also accrue to the beneficiaries. In our case, it is not clear whether any bribe has in fact been given and received. We are told that Alan is 'reluctant' to accept Getahead's offer and the fact that he investigated that company would seem to suggest that he pursues their employment as investment managers for reasons that are entirely proper. Indeed, a bribe is traditionally defined as 'a gift accepted by a fiduciary as an inducement to him to betray his trust' (*Reid*) and, in this case, it is not clear that Alan has been induced by Getahead's gift or that he has actually betrayed his trust, that is, he may not have breached his fiduciary duties. It is not conclusive that no loss was caused to the beneficiaries as a result of these dealings, for a payment may still be a bribe even if every person benefits (*Reading v Attorney General* (1951)). Nevertheless, it may well be that the law on bribes is not in issue here but, in any event, that is not the end of the matter.

It is clear from cases such as *Williams v Barton* (1927), *Reading v Attorney General* (1951) and *Regal (Hastings) Ltd v Gulliver* (1942) that any personal gain received by a trustee by virtue of his fiduciary position must be held on constructive trust for the beneficiaries, even if there was no dishonesty, again as was emphasised in *LSE v Pearson*. In fact, since *Reid*, it is now clear that the difference between bribes and perfectly honest payments to trustees is that bribes will trigger a greater range of remedies than purely honest payments. Both, however, will involve the imposition of a constructive trust on the recipient. It follows that Alan may well find himself to be a constructive trustee of the shares he has received in Getahead plc because, even if they are not a bribe, they have been received as a consequence of his position as trustee. So, also, with their increase in value (*Regal (Hastings) Ltd*) and Crown Dilmun v Sutton (2004).

Finally, for the sake of completeness, we should note that, if this were a bribe, then any contract between Getahead plc and the trust can be set aside at the option of the beneficiaries (*Bartram v Lloyd* (1904)) and the briber can be sued in fraud or for money had and received. If, on the other hand, this is not a bribe, Getahead plc will not suffer the intervention of equity, and the constructive trust will fall on Alan alone because of the unauthorised profit. Again, as in the previous discussion, if Alan has behaved honestly, he may receive equitable compensation for his diligence, although in *Guinness plc v Saunders* (1990) it was emphasised that this jurisdiction should be exercised sparingly.

(c) The leasehold reversion

In *Keech v Sandford* (1726), it was established that, if a trustee holds a lease on trust for beneficiaries, then the trustee is barred as a matter of law from taking a renewal of the lease for himself, even if the landlord would not have granted a renewal to the beneficiaries as such. Any lease which the trustee may acquire in this way would be held on constructive trust for the beneficiaries, even though no breach of trust has been committed. Similarly, it also appears that a trustee may be precluded from purchasing the freehold reversion of a lease, at least where the lease was renewable by custom or the trustee obtained the chance of purchasing the reversion because of his position as trustee (*Griffith v Owen* (1907)). In *Protheroe v Protheroe* (1968), the court went further, holding that a trustee purchasing the reversion of a trust lease would be subject to a constructive trust, irrespective of the type of lease involved or the manner in which the opportunity arose (and see, also, *Popat v Shonchhatra* (1996)). Consequently, assuming *Protheroe* to state the law accurately and it to be true that a constructive trust will be imposed on Alan automatically, it would appear that he must hold the freehold reversion on trust for Henry and Oliver and must account for the profit he has made (or will make) on its resale (*Re Thompson* (1934)).

The strict approach of the *Protheroe* rule has attracted some criticism, not least because it fails to take account of the many and varied circumstances in which a trustee or fiduciary may become privately entangled with trust property. Perhaps, then, it might be possible to argue that a trustee should not be bound to hold a freehold reversion on constructive trust for the beneficiaries if the circumstances reveal no potential conflict of interest and duty. This may now be the position in respect of the 'self-dealing' rule, which occurs when a trustee or fiduciary seeks to purchase the trust property itself: *Holder v Holder* (1966). There seems little objection to extending it to the *Protheroe* type situation. In other words, it can be argued that it is appropriate to disqualify a trustee from obtaining the freehold reversion of a trust lease only when the transaction is inequitable or when the trustee has taken advantage of his privileged position. Therefore, in our case, the fact that Barnaby and Alan were advised not to purchase the reversion on behalf of the trust, and that Alan secured it on the open market at auction, could be used to discount the possibility that he (Alan) be a constructive trustee of the reversion.

Finally there is always the possibility that Alan will be caught directly by the original rule in *Griffith v Owen* (1907), irrespective of its extension by *Protheroe*. So, if Alan had acquired either the knowledge or the opportunity to purchase the reversion in his capacity as trustee, he will be called to account for that reason alone (see, also, *Boardman v Phipps* (1967)) and he may find it difficult to avoid a constructive trust by pleading the fairness of his transaction. In the end, the court must exercise its discretion, for the imposition of a constructive trust is never automatic. Thus, even if Alan did learn of the opportunity to purchase the reversion when acting as trustee and is thereby fixed with a constructive trust, the circumstances will be relevant in determining whether he is entitled to receive equitable remuneration within the principle of *Boardman v Phipps* (1966). After all, Alan has taken the risk in the open market against the advice of Getahead plc and it appears that the trust will profit from that risk.

Question 32

The principles concerning the imposition of a constructive trust on an owner of real property in circumstances of co-habitation are generous to the claimant. In fact, they are so generous that it would cause little difference to adopt statutory co-ownership of such property.

Discuss.

Answer plan

- Role of constructive trusts: *Pettitt v Pettitt* (1970), *Gissing v Gissing* (1971), *Lloyds Bank v Rosset* (1991);
- the elements of a successful claim to co-ownership by means of a constructive trust;
- a remedy for inequitable conduct, but widely or narrowly defined: *Burns v Burns* (1984); *Grant v Edwards* (1986); or *Lloyds Bank v Rosset* (1991);
- difficulties in quantifying the beneficial interest: restitutionary or remedial constructive trust: *Midland Bank v Cooke* (1996);
- whether statutory co-ownership would serve the same purposes as the law of constructive trusts.

Answer

One of the most common uses of the constructive trust in English law is as a device for settling disputes about the ownership of real property. For a variety of reasons, a property shared by a couple as their home may, at law, be owned only by one of them – often the man – although it matters little whether the couple are married or not, or heterosexual or not, for the law of constructive trusts to be applicable (*Tinsley v Milligan* (1993)). In this context, constructive trusts are not used as an arm of the family court but, apparently, as a remedy for inequitable conduct (*Gissing v Gissing* (1971)).

Disputes of this nature arise typically when the legal title to the house is held by one party to the relationship (or, occasionally, jointly with a non-occupier – *Grant v Edwards* (1986)) and the other occupier (the claimant) seeks to rely on words or deeds to prove that he or she should be entitled to a share of ownership. This usually follows a breakdown in the parties' relationship or some financial catastrophe which requires the property to be sold and the proceeds distributed. If the claim is successful, the legal owner will henceforth hold the property on trust for himself and the claimant, in whatever portions the court decides. Indeed, should the claimant have made direct contributions to the purchase price of the property (by lump sum or mortgage payments), then, in the absence of any other explanation (such as a loan or gift to the legal owner), an interest by way of resulting trust will arise and there will be no need to resort to the principles of constructive trusts, *Drake v Whipp* (1996). The resulting trust route is fairly clear and, although the evidence may be disputed, the parties know in advance and with some certainty exactly how the claimant may establish an interest and how the legal owner may avoid granting one. Unfortunately the same may not be true if the claimant has to resort to the constructive trust as a means of claiming that interest.

As originally conceived by the House of Lords in *Pettitt v Pettitt* (1970), the law of constructive trusts as applied to real property was hedged around with limitations and was quite circumspect. According to *Pettitt* itself and *Gissing v Gissing* (1971) which followed shortly thereafter, the imposition of a constructive trust was possible only when the claimant could establish that there had been a common intention between owner and claimant that they should share the ownership of property, which common intention had been relied upon by the claimant to her detriment. This common intention had to be real (not invented by the court) and would arise from an express oral assurance about ownership relied upon detrimentally. Moreover, even then, a constructive trust would not be imposed on the legal owner of the property unless this was necessary to remedy his inequitable conduct (*Gissing v Gissing*).

However, this apparently clear direction from the House of Lords soon began to be exploited by lower courts eager to do practical justice for deserted partners who could not rely on the divorce jurisdiction. In the 1970s, under the influence of Lord Denning in the Court of Appeal, constructive trusts began to be used widely as a device for granting an interest to claimants (usually deserted female lovers) in the property of their co-habitee. It soon became apparent that the *Pettitt* decision could be 'adjusted' to justify nearly any re-ordering of property rights that seemed appropriate to the judge. Cases such as *Falconer v Falconer* (1970), *Heseltine v Heseltine* (1971) and *Eves v Eves* (1975) showed that the constructive trust route to a share of ownership could, in fact, be used to satisfy a claimant whenever the court thought it just and equitable to do so. For example, it is but a small step from requiring an express oral assurance as evidence of a common intention to inferring a common intention from the general conduct of the parties. It is then an even smaller step to inferring a common intention about ownership on the basis that it was what the parties 'would have done' had they thought about it.

In reality, at the heart of this expansion of the role of constructive trusts was a dispute over what kind of conduct could give rise to the common intention sufficient to support the claim. Thus, in *Burns v Burns* (1984), the unmarried Ms Burns was denied a share in her partner's property because she had made neither a contribution to the purchase price of the house (that is, there was no resulting trust) nor had she been promised any interest in it. This was despite the fact that the couple had co-habited for 17 years and that Ms Burns had given up the chance of earning an income in order to raise the couple's children. Similarly, in *Lightfoot v Lightfoot-Brown* [2004] All ER (D) 92, the court decided that there was no evidence of a constructive trust where capital payments were made for the benefit of the family home without any discussion between the parties. In contrast, in *Grant v Edwards* (1986), the judgments suggest that a common intention could be inferred from the conduct of the parties, including the performance of everyday domestic duties, even though, in that case, the legal owner had made an express oral assurance to the claimant.

In itself, the fact that there was a difference between the traditional approach of *Burns* and the expanded jurisdiction of *Grant* is not critical. However, the clear consequence of *Grant* is that a court could, if it wished, 'discover' the common intention and impose a constructive trust simply because the parties shared the occupation of the property and jointly undertook normal obligations of cohabitation – such as house cleaning, child rearing and payment of household expenses. This is very different from the relative objectivity of the *Pettitt* requirements and would have the result that neither party could predict with *any* degree of certainty when a constructive trust would be imposed. Nor can the legal owner so order his affairs so as to *avoid* behaving inequitably. In short, *Grant* indicated a change from reliance on principle to reliance on discretion and was an attempt to turn the constructive trust into a truly remedial institution, much as Lord Denning envisaged in *Eves v Eves* (1975). If matters had remained as this, statutory co-ownership would have been a blessing: at least it would have brought certainty.

However, this is not the end of the matter. In 1991, the House of Lords in *Lloyds Bank v Rosset* attempted to return the law to the spirit of *Pettitt* and to establish reasonably clear guidelines for the future use of constructive trusts. According to Lord Bridge in *Rosset*, a constructive trust to achieve co-ownership would be imposed when an express oral promise or assurance as to shared ownership had been made and had been relied on by the claimant in circumstances resulting in detriment. Importantly, Lord Bridge doubted whether anything other than an express oral assurance could raise a constructive trust (except payments to the purchase price of the property: also known as a resulting trust). Lord Bridge went on to justify this return to orthodoxy by making it clear that an agreement to share the common obligations of co-habitation was not the same as an agreement to share the ownership of property and so signalled that a constructive trust should not be imposed to 'do justice' in the absence of objective facts requiring its imposition.

However, Lord Bridge in his guidelines omitted to mention the significance of indirect contributions. These involve an arrangement between the parties to the effect that the claimant agrees to undertake the household expenses on condition that the legal owner pays the mortgage instalments. In short, a link between the mortgage payments and the expenses undertaken by the claimant is required to be established and the claimant's expenses are required to be of a substantial nature, see Lord Pearson in *Gissing v Gissing*. Despite Lord Bridge's omission, it is clear that he did not intend to overrule such evidence. A recent illustration of such contributions and their effect is *Le Foe v Le Foe* [2001] All ER (D) 325. In this case the court construed the Rossett principles and concluded that the claimant would be entitled to an interest by way of indirect contributions in exceptional circumstances.

In addition, Lord Bridge's statement in *Rosset* equates the interest of the spouse with that of a cohabitee. This ignores the significance of s 37 of the Matrimonial Proceedings and Property Act 1970, (substantial improvement of property by one spouse). In addition, on a divorce, judicial separation or nullity decree the court has a discretion to award a spouse an interest in the house under ss 23–25 of the Matrimonial Causes Act 1973. This discretion is not limited by the *Rosset* principles.

This should have settled matters. Constructive trusts remedy assurances unconscionably denied; they do not allow the manipulation of property rights for other (albeit worthy) reasons. This is consistent with later House of Lords authority discussing constructive trusts generally, as in *Westdeutsche Landesbank Girozentrale v Islington LBC* (1996), where Lord Browne-Wilkinson stated that constructive trusts were imposed where a person's conscience was bound, not because there might be justice in doing so. Nevertheless, difficulties remain. In *Midland Bank v Cooke* (1996), an interest in property was established by means of payments towards the purchase price (a resulting trust), but the claimant's share of ownership was quantified on the basis of the parties' entire conduct and was not proportionate to the amount paid (see the contrary result in *Huntingford v Hobbs* (1993)). This is again the use of a wide discretionary constructive trust (see, also, the earlier *Hammond v Mitchell* (1992)) and, in *Cooke*, appears to have been imposed despite clear evidence that the parties never agreed how the property was to be owned. It is difficult in such cases to see why the legal owner's conscience was affected at all, save only to the extent that he had used another's money to pay the purchase price. It is pure remedy, not restitution.

In conclusion then, it is not true that the imposition of a constructive trust now lies squarely in the discretion of the court, although the stricter rules of *Rosset* are easily attacked if the court so wishes (as in *Cooke*). So, in present circumstances, there is no *need* for statutory co-ownership because the law remains reasonably certain. However, that does not mean that statutory co-ownership should not be imposed *as a result of a deliberate choice*. But, this is a choice for Parliament to make and should not be rendered otiose by a return to the discretionary, uncertain and unstable use of the constructive trust advocated in some cases. In fact, the matter is under active consideration by the Law Commission as part of their review of the rights of homesharers. Of course, the constructive trust (like equity itself) retains an inherent flexibility. That is not the same, however, as having completely open ended rules and uncertain legal concepts.

Question 33

Cassandra is the registered proprietor of a large house in London. In 1999 she met Donald, a young merchant banker, and soon she had invited him to live with her. Donald willingly accepted, not least because he was about to be evicted from his own flat through his inability to pay the rent. At first, Donald insisted that he share the expenses of running the house, but it soon became clear to him that Cassandra had more money than sense, and he accepted her generosity without complaint. After some time, Cassandra began talking about 'the future', and although he was not entirely committed to the relationship, Donald played along, especially as Cassandra had told him that the house was as good as his own now that they were together. This slice of luck encouraged Donald to abandon even that little financial caution that he possessed, and he had soon spent nearly all of his savings on various luxury, but unnecessary, items of furniture for the house and far too many visits to the Casino. By this time, Cassandra was becoming a little annoyed at Donald's behaviour, and after one terrible row, in which she had told him to leave, Donald promised to mend his ways. Subsequently, he became altogether more responsible and even began to redecorate the house at his own expense and overhaul the garden. Unfortunately for him, this had come too late for Cassandra, and this month she has decided to throw Donald out.

Donald is devastated and comes to you for advice as to whether he can claim a share in the house.

Answer plan

- General principles of acquisition of beneficial interests through constructive trusts;
- the legal owner as constructive trustee;
- the need for a promise, reliance and detriment, *Lloyds Bank v Rosset* (1991);
- quantifying the share; and
- whether a remedy can be refused on general equitable principles.

Answer

This question concerns the acquisition of beneficial interests in property belonging to another through the medium of constructive trusts. In concrete terms, the problem revolves around a contest between the legal owner of the property – Cassandra – and the person who may be able to claim an interest in the property under a constructive trust – Donald. If he is successful, Cassandra will hold the legal title on trust for both of them, in such shares as the court determines.

By way of introduction, it is important to note that, in our case, there is no express conveyance of the house to Donald as owner, and no express written declaration of trust by Cassandra in his favour. There is no written declaration within s 53(1) of the Law of Property Act (LPA) 1925. So, if Donald is to have any interest in Cassandra's property, it is clear that this must be established under the principles elaborated in *Pettitt v Pettitt* (1970) and codified by the House of Lords in *Lloyds Bank v Rosset* (1991): he must rely on a constructive or resulting trust, as these are exempt from the requirement of writing by s 53(2) of the LPA 1925. Following *Rosset*, a person claiming an equitable interest in property, legal title to which is vested in another, must be able to show either some contribution to the purchase price of the property (that is, a resulting trust) or must prove some oral assurance that he or she was to have an interest in the property which they have relied upon to their detriment. On the facts as stated, it seems clear that when Donald met Cassandra, Cassandra was sole legal owner of the property and that it was not subject to any mortgage. The property belonged to Cassandra absolutely and had already been paid for. It follows, therefore, that Donald cannot pursue the resulting trust path to an equitable interest – there is no purchase price to which he can make a contribution. It would seem, then, that Donald must rely on the doctrine of constructive trusts: he must plead a promise or oral assurance plus detrimental reliance in order to establish that it would be inequitable for Cassandra to deny him a share in the property. There are a number of factors to consider here.

First, it is clear that Donald readily moves into the house at Cassandra's instigation. However, there is no suggestion at this stage that Cassandra has made any promise or assurance in relation to ownership of the property. As Lord Bridge made clear in *Lloyds Bank v Rosset* (1991), the obligations of common or shared *occupation* of property are not identical with the *obligations* of shared ownership and consequently it is extremely unlikely that a court would be prepared to divine a promise of shared ownership from facts such as ours. Indeed, because in *Rosset* Lord Bridge went so far as to suggest that it was virtually impossible *as a matter of principle* to infer a promise from conduct *per se*, there seems little upon which Donald can base a claim at this stage. Even if by some intellectual gymnastics it is possible to discover a promise made to Donald, there is no evidence of detrimental reliance. Although Donald does vacate his current residence, and even though such action has, in the past, been held to constitute detriment

(*Tanner v Tanner* (1975)), it is clear that his actions are prompted by his own circumstances and have little to do with whatever Cassandra may or may not have promised.

Secondly, there is little chance that Donald may claim an interest just because he has insisted on paying household expenses. The payment of household expenses is not equivalent to payment of the purchase price of property (*Burns v Burns* (1984)) and (as above) there is no oral assurance to which this expenditure can be linked as detrimental reliance. Indeed, such statements that Cassandra does make (see below) are made *after* Donald spends money. In other words, these monetary payments are not made to the acquisition of the property, nor are they in reliance on a promise. There is no interest to be found on these facts (*Burns v Burns* (1984) and *Lloyds Bank v Rosset* (1991)).

Finally, however, it appears that Cassandra does make a promise of sorts to Donald and it is a matter of construction whether this is sufficient to raise an interest in his favour by way of a constructive trust. First, a problem exists with intention: does Cassandra intend to grant Donald a share in the property by her references to 'the future' and her apparent statement that the house is 'as good as' his? Fortunately for Donald, although *Gissing v Gissing* (1971) suggests that an oral promise (the 'common intention') must be real rather than imagined, it is likely that a court would consider an assurance to have been made if a reasonable person would have believed that the property owner was making a statement about ownership of the property or, indeed, if the actual claimant honestly so believed. In our case, we do not know what Cassandra actually meant, but a reasonable person in Donald's position might well conclude that this was an assurance about the ownership of the shared home. Such a view is clearly supported by *Midland Bank v Cooke* (1996) which, although distinguishable because in that case there were some payments towards the purchase price, suggests that the court will take a generous view of what the parties 'intended'. Consequently, Cassandra may find herself having assured Donald that he had a share in the property, even if this was not actually her intention (see, for example, *Eves v Eves* (1975), where the real intention was to deny an interest). Furthermore, it seems clear from the facts that Donald has relied on this assurance in that he has spent his savings on various items of furniture and visits to the Casino.

With reference to the alleged detriment, Cassandra might claim that this kind of detrimental reliance is insufficient to found an interest by way of a constructive trust because it was unrelated to the property (money spent at the Casino) and part was not necessary for the use and enjoyment of the property (luxury furniture). Indeed, certain cases, such as *Gissing* and *Christian v Christian* (1981), suggest that the detriment suffered as a result of the promise or assurance must be related to the property over which the interest is claimed; for example, spending money on improvements. However, an alternative view is that all that is required is detriment which has been caused by the promise, the nature of such detriment being immaterial. This second approach has much to commend it, especially since it is consistent with the theory that the essence of the constructive trust in these cases is the fact of a promise made and then inequitably denied. The detriment is, on this view, merely the trigger for the trust, not the reason for its existence in the first place. So, following this approach, Donald appears to have a reasonably strong claim to an equitable interest in Cassandra's property. He can show an assurance, reliance and detriment. This means that Cassandra's subsequent attempt to evict him – which may be seen as an attempt to withdraw the promise – comes too late (*Turton v Turton* (1987)). By that time, the equity may have been raised in his favour.

Finally, however, as adviser to Donald, one must issue a word of caution. Although it appears, on a strict application of the *Rosset* principles, that he can claim an interest in Cassandra's property, the court might seek to deny him this by referring to the origins of its equitable jurisdiction in cases such as this. Undoubtedly, the constructive trust is a flexible tool that serves many purposes and can be used in many ways: for example, in

Cooke it was used with maximum flexibility in order to achieve what the judge believed to be an equitable result. This was despite the apparent contradiction with *Rosset*. In some cases, constructive trusts appear to treat morally innocent people harshly, but only then in order to do equity to another person who has a greater claim. Yet, what constructive trusts will not be used for is to enable an undeserving litigant to gain a windfall which is not merited: the trust fixes on the conscience of the legal owner of property, it will not be imposed mechanically to assist the undeserving (*Westdeutsche Landesbank Girozentrale v Islington LBC* (1996)). The very essence of the constructive trust is that it is not rigid in application and does not have hard and fast rules. As much was stated by Lord Diplock in *Gissing v Gissing* and is a feature of the use of constructive trusts in later cases, including those cases difficult to reconcile with each other such as *Lloyds Bank v Rosset* and *Midland Bank v Cooke*. Thus, if the constructive trust is rightly to be regarded as a means of remedying inequitable conduct in circumstances where the conscience of the legal owner is affected, a court may well take the view that Donald should not be able to rely on it to claim a benefit which he appears not to deserve.

Note

The previous two questions consider an aspect of constructive trusts that is often taught as part of courses on land law. It is closely related to the law on resulting trusts and textbooks on land law should be consulted for a fuller analysis. Question 32 is interesting because it illustrates the danger of becoming too rigid in the use of constructive trusts. The question requires a knowledge of the relevant law but also an understanding of the role and purpose of constructive trusts in these type of cases. As will be apparent, the general theory of trusts put forward in *Westdeutsche Landesbank Girozentrale v Islington LBC* is very important.

7 Constructive Trusts 2:

The Liability of Strangers to the Trust

Introduction

We have seen already in previous chapters that to accept the office of trustee is to open oneself and one's conduct to the closest scrutiny. Not only is the trustee expected to behave at all times with the utmost propriety, but there are also circumstances when even the morally innocent fiduciary may find himself subject to the coercive jurisdiction of the court. Furthermore, it is not only trustees proper who may find themselves in this position, for the reach of a court of equity is both long and powerful. As we shall see in this and the following chapters, third parties may all too easily become embroiled in the trust's affairs and, as far as the various remedies of the beneficiaries are concerned, it is often irrelevant whether these 'strangers to the trust' are innocent, negligent or downright dishonest.

The problems considered in this chapter relate to the liability of a person who is a stranger to the trust – broadly defined as a person who was not originally appointed a trustee or to a fiduciary position. In very general terms, any person who interferes with the operation of the trust or who assists the trustee in a breach of his trust duties may find himself fixed with a constructive trust and answerable to the court and the beneficiaries for any misapplication of the trust property. Of course, it is not in every situation that a stranger to the trust is held liable to the beneficiaries as a constructive trustee. Yet in appropriate cases, when the conditions established by the case law are fulfilled, the constructive trust swings into operation and provides a most powerful remedy.

In simple terms, a stranger to the trust may become a constructive trustee in four situations:

(a) by dishonestly assisting the trustee in a breach of trust;

(b) by receiving trust property for his own use in the knowledge that it was transferred in breach of trust;

(c) after having received trust property in conformity with the terms of the trust, by knowingly dealing with that property in breach of the terms of the trust; and

(d) by inducing the trustee to commit a breach of trust.

Together, these different examples of the constructive trust give the beneficiary some hope of redress in the event of a breach of trust, even if the trustee has escaped the clutches of the court or no longer has the trust property. One note of caution ought to be mentioned. Millett LJ in *Paragon Finance v Thakerar* [1999] 1 All ER 400, opined that the liability of an accessory is strictly not as a constructive trustee because he does not acquire the trust property. His liability is to account to the beneficiaries for any benefits received. This is a 'personal' liability to account rather than an *in rem* liability. Once again, as with so much in the law of trusts, the 'rules' are to be found in case law, although there is some doubt whether the growing volume of case law actually has done anything to clarify the law.

Question 34

Analyse the circumstances in which a 'stranger' may be liable as a constructive trustee for intermeddling with the management of a trust.

Answer plan

- The nature of a stranger's liability as constructive trustee and its necessity;
- knowing receipt or dealing;
- dishonest assistance; and
- lack of clarity: position of principle.

Answer

In general terms, constructive trusts arise by operation of law rather than as a result of the express or implied intention of the settlor or other person (*Westdeutsche v Islington LBC* (1996)). They are imposed upon the owner of property in order to satisfy principles of equity, fairness and good conscience. In fact, it is quite possible for an existing trustee to become a constructive trustee of property other than the original trust property, which he will then hold on the same or substantially similar terms to those which already bind him. A good example of this is *Keech v Sandford* (1726) and see a modern example involving persons in a fiduciary position in *Hooper v Gorvin* (2001). However, another very powerful form of the constructive trust is that which is imposed on a person who is not already in a fiduciary position – a stranger to the trust. In these cases, the court will impose the obligations of a trustee on a person because that person has so conducted himself in relation to the trust's affairs that in all conscience he should be held accountable to the beneficiaries for any breach of trust that may have occurred. Although there have been suggestions that some instances of stranger liability should be triggered irrespective of the 'fault' of the stranger (that is, liability should be strict, based on principles of restitution) at present the liability is 'fault' based although, as discussed below, there are disagreements as to which type of 'fault' is required (intentional wrongdoing, recklessness or negligence) and in which circumstances.

In recent years, the incidence of claims concerning strangers to the trust has increased considerably, not least because of the complicated financial arrangements that can accompany investment of trust funds. However, although these cases have highlighted the effective use of the constructive trust as a remedy for inequitable conduct, they have done little to clarify the principles upon which the imposition of liability is based. While it is understandable that individual judgments should concentrate on the liability of the particular defendant, the lack of a consistent exposition of the underlying rationale for the imposition of a constructive trust on a stranger makes it difficult to generalise or to predict the liability (if any) of defendants in future cases. Consequently, there is much in this area of the law that is uncertain and some important questions remain to be answered. With that in mind, it is possible to analyse the liability of strangers as constructive trustees in the following way.

First, a stranger to the trust may become a constructive trustee because he or she has assumed the duties of a trustee. In other words, if a stranger takes it upon himself to meddle with the trust property as if he were a trustee, equity will treat him as such a trustee (*Mara v Browne* (1896)). This is trusteeship *de son tort* and the essential point is that the person fixed with liability as a constructive trustee has stepped willingly into the shoes of the original trustees or fiduciaries, as in *James v Williams* (1999). It is effectively self-appointed trusteeship. Importantly, it is reasonably clear that the trustee *de son tort* does not attract liability to account to the beneficiaries merely by assuming the duties of a trustee. The 'trustee' is assimilated to the position of the original trustees and so there must be a breach of the terms of the trust or instances of unauthorised profits, bribes, etc, before liability can arise although given that properly appointed trustees may become liable for maladministering the trust even in the absence of fault, the *trustee de son tort* can easily find himself in breach and liable for damages (*Selangor United Rubber Estates v Craddock (No 3)* (1968)).

Secondly, equity will impose a constructive trust on a stranger who has received trust property for his own benefit in breach of the terms of the trust. This form of liability is often referred to 'knowing receipt or dealing' with the trust property (*Baden Delvaux and Lecuit v Société Génerale pour Favouriser le Développement du Commerce et de l'Industrie en France SA* (1983); *Houghton v Fayers* (2000)). It is important to realise, however, that the essence of the liability is that the stranger has received property for his own benefit to which he has no right. Consequently, he may be held accountable as constructive trustee for that property or its value to any person having a better claim – that is, the beneficiaries of the trust. In this sense, the imposition of the constructive trust is not necessarily triggered by the personal conduct of the stranger, but arises from the greater claim of another to the property. In this sense, the liability is restitutionary and not punitive. Of course, it will not be every stranger who receives trust property who will be liable as a constructive trustee, for clearly some transfers will be perfectly legitimate and some strangers will be shielded from liability because of the facts of the case – being, usually, the legitimacy of the circumstances in which the property was transferred.

It seems, then, that there are three primary conditions for the imposition of this liability: *Houghton v Fayers*. First, and obviously, there must be disposal of assets in breach of trust or breach of fiduciary duty, and in the absence of such breach no liability for 'receipt' can arise (*Brown v Bennett* (1998)). Secondly, the stranger must either have lawfully received property and thereafter applied it for his own purposes in a manner inconsistent with the terms of the trust (inconsistent dealing: *Karak Rubber v Burden* (1972)) or, in the alternative, have received trust property for his own benefit, (knowing receipt: *International Sales Ltd v Marcus* (1982)). A good factual example of the 'inconsistent dealing' liability is where an agent of the trustee (for example, a stockbroker) lawfully receives trust monies but then applies them for his own benefit in a manner inconsistent with the terms of the trust; and an example of the latter is where a stockbroker is given trust monies for his own benefit, this time with the transfer itself being in breach of trust. However, in both cases, it is not enough that the transferee has simply utilised the trust property for his own benefit. Thirdly, it seems that the transferee must have some degree of knowledge or notice of the fact that the transfer (or inconsistent dealing) was in breach of trust (*Polly Peck International plc v Nadir* (1992); *Westdeutsche Landesbank Girozentrale v Islington*

LBC (1996)). This insistence that the stranger be guilty of some degree of 'fault' (in the sense of having some 'knowledge' of the breach) is somewhat at odds with the restitutionary nature of liability – after all, if the root of liability is that X has Y's property, why should Y's state of mind be relevant? – but at present it seems securely established in the case law: *BCCI (Overseas) Ltd v Akindele* (2000). What is clear, however, is that a stranger can have no liability if the property was never held on trust in the first place: *Box v Barclays Bank* (1998).

Unfortunately, the precise degree of knowledge required for liability for knowing receipt/inconsistent dealing is uncertain. On the one hand, it has been suggested that, before liability can arise, the recipient must either know or be reckless as to whether the transfer to him or subsequent use of property is in breach of trust. This degree of knowledge equates to the first three of Peter Gibson LJ's infamous categories of knowledge in *Baden Delvaux* (1983) and necessarily has the effect of restricting the circumstances in which a stranger may be liable. It has been applied in cases such as *Carl Zeiss Stiftung v Herbert Smith & Co (No 2)* (1969), *Re Montague* (1987) and, in a commercial context, in *Cowan de Groot Properties v Eagle Trust plc* (1992); *Eagle Trust v SBC Securities (No 2)* (1992). Alternatively, other cases suggest that liability should exist if the stranger is simply negligent with regard to the facts of a breach of trust: in other words, if he should have known that the transfer of trust funds or his own subsequent dealings with them were in breach of trust. This ensures that liability will arise when *any* of the five categories of knowledge in *Baden Delvaux* exists. Cases such as *International Sales Ltd v Marcus* (1982), *Belmont Finance Corporation v Williams Furniture (No 2)* (1980) and the closely argued judgment of Millet J at first instance in *AGIP (Africa) Ltd v Jackson* (1992) support this view. It is implicit in the recent judgment of Ferris J in *Box v Barclays* (1998). Indeed, if it is true that the essence of liability for knowing receipt/inconsistent dealing is that the stranger has received property for his own benefit to which he was not entitled, then (in the absence of a pure 'no fault' restitutionary liability) it is quite appropriate that he should be obliged to return it unless he was innocent of all participation in a breach of trust and it should make no difference whether the alleged transaction in breach arose out of a 'commercial' or 'private' trust. Of course, what a 'reasonable' person should have known or enquired about may vary according to the circumstances – and the nature of the transaction may affect this – with strangers acting commercially being under a lesser duty to enquire and hence a lesser chance of liability (*El Ajou v Dollar Land Holdings*, first instance (1993)). Yet, in principle, negligence should not be a defence to a claim by a person with a better title. In *BCCI v Akindele* (2000), the Court of Appeal tried to overcome these difficulties by noting that the state of knowledge 'must be such as to make it unconscionable' for the recipient to retain the benefit. This reformulation by Nourse LJ clearly is intended to avoid the controversy surrounding the '*Baden* categories' and the uncertainties produced by the 'knowledge/notice' distinction. However, it is not certain that 'unconscionability' is any less opaque than previous attempts to identify the 'core' reason for liability. In fact, in *Lipkin Gorman v Karpnale* (1991), the House of Lords *may* have gone further and suggested that this liability should be strict and could be triggered simply by the receipt or inconsistent dealing with the trust property, irrespective of the state of knowledge of the stranger. Such a view clearly establishes the restitutionary nature of this liability, especially as the House of Lords would also allow a 'change of position' defence to the strict liability in appropriate cases. It has not yet been accepted and recent cases (*Westdeutsche; Box v Barclays*) may have ruled out strict liability for the foreseeable future.

Moving now to examine the third general set of circumstances in which a stranger may be made liable as constructive trustee for intermeddling with the trust funds, we come to liability for 'knowing assistance'. A stranger may be liable as constructive trustee for dishonestly assisting a trustee to commit a breach of trust (*Barnes v Addy* (1874); *Royal Brunei Airlines v Tan* (1995)). It is important to realise here that, unlike knowing receipt/inconsistent dealing, the stranger may never receive the trust property and, even if he does, it is not for his own benefit. Consequently, this is a form of secondary liability, usually resorted to when for some reason the trustee who has committed the fraudulent breach of trust cannot be found or has insufficient funds to satisfy the claims of the beneficiaries. In addition, the stranger's liability is to account for the profits. Strictly he is not a constructive trustee for he does not receive the trust property but merely assists in a breach of trust, see Millett LJ in *Paragon Finance v Thakerar* [1999] 1 All ER 400.

However, the liability belongs to the stranger alone – it is for his misconduct that he is liable – and hence it is no longer true that the stranger can be liable only if the trustee himself has behaved fraudulently. This was established by the Privy Council in *Tan*, overruling early cases that linked the stranger's liability to the fraud of the trustee. Of course, it remains true that the stranger must himself be culpable. Previously, this was expressed in terms of whether the assistor had 'knowledge' of the breach of trust, such knowledge generally being thought to exist only when the first three *Baden* degrees existed (*AGIP v Jackson*; *Polly Peck International plc v Nadir*; *contra Selangor United Rubber Estates v Craddock (No 3)* (1968)). In *Tan*, however, Lord Nicholls, for the Privy Council, made it clear that this was a misleading approach. What was required was for the assistor to be 'dishonest' before liability could arise which, apparently, is a concept with which the courts are familiar and which therefore will be easier to apply. The end result is that a stranger will be liable as constructive trustee for dishonestly assisting a trustee in a breach of trust, and this formulation is now the established standard (for example, *Brown v Bennett* (1999); *Jyske Bank v Heinl* (1999); *Ferrotex v Banque Français de l'Orient* (2000)).

Necessarily, this leaves some questions unanswered. As the later case of *Brinks v Abu-Saleh (No 3)* (1995) illustrates, not only must the defendant be proved to have factually assisted in a breach of trust (which was not established in that case). In *Twinsectra v Yardley* [2002] 2 All ER 377, the majority of the House of Lords adopted the criminal law test for dishonesty (as laid down by Lord Lane CJ in *R v Ghosh* [1982] QB 1053) namely, the defendant's conduct is dishonest by reference to the ordinary standards of reasonable and honest people *and* that he himself realised that his conduct was dishonest by those standards. This involves both objective and subjective questions. Further, there are significant issues concerning the standard of proof required for dishonesty. In *Jyske v Heinl* it was held that the standard of proof involved a high level of probability greater than a 'balance of probabilities' and the inability of the claimants to meet this meant that the 'assistance' claim in *Akindele* was unsuccessful.

Finally, it is clear that the above circumstances in which a constructive trust may be imposed on a stranger cannot be regarded as exhaustive. For example, a stranger will be liable as a constructive trustee if he induces a trustee to commit a breach of trust (*Eaves v Hickson* (1861)). Again, it is notoriously difficult to determine whether the activities of a stranger fall under 'knowing receipt' or 'dishonest assistance' for the matter often turns on whether the trust property was received for the transferee's own benefit. Consequently, some of the earlier 'receipt' cases may be better described as 'assistance' cases, which could explain some of the confusion already alluded to between the different tests of knowledge for each form of liability. In fact, following the decision in *Lipkin Gorman v Karpnale* (1991), and despite obvious judicial reluctance, we could argue that the separation of constructive trust liability into these different categories is redundant. Instead, the principle might be that a person can be made liable as constructive trustee for intermeddling with trust property whenever this is necessary to reverse an unjust enrichment, having regard to the defendant's status as a *bona fide* purchaser for value or any defence of change of position. The case of *Westdeutsche Landesbank Girozentrale v Islington LBC* (1996)) has not helped in this regard, save only that we know that the House of Lords is not yet ready for the purely remedial constructive trust that exists in some other common law jurisdictions.

Note

It is a perfectly respectable answer to conclude that the law is in a state of flux and is uncertain as to its practical application (even if the principles are clear). A question such as this cannot really be answered adequately in an examination setting, as there are many more issues which we could consider. Consequently, a general answer is sufficient, provided that there is ample reference to case law.

Question 35

The liability of a stranger for meddling with trust property should be strict. Then, subject only to the defence of change of position, the courts could determine in all the circumstances whether the defendant should return property to the beneficiaries without having to agonise about the defendant's state of mind.

Discuss.

Answer plan

- Basis of liability for knowing assistance and dishonest receipt;
- confirmation that some degree of fault is required: *Royal Brunei Airlines v Tan*, *Westdeutsche Landesbank Girozentrale v Islington LBC* (1996);
- the restitution angle and the change of position defence;
- confusion of language: the problem of semantics;
- confusion of facts: receipt or assistance;
- the application of law to facts – a recipe for different interpretations of the law.

Answer

The possibility that strangers to a trust – that is, persons not appointed trustees – may be fixed with the obligations and liabilities of constructive trusteeship is settled law. Indeed, now that it is virtually inevitable when investing and transferring trust funds that the trust monies will pass through the hands of others (be they professional advisers, banks, stockbrokers or other agents of the trustees), the chance that a stranger will incur this liability – or that a beneficiary will claim that he has – has increased considerably. Likewise, dishonest and fraudulent trustees are not a modern phenomenon, and the possibility that they might be tempted to transfer the trust monies in breach of trust to a friend or confidant is not remote. Of course, in most of these cases, the trustee will be liable personally to the beneficiaries for any loss occasioned by a breach of trust and it may well be that the trustee has the resources to meet these claims. Yet, in many instances, the loss to the trust will be beyond the trustee, or the trustee may have fled the jurisdiction, and this is where the use of constructive trusts becomes vital. In those instances where the loss cannot be recovered from the trustee, constructive trusts enable the beneficiaries to seek redress from someone who has meddled with the trust's affairs or who has been involved in the breach of trust. Such is the power of this remedy that the constructive trustee will be liable not only to return any trust property that he retains (that is, it is held on trust), but also to recompense the beneficiaries personally from his own resources to the full value of their loss.

Traditionally, there are two main grounds for fixing a stranger with liability as constructive trustee – when the stranger has assisted the trustee in a breach of trust and when the stranger has received trust property for his own benefit in breach of trust (*AGIP (Africa) Ltd v Jackson* (1992)). In addition to these, there are a further two less well used circumstances in which liability for a stranger can arise. These are constructive trusteeship as a result of inducing a breach of trust (*Eaves v Hickson* (1861)) or where the defendant, after having lawfully received trust property, deals with it inconsistently with the terms of the trust (*Neste Oy v Lloyds Bank* (1983)). Again, traditionally, liability for constructive trusteeship (in all these forms) is said to turn first on evidence of factual involvement (receipt, assistance, inducement, etc) plus some degree of knowledge on the part of the stranger.

There is little doubt that, at present, some element of 'fault' on the part of the stranger is required to establish liability (see, for example, *BCCI v Akindele* (2000)). In *Baden Delvaux and Lecuit v Société Génerale pour Favouriser le Développement du Commerce et de l'Industrie en France SA* (1983), Peter Gibson J described five degrees or types of knowledge which he thought could be relevant in fixing a stranger with a constructive trust. First, there is actual knowledge of the relevant facts; secondly, the stranger may wilfully shut his eyes to the obvious; thirdly, the stranger may wilfully and recklessly fail to make such enquiries as an honest and reasonable man would make; fourthly, the stranger may have knowledge of circumstances which would indicate the relevant facts to an honest and reasonable man; and, fifthly, the stranger may have knowledge of circumstances that would put an honest and reasonable man on enquiry so that he would be liable if he failed to ask the relevant questions. However, what Peter Gibson and, indeed, other judges in other cases have not made clear is what degree of knowledge is required for which type of liability. Further, it is readily apparent that the distinction between each category of knowledge may be very fine indeed and, what is more, although the 'five degrees of knowledge' are often used as a baseline in other cases, many judges prefer their own formulations or variations of Peter Gibson's categories (see, for example, *AGIP (Africa) Ltd v Jackson* (1992); *Re Montague* (1987); *Eagle Trust plc v SBC Securities* (1992); *BCCI v Akindele* (2000)).

Recently, case law has attempted to clarify the position but not, as the question seems to hope, by removing the 'fault' element from liability. Liability in 'assistance' type cases is premised on the assumption that a stranger may be required to compensate the beneficiaries for loss, even though the stranger has never received the trust property and certainly does not now have it. The property was not given to the stranger for his own benefit (*Barnes v Addy* (1874)). Thus, as was made clear at first instance in *AGIP (Africa) Ltd v Jackson* (1992), the essence of the liability is that of someone who facilitates the breach of trust of another and who may take no benefit from the trust property itself. Consequently, it is apparent that such liability should never be triggered by simple factual assistance, but only where such assistance is tainted by personal fault. Further, as is made clear by the Privy Council in *Royal Brunei Airlines v Tan* (1995)), the stranger may be liable only where 'dishonest': mere negligence, or a deliberate but honest assistance is not sufficient to found liability (see, for example, *Ferrotex v Banque Français de l'Orient* (2000), where an awareness that a person had been dishonest in other business activities was not sufficient to found 'dishonesty' in relation to the transfer in breach of trust). The dishonesty test now replaces the old tests of knowledge based on the *Baden* categories for assistance liability. However, although *apparently* simpler, no agreed meaning of what amounts to dishonesty, or how it is proven, has emerged. *Brinks v Abu-Saleh* (1995) suggests that dishonesty implies some knowledge on the part of the stranger, but it is not clear whether this is of the existence of a trust, or of the fact of breach, or of the fact that the property is another's, or if it has some other meaning. *Armitage v Nurse* (1997) implies that dishonesty arises from intentional or reckless knowledge, but this was held in a different context (see Chapter 9). The test today for dishonesty in this context was laid down by Lord Hutton in *Twinsectra v Yardley* [2002] 2 All ER 377. This involves the criminal law test for dishonesty (as laid down by Lord Lane CJ in *R v Ghosh* [1982] QB 1053) namely, the defendant's conduct is dishonest by reference to the ordinary standards of reasonable and honest people *and* that he himself realised that his conduct was dishonest by those standards. In *Jyske Bank v Heinl*, it was held that proof of dishonesty involved a high level of probability. So, in that case, it was *not* enough that H appreciated that there was a very real possibility of fraud; what was required was that he 'knew' it. In fact, these are questions which can only be worked out on a case by case basis – hopefully by employing the 'common sense' approach to the meaning of dishonesty which Lord Nicholls in *Tan* believes is possible. However, what is clear is that liability for assistance is fault based and will remain so.

Turning then to 'knowing receipt', it seems clear that the essence of the liability of the stranger in these cases is that he has received trust property for his own benefit: *per* Millet J in *AGIP (Africa) Ltd v Jackson* (1992). Liability is triggered by the personal 'gain' of the stranger at the expense of the beneficiaries (ie, in breach of trust: *Box v Barclays* (1998)) and comprises an obligation to return the property or account for it out of his own resources. Consequently, the liability is primarily restitutionary: to return property which belongs to another. With this in mind, the crucial question is whether the stranger – who has received the property for his own benefit – will be liable only when they were at 'fault' (that is, had some degree of 'knowledge') or whether the liability is strict – so that even an innocent can be liable – subject to a defence of change of position. At present, it seems that liability is fault based: see Lord Browne-Wilkinson (*obiter*) in *Westdeutsche Landesbank Girozentrale v Islington LBC* (1996) and, firmly, the Court of Appeal in *BCCI v Akindele*. Yet, as noted below, this has been challenged, although there is little unanimity among the cases for what degree of knowledge is required. It has been suggested in cases such as *Carl Zeiss Stiftung v Herbert Smith & Co (No 2)* (1969), *Re Montague* (1987) and *Cowan de Groot Properties v Eagle Trust plc* (1992) that liability arises only when the stranger had 'want of probity', probably meaning intention or recklessness as to whether the property was transferred in breach of trust and some case law suggests that mere negligence might be too low a standard in so called 'commercial' cases where the strangers are professional advisers merely executing the wishes of the trustee (*Cowan de Groot Properties v Eagle Trust plc* (1992); *Polly Peck International plc v Nadir (No 2)* (1992)). Alternatively, other cases suggest that liability should exist if the stranger is simply negligent with regard to the terms of the trust: in other words, if he should have known that the transfer of trust funds or his own subsequent dealings with them were in breach of trust. This ensures that liability will arise when *any* of the five of the categories of knowledge in *Baden Delvaux* exists. Judgments in cases such as *International Sales Ltd v Marcus* (1982), *Belmont Finance Corporation v Williams Furniture (No 2)* (1980), at first instance in *AGIP (Africa) Ltd v Jackson* (1992) and *Box v Barclays* (1998) support this view. Different again is the approach in *Akindele*, where Nourse LJ seeks to avoid this past confusion by saying that the recipient must be 'unconscionable' before liability can arise. How this differs from 'knowledge' or 'notice' is unclear, although it seems certain that it does presuppose some element of fault. Indeed, if it is true that the essence of liability for knowing receipt is that the stranger has received property for his own benefit to which he was not entitled, then it is quite appropriate that he should be obliged to return it unless (possibly) he was innocent of all participation in a breach of trust.

This doubt about the practical application of the test of 'fault' required to fix a stranger with liability for 'knowing receipt' raises a more fundamental point: viz, whether liability should depend on any fault at all. After all, if liability is triggered by receipt and the obligation is to account for its value (or return it if still held), then should not merely innocent recipients also be liable? Of course, recipients would need a defence, as every circumstance in which X might receive Y's property could not found liability (for example, if X were a *bona fide* purchaser for value). This approach – generally thought to be purely restitutionary – is indicated by the House of Lords in *Lipkin Gorman v Karpnale* (1991) and has been argued forcefully academically. That case turns on recovery of property at law – that is, the claimant is not a beneficiary of a trust but is chasing his legal title – but it suggests that the liability of a stranger should exist without proof of any degree of knowledge. Certainly, that was the position with the claim at law and many would argue that there is no reason for any difference merely because the beneficiaries of a trust are pursuing a claim in equity. Lest this is thought to be unfair to the innocent stranger, it is balanced by the recognition of a general defence – 'change of position'. This would be available to any stranger to defeat the imposition of a constructive trust, if the court thought fit, depending on whether the stranger has changed his position in reliance on receipt of the money. As is evident, this introduces an element of discretion into the fixing of receipt liability but it is not at all clear whether the 'knowledge' based test really is any more objective.

At present, then, there is no doubt that liability in assistance type cases (and inducement cases where the inducer never receives the trust property for his own use) is fault based – that fault being dishonesty. In receipt based cases (including lawful receipt tainted by subsequent actions in breach of trust), recent case law firmly maintains fault as the basis of liability. However, whether this is logical (see the strict liability position with claims made at law) is open to question, and whether it will survive in the face of powerful restitutionary arguments remains to be seen. However, if questions of 'knowledge' are dispensed with, greater judicial attention will need to be focused on the meaning of the counter-balancing 'change of position' defence.

Note

This question reflects the academic debate which is raging over the scope of, and proper conditions for, the granting of equitable remedies consequent on a breach of trust. It is large issue. It is also relevant in such questions to note the practical constraints under which judges operate and anybody who has read the facts of a commercial 'receipt' or 'assistance' case knows how convoluted the transactions can be.

Question 36

William is the trustee of the Duke of Normandy's Trust Fund and holds various property on trust for the beneficiaries, Harold and Matilda. The following events occur:

(a) William decides to employ the services of a stockbroker to help him invest the trust property, and he transfers £50,000 of alpha stock to Richard with instructions to invest in Blue Chip plc, an authorised investment. Richard thinks this is a poor choice and persuades William to allow him to invest half the amount in Stockbroker Finance, a company that has been tipped to 'boom or bust';

(b) William also decides to sell to Jerry half of the freehold property held on trust for a knockdown price in return for 'an introduction fee' of £5,000. Jerry develops the site for an enormous profit, selling luxury houses to wealthy businessmen;

(c) Harold and Matilda become suspicious of these developments and suggest to William that Catchcon Ltd, a well known firm of auditors, check the Trust account. William fears that they will find something amiss and immediately asks his accountant (Sharp) to 'use the remaining £100,000 of the Duke of Norfolk Trust Fund to purchase travellers' cheques in my name'. The accountant agrees after speaking to William on the telephone and telling him that such an unusual transaction would require a higher fee than usual.

William is now in the Bahamas, and it appears that Stockbroker Finance plc has gone into liquidation. Harold and Matilda urgently seek your advice as to whether they have any remedies.

Answer plan

- Liability as a constructive trustee for: knowing receipt;
- duty to account for dishonest assistance and inconsistent dealing;
- level of knowledge required; meaning of dishonest;
- appropriate remedy;
- bribes; and
- profits.

Answer

It is clear from the facts of this problem that William has committed a series of breaches of trust. Unfortunately for the beneficiaries, he is outside the jurisdiction and the prospects of recovering the lost trust monies from him in a personal action for breach of trust must be remote. Furthermore, it also appears that little of the trust property is in traceable form: Stockbroker plc has gone into liquidation and no mention is made of its assets; Jerry has used the former trust land to build houses which he has sold on to (presumably) innocent purchasers and nothing is said of the money he received on sale. Consequently, with the likely failure of the personal action against the trustee for breach of trust, and with doubts as to the efficacy of the tracing remedy, Harold and Matilda should turn to those persons who have been instrumental in a practical way in these affairs.

As is well known, it is perfectly possible for a non-trustee – a stranger to the trust – to become liable as constructive trustee for intermeddling in some way with the affairs of the trust. This liability has many different aspects and the precise conditions for the establishment of a constructive trust will vary from situation to situation. In general, a stranger may be liable as a constructive trustee if he has either knowingly induced a breach of trust (*Eaves v Hickson* (1861)), dishonestly assisted in a breach of trust (*Royal Brunei Airlines v Tan* (1995)), knowingly received trust property for his own benefit in breach of trust (*Belmont Finance Corporation v Williams Furniture (No 2)* (1980); *BCCI v Akindele* (2000)) or knowingly dealt with trust property in his possession in breach of the terms of the trust (*William-Ashman v Price* (1942)). The consequences of being fixed with a constructive trust are that the stranger is under a duty to return to the beneficiaries any trust property which he still retains and, additionally, to make up any shortfall out of his own assets. Further, because a constructive trustee is also personally liable to the beneficiaries for any loss they have suffered – that is, he must satisfy a claim out of his own funds if necessary – this makes this remedy particularly attractive to beneficiaries who have no hope of recovery from the original trustee and little chance of maintaining a successful claim to the trust property *per se* through a tracing claim.

Turning to consider the particular facts of this problem, it may well be that Harold and Matilda will be able to claim successfully that the 'stranger' who dealt with each aspect of the trust property should be clothed with a constructive trust. First, let us consider the position of Richard and the investment in Stockbroker Finance plc. It is perfectly acceptable for William to employ the services of a professional adviser or agent when investing the trust property (s 11 of the Trustee Act 2000). As we are told, when the £50,000 is transferred, this is perfectly in accordance with the terms of the trust. Importantly, then, Richard has not received the money in breach of trust, and nor has he assisted William in a breach of trust. This eliminates any constructive trust liability on these grounds (see, for example, *Brown v Bennett* (1998) and *Box v Barclays* (1998)). However, it is possible that Richard may be liable as constructive trustee in respect of those part of the trust funds invested in Stockbroker Finance plc for either of two further reasons. First, Richard may be regarded as a constructive trustee because he may have induced William to commit a breach of trust, provided that (a) the investment in Stockbroker Finance plc was indeed a breach of trust; and (b) Richard had a sufficient degree of knowledge of the terms of the trust to trigger liability (*Eaves v Hickson* (1861)).

As to (a), it is not clear from the facts of the problem whether the investment in Stockbroker Finance plc was legitimate or not, although the presumption is that the investment breached William's duty of care under s 1 of Sched 1(1) to the Trustee Act 2000, given the need for Richard to persuade William of this course of action and the volatile nature of Stockbroker's shares. Again, as to (b), it is not clear from the facts whether Richard had sufficient knowledge to found liability. In principle, it is reasonably clear that mere negligence on Richard's part as to whether the investment was legitimate (that is, was a breach of trust) is not sufficient to found liability for knowing inducement. What appears to be necessary is either actual knowledge that it was a breach of trust to invest in Stockbroker or a reckless disregard of whether it was a breach. 'Knowledge' within any of the first three of the *Baden* categories is required (or possibly, after *Tan*, even 'dishonesty'). This may or may not exist in our case and liability will depend on a thorough examination of the facts and circumstances of the case.

Secondly, however, if it is unclear whether Richard actually *induced* William to commit a breach of trust, as opposed to merely facilitating its achievement, it may be possible to fix Richard with a duty to account for dealing inconsistently with trust property in the knowledge that the dealing was in breach of trust. This is a form of secondary liability as it seems clear that Richard has never received the trust property for his own benefit. Under the pre-*Tan* approach liability would seem to depend on finding that Richard had intention or recklessness with regard to the existence of a breach of trust (the 'old' rules for what was called 'knowing assistance'). However, given that this form of inconsistent dealing is, in essence, another form of assistance liability, it may be correct to assume that liability exists only in conjunction with dishonesty (*Tan*). By the same token, although it will not be necessary to prove that there has been a fraudulent breach of trust by the trustee (which almost certainly there was not, because of William's reluctance), it is necessary to prove a breach and that Richard factually assisted it. The second is established; the first depends on the legitimacy of William's investment in terms of his duty of care. Even then, we must ask whether Richard really was 'dishonest' (on which, see *Brinks v Abu-Saleh (No 3)* (1995) and *Jyske Bank v Heinl* (1999)). The test for dishonesty as laid down in *Twinsectra v Yardley* [2002] 2 All ER 377, involves a two step approach as declared by Lord Lane CJ in the criminal law case, *R v Ghosh* [1982] QB 1053. The first step is whether Richard's conduct was dishonest by reference to the ordinary standards of reasonable and honest people *and* whether he realised that his conduct was dishonest by those standards. Perhaps he was only negligent and so liable only in tort (*Box v Barclays Bank* (1998)).

The second element of the problem raises similar issues, although now it is a question of whether the liability of Jerry (if any) lies in knowing receipt or dishonest assistance. It seems clear from the facts of the problem that the land was 'sold' to Jerry for his own personal use. For example, title to the land did not remain with William (although this is not conclusive) and Jerry cannot be regarded as William's agent. This seems to be a case of knowing receipt, being a case whether the stranger has received trust property for his own use (*AGIP (Africa) Ltd v Jackson* (1992)). As such, if Jerry is to be fixed with a constructive trust, and thereby be required to satisfy the claims of Harold and Matilda out of his own resources, it is clear that he must have acted with some degree of knowledge. This requires an understanding that the actions of William were in breach of trust (*Westdeutsche v Islington LBC* (1996)), expressed in *Akindele* as to whether it would be 'unconscionable' for Jerry to retain the benefit. Initially, of course, Jerry will claim that he is a *bona fide* purchaser for value of the freehold land and, in consequence, is not liable to the beneficiaries either as a constructive trustee or in tracing (*Re Diplock* (1948)). However, as the facts indicate, Jerry purchases the property for 'a knockdown price' and gives William an introduction fee. Although one must not speculate unduly, the clear inference here is that Jerry is not *bona fides*. Of course, mere suspicion on his part that William is engaged in a breach of trust may not be sufficient to establish Jerry's liability; he must have 'knowledge' of the relevant facts and be 'unconscionable'. Unfortunately, what this means in practice is uncertain. The logic of the situation suggests that simple negligence (that is, any of the five categories of knowledge in *Baden*) should suffice and this is supported by *dicta* in several cases (*International Sales Ltd v Marcus* (1982); *Belmont Finance Corporation v Williams Furniture (No 2)* (1980); *AGIP (Africa) Ltd v Jackson* (1992); *Box v Barclays* (1998)). However, other authority has moved away from such an approach and has placed more emphasis on the 'want of probity' or deliberate fault of the stranger (that is, intention or recklessness). The case for restricting liability in this fashion is strongly argued in *Re Montague* (1987), and a spate of cases involving the alleged liability of professional financial advisers has tended to confirm this view (*Cowan de Groot Properties v Eagle Trust plc* (1992); *Polly Peck International plc v Nadir (No 2)* (1992)). In these so called 'commercial' cases, the powerful nature of the constructive trust was emphasised and there were fears that commercial transactions would be hampered if mere negligence could trigger the personal liability of the stranger, especially as the stranger might well be liable in any event for breach of contract. As yet the matter is unclear and the decision in *Akindele*, that it is better to think in terms of unconscionability, may not prove any more helpful. In our case, while there is no doubt that Jerry was negligent, there is also evidence to suggest that he was, at best, reckless and, at worst, that he conspired with William to defeat the rights of the beneficiaries, all for personal gain. In such circumstances, there is a good chance that he would be held liable as constructive trustee for knowing receipt. Likewise, if William had been in the jurisdiction, he would have been accountable as constructive trustee for the 'introduction fee' as having derived a profit from his position as trustee (*Williams v Barton* (1927); *Box v Barclays* (1998)). Further, if this was a bribe, William would be accountable under *Attorney General for Hong Kong v Reid* (1992), as applied in *LSE v Pearson*.

The third element of the problem raises similar difficulties. William has clearly embarked on a fraudulent and dishonest course of action which has breached the terms of the trust. The only question is whether Sharp, the accountant, is liable for assisting in this breach of trust. The authorities were fully explored and analysed in *AGIP (Africa) Ltd v Jackson* (1992) and then explained clearly by the Privy Council in *Tan*. It is now relatively clear that the accountant will be accountable for such profits directly connected with knowingly assisting in a breach of trust if he was 'dishonest' and his actions did indeed facilitate the breach. Of course, there are difficulties over the meaning of dishonesty (see *Teinsectra v Yardley* (2002), *Brinks v Abu-Saleh (No 3)* and *Jyske v Heinl* (1999) for a discussion of what 'dishonesty' might mean). In this problem the facts are equivocal. Sharp's higher fee and realisation that the transaction was 'unusual' may be evidence of dishonesty or it may simply be evidence that Sharp appreciated the possibility of fraud – which appears not to amount to dishonesty – *Jyske*. Undoubtedly, the accountant will attempt to plead that he was merely carrying out his contract with William – in much the same way as the bank claimed to avoid liability in *Lipkin Gorman v Karpnale* (1991), but this will not be enough if the court determines – as in *AGIP* – that the strangers were materially involved in the fraud or at least did not care about the possibility that a fraud was being perpetrated (compare *Jyske*). All in all, this stranger may well find himself liable to Harold and Matilda for the balance of the fund that William has taken with him to the Bahamas.

Question 37

Arnold is the agent of Tarquin, the trustee of a settlement in favour of 'the children of Sarah'. Tarquin instructs Arnold to pay £5,000 to Len, who, Tarquin says, is the illegitimate child of Sarah and himself. Tarquin also instructs Arnold to invest £10,000 in the stock exchange in Tarquin Enterprises Ltd, to buy £5,000 worth of tickets in the national lottery (all of which lose) and to transfer £10,000 to Clarence as payment for services rendered to the trust. One year later, Tarquin goes missing with the remaining trust fund monies. Moreover, it transpires that Len is in fact the child of Tarquin and Sandra (Arnold's sister) and that the money has all been spent. Tarquin Enterprises have gone bust due to a dramatic withdrawal of cash from their bank account.

Advise the children of Sarah as to their remedies, if any, against Arnold and Clarence.

Answer plan

- Liability as a constructive trustee for: knowing receipt and dishonest assistance;
- level of knowledge or dishonesty required: whether satisfied; and
- profits.

Answer

The facts disclosed by this problem relate to an area of the law of trusts that appears to be growing in popularity, at least with beneficiaries who perceive a breach of trust on the part of their trustees but who, for one reason or another, have no trustee to sue personally. In our particular case, it seems that 'the children of Sarah' – the beneficiaries of the trust – would be unable to pursue an action in breach of trust against Tarquin (their trustee) because he has disappeared. Consequently, they must resort to alternative remedies, which, in this case, means attempting to establish that strangers to the trust are fixed with constructive trusteeship because of their interference or involvement with the activities which have caused loss to the trust estate. Importantly, it must be remembered that the liability of the strangers – Arnold and Clarence – can exist only if there has actually been a breach of trust: *Brown v Bennett* (1998). The familiar liability of 'dishonest assistance' and 'knowing receipt' can arise only if the dealings with the trust property disclose a breach of the terms of the trust. There is no liability for the strangers if they are involved in activities which are consistent with the terms of the trust, even if those activities go wrong and cause a loss to the trust estate (see, for example, *Box v Barclays Bank* (1998)).

It is stated in the facts of the problem that Tarquin holds the property on trust for a certain specified class of persons – the children of Sarah. Necessarily, any distribution of the trust property to persons outside of this class will be a breach of trust, for which Tarquin will be liable, even if he has made an honest mistake (*Re Diplock*). Consequently, a stranger may be liable as constructive trustee if he has assisted in or induced the breach of trust, as per the conditions laid down in *Barnes v Addy* (1874) and explained in *Royal Brunei Airlines v Tan*. Prima facie then, the distribution of £5,000 to Len is a breach of trust that may generate liability for Arnold. However, this is the only unequivocal breach of trust disclosed by the facts of the problem. For example, it may well be that investing in Tarquin Enterprises Ltd is perfectly within the investment powers of the trust (see, for example, ss 3, 4 and 6 of the Trustee Act 2000) and, if it were, it would be almost impossible to establish Arnold's liability as a stranger. Indeed, whereas Tarquin might be liable for his particular choice of investment – even though it was within his investment powers generally (breach of duty of care: s 1 of the Trustee Act 2000) – Arnold would not be liable as a stranger unless Tarquin's direction to him was part of a design to escape with the trust funds and Arnold dishonestly assisted in this (*Tan*; *Brinks v Abu-Saleh (No 3)*). Likewise, although it is unlikely, the trust instrument might authorise the purchase of lottery tickets (this would seem to be excluded from the statutory power of investment under the Trustee Act 2000 – see s 4 of that Act) and Clarence may well have rendered services to the trust in this regard for which he has been paid legitimately. So, without more, it is impossible to determine whether these events disclose a breach of trust. Consequently, the liability of Arnold and Clarence can be discussed only on the assumption that the activities of Tarquin do disclose a breach of trust and would have generated his personal liability. Even then, in itself, this is not enough to establish the liability of the strangers: we must also examine actions of the stranger.

As far as the wrongful distribution of the trust monies is concerned, it has been noted above that this, at least, is a clear breach of the terms of the trust (*Re Hulkes* (1886)). Moreover, given that Arnold is Tarquin's agent and only has possession of the £5,000 in order to deal with it at Tarquin's direction, he (Arnold) cannot be liable for knowingly receiving trust property; Arnold has not received trust money for his own benefit (*AGIP (Africa) Ltd v Jackson* (1992)). If any liability exists, it will lay in 'dishonest assistance' for clearly Arnold has participated in Tarquin's act which is revealed to be a breach of trust. In order to maintain a successful action against Arnold on this ground, two essential conditions must be fulfilled. First, it must be established that Arnold has assisted Tarquin in a breach of trust. This is a factual matter and, as *Brinks* shows, the mere offering of aid to a person committing a breach of trust may not in law amount to 'assistance'. Assistance implies positive help although, in this case, it is not difficult to establish. Also, following *Tan*, it is no longer necessary to prove that the trustee's breach itself was fraudulent and dishonest. *Tan* makes it clear that the liability is the stranger's and the state of mind of the trustee cannot colour it. A 'simple' breach of trust is enough. Secondly, *Tan* also makes it clear that the stranger's assistance must be coloured by his own 'dishonesty' before liability can arise. This test now replaces the old tests of knowledge based on the *Baden* categories. In *Twinsectra v Yardley* [2002] 2 All ER 377, the majority of the House of Lords adopted the criminal law test for dishonesty (as laid down by Lord Lane CJ in *R v Ghosh* [1982] QB 1053) namely, the defendant's conduct is dishonest by reference to the ordinary standards of reasonable and honest people *and* that he himself realised that his conduct was dishonest by those standards. This involves both objective and subjective questions. Likewise, although we know dishonesty requires a high standard of proof (*Jyske v Heinl*), each case will be unique to its own facts. In our case, we do not know with certainty Arnold's state of mind or motives, but it might be significant that Len's mother is Arnold's sister. While not conclusive, this does suggest some participation in Tarquin's fraud and, if this is true, Arnold will be liable as constructive trustee and will be ordered to repay the £5,000 to the trust fund which Len has now dissipated.

Much the same considerations apply to the two further 'investments' made by Arnold on Tarquin's instructions except that, in both cases, there is no clear evidence of a breach of trust. This makes it impossible to be certain whether the strangers will be fixed with a constructive trust for dishonestly assisting Tarquin in his activities. Of course, as above, the possibility that a breach of trust has occurred can be inferred from the nature of the investments ordered by Tarquin, as it is hardly likely that the trust deed authorises investment in one of the trustee's own companies or in a purely speculative lottery and such investments may well be outside ss 3 and 4 of the Trustee Act 2000. Yet this is only a rebuttable presumption. With that in mind, it is again necessary to assess Arnold's state of mind in order to determine whether the beneficiaries have a remedy in dishonest assistance in respect of these lost trust funds. Unfortunately, there is nothing in the facts of the problem to help us here and, as we have seen, the fact that no reasonable person would have acted as Arnold did (that is, Arnold was negligent) is not enough to trigger the powerful constructive trust in assistance cases (*Tan*). In the absence of further evidence, the matter must rest there.

The third stage of the beneficiaries proceedings against the 'strangers' will be an attempt to fix Clarence with constructive trusteeship, this time on the basis of 'knowing receipt'. If this liability is successfully established, Clarence will be required to return the £10,000 to the trust and any profit that it has generated while in his hands (*English v Dedham Vale Properties* (1978)). As a first step, it is apparent that Clarence has received the £10,000 for his own use and benefit, thus establishing clearly that this is a case of 'receipt' (*AGIP (Africa) Ltd v Jackson* (1992); *BCCI v Akindele*). Yet, before Clarence can be liable, it must be established both that the transfer to Clarence was in breach of trust and that Clarence had sufficient 'knowledge' of this to make him liable: that is, it is unconscionable for him to retain the benefit (*Akindele*). In fact, although these are separate criteria, it often happens that they are interwoven, as they are in this case. So, if it is true that Clarence has rendered services to the trust, the payment of £10,000 may well be legitimate (that is, there is no breach) – s 14 of the Trustee Act 2000 – and, even if the payment is not legitimate *per se*, Clarence could easily be a *bona fide* purchaser for value (having 'paid' for the money with his services) and thus not be liable. On the other hand, if the transfer to Clarence was in breach of trust – perhaps as part of a scheme to defraud the beneficiaries – Clarence's position must come under much closer scrutiny. If a breach has occurred, Clarence will be liable if he had 'knowledge' of the relevant facts. There is no agreement in the case law as to which level of knowledge is required for 'receipt' liability. Some cases (for example, *Cowan de Groot Properties v Eagle Trust plc* (1992)) suggest that either 'actual knowledge' or 'recklessness' must exist in order to establish liability and, even if we can distinguish some of these cases on the ground that they involved a 'commercial' transaction where the court was reluctant to impose a liability on professional advisers over and above their contractual responsibilities, the private trust case of *Re Montague* (1987) also argues powerfully in favour of a minimum standard of 'want of probity'. On the other hand, other cases (*International Sales*

Ltd v Marcus (1982); *Belmont Finance Corporation v Williams Furniture (No 2)* (1980); *Box v Barclays* (1998)) indicate plainly that receipt liability can be triggered by mere negligence and this was also the view of Millet J in his very thorough judgment in *AGIP (Africa) Ltd v Jackson* (1992). Possibly, it is the meaning to be given to the 'unconscionability' test put forward in *Akindele*, but this remains to be seen. In fact, the reasoning in *AGIP* is based on the fact that liability for receipt is essentially a restitutionary liability – a liability to return that which the defendant has, to the person to whom it rightfully belongs. If this is the correct view, it is entirely appropriate that negligence (or, perhaps, mere innocent possession) can trigger liability, as otherwise a recipient could retain property he had received beneficially because he had failed to meet standards of reasonable conduct. In our case, it is not clear whether Clarence has any knowledge of the breach of trust; he may be innocent. An enquiry must be made as to Clarence's understanding of Tarquin's actions and, it is submitted, that the better view is that he will be liable as constructive trustee if he was merely negligent or worse: that is, if any of the five categories of knowledge identified in *Baden Delvaux and Lecuit v Société Génerale pour Favouriser le Développement du Commerce et de l'Industrie en France SA* (1983) are present.

To conclude, much turns in this case on precise proof of facts which are not apparent from the problem. These are, principally, whether there were breaches of trust and whether the *mens rea* conditions are satisfied. In appropriate cases, the powerful constructive trust will be imposed and the strangers will be held personally responsible for any loss to the trust fund. This will be in addition to the obligation to return any trust property that they do retain, along with any profits that that property has generated in the meantime.

Note

These two problem questions are quite general and one should not shy from stating that the precise answer depends on facts which are not made apparent in the question. Of course, this means that the answer requires a discussion of the principles behind the rules.

8 The Law of Tracing

Introduction

One of the most effective remedies available to a beneficiary who has been deprived of the trust property as a result of a breach of trust by the trustee is to be found in the law of tracing. 'Tracing' of trust property – either 'at law' or 'in equity' – enables a claimant to follow the ownership of property into whosoever's hands that property falls and to recover it to the extent that the defendant still possesses it. Most importantly, it is clear that a claimant who relies on a tracing remedy is tracing his or her ownership of the property irrespective of the form the property has taken in the hands of the defendant. For example, if the trustee wrongly distributes trust property – being cash – to X, and X uses that cash to purchase a car, the claimant may trace his ownership through the cash into the car and recover it from X. It should also be noted at this early stage that the remedies of tracing and the liability of a stranger as constructive trustee (Chapter 7) are frequently complimentary. So, a third party who has received trust property with 'knowledge' that there has been a breach of trust may be a constructive trustee and subject to the tracing remedy. In the former case (that is, that of constructive trusteeship), he must hold the trust property for the beneficiaries *and* is subject to a personal liability. As we shall see in the case of successful tracing, the defendant may be entirely innocent but must still return the property in its present form to the rightful owners.

In addition, it is reasonably clear that tracing in equity is a 'proprietary' remedy in the sense that a successful claimant is asserting his right to the property *per se*: hence, if the defendant is bankrupt, the claimant may recover 'his' property (assuming it exists and is identifiable) and he is not treated as a general creditor and does not have to take only a share of the defendant's assets. It is a matter of 'hard nosed property rights': *Foskett v McKeown* (2000). Obviously, such a powerful remedy cannot go unchecked and it should come as no surprise that the availability of the remedy of tracing in equity is restricted to certain situations. Unfortunately, the precise circumstances in which tracing is available are not universally agreed – either academically or judicially – nor, indeed, is there agreement as to whether tracing 'at law' and tracing 'in equity' are as similar as they first appear. These issues, as well as problem questions testing an awareness of how tracing works in practice, are the staple of examinations.

As inferred already, there are two forms of tracing: tracing 'at law' (common law tracing) and tracing 'in equity'. Tracing at law is available to any person who has legal title to property and its primary purpose is to identify the person whom the legal owner should sue, that being the person into whose hands the property has passed. Once the defendant has been identified, the claimant may then sue on a variety of causes of action as circumstances dictate. These are the action for 'money had and received', being appropriate where the property traced was money, and an action in conversion or for wrongful interference, where the property consists of goods or other kinds of property. We should note, however, that recent case law has tended to 'deconstruct' claims in tracing – especially at law – and to regard the claim as an example of a general restitutionary liability, whereby the defendant should return property to the claimant if the defendant has been unjustly enriched at the claimant's expense, to the extent of the unjust enrichment, in circumstances where there is no defence of change of position (*Trustee of the property of FC Jones v Jones* (1996)). In addition, as we shall see, there is one serious limitation on the effectiveness of tracing at law for it is impossible to trace at law if the original property has been mixed with any other property (as opposed to having been exchanged for any other), although, again, this may be changing.

Fortunately, tracing into a 'mixed fund' is perfectly possible in equity. Moreover, given that tracing at law requires the claimant to have *legal* title to property, it is clearly not available to a beneficiary under a trust who, after all, has only an equitable title. Consequently, most of the issues examined in this chapter will focus on tracing in equity, that being the remedy available to a beneficiary under a trust and that being the remedy that *does* permit a claim to be made even though the trust property has been mixed with some other, even if it has been mixed with that of the trustee himself: *Foskett*). Finally, we shall see that another aspect of the proprietary nature of tracing in equity is that it entitles the claimant both to the property which the defendant has in his possession and to any increase in its value that it may have acquired in the meantime (*Foskett*: entitled to benefits of life insurance because premiums were paid with beneficiaries' money). Until recently, this has not been possible in law, but once again, the move to a generally restitutionary approach may make even this possible (*Trustee of the property of FC Jones v Jones*).

 ───── **Question 38** ─────

What are the essential requirements for a successful tracing claim at law and in equity?

 Answer plan

- The purpose of a tracing claim, both at law and in equity;
- conditions for both claims; and
- differences between them: in establishing the remedy and in respect of the defences available to a defendant.

 ───────── **Answer** ─────────

A tracing claim is a method of asserting ownership to property. Literally, the legal or equitable owner of property may 'trace' his or her ownership through the hands of the different persons who have possessed it and may recover it from the person who currently possesses it. Tracing 'at law' (common law tracing) is a means of following the legal title to property, while tracing 'in equity' signifies a similar right of the equitable owner, such as a beneficiary under a trust. Moreover, such is the power of the tracing claim that the claimant's property need not be in the same form as that when he or she lost possession: the claimant is tracing a right of ownership and may enforce that *right of ownership* against any property which has been exchanged for the original property. It is a matter of 'hard nosed' property rights: *Foskett v McKeown* (2000). For example, if a beneficiary wishes to trace her equitable ownership of £500, her claim will survive if that £500 has been turned in £500 worth of shares or some other identifiable property. Tracing, both at law and in equity, is not defeated by a change in the external appearance of the claimant's property, but will run against any property which can be identified as encapsulating the claimant's rights of ownership.

It will be apparent from this brief introduction that tracing can be a powerful weapon in the hands of a legal or equitable owner who has been improperly deprived of her property. As we shall see, tracing enjoys distinct advantages over other remedies designed to recover ownership of property, not least of which is the ability to subsist through changes in the form of property. However, it should come as no surprise to learn that there are certain preconditions to a successful tracing claim and, importantly, these differ depending on whether the claim is made 'at law' or 'in equity'. Indeed, we can go further and note that tracing at law and tracing in equity are regarded by some commentators as so distinct that they should properly be regarded as quite separate remedies for the recovery of property and not merely as two different examples of the same principle. Others, however, believe that the existence of different conditions for the two types of claim are anomalous and mask the true restitutionary basis of the actions. This view seems to be gathering pace (although not yet judicially: see the views of the majority in *Foskett* denying this approach), but for the purposes of this answer, tracing at law and in equity will be considered separately.

Common law tracing is a means of following legal title to property through successive persons until the property (or its present equivalent) is identified in the hands of the person against whom the concrete remedy for recovery is pursued. In essence, it is a means to an end, not the end itself (*AGIP (Africa) Ltd v Jackson* (1992); *Trustee of the property of FC Jones v Jones* (1996)). When the present possessor of the property in which the claimant's legal title subsists is identified, the claimant has a choice of remedies against that possessor. If the property is money, then the action will be against the present recipient for 'money had and received' (*Lipkin Gorman v Karpnale* (1991)), whereas if the property is a specific item, then the action will lie in tort for wrongful interference with goods or conversion. In the former case, the amount of the money 'had and received' by the defendant will be returned to the claimant and, in the latter case, the defendant will pay damages representing the value of the item or, in exceptional cases, the item itself may be returned at the discretion of the court. Importantly, however, because tracing at law is simply a means of identifying the defendant, who is then subject to a specific remedy, it is reasonably clear that the liability of the defendant is personal, not proprietary. In other words, the person identified as the defendant through common law tracing is personally liable to the claimant for either money had and received or wrongful interference with goods and must, therefore, pay the claimant whether or not he still retains the property in question. As was made clear by the Court of Appeal in *AGIP (Africa) Ltd v Jackson* (1992), liability exists because the defendant has received property to which another has a better legal title. It does not exist because the defendant has retained that title. Likewise, the defendant's honesty or dishonesty is irrelevant and, subject to what was said by the House of Lords in *Lipkin Gorman v Karpnale* (1991), the defendant cannot escape liability by pleading that he is a *bona fide* purchaser for value, except, possibly, where legal title to money passes with an exchange for value. Of course, there are limits to the ability to trace at law, one of which is particularly important in the context of the law of trusts.

In the first place, tracing at law (and in equity) requires the property to be in identifiable form. If it has been destroyed, or money has been dissipated, then tracing is of no use: the property and the *legal* title to it are extinct. Secondly, tracing at law requires the claimant to have had legal title to property. Therefore, as a matter of principle, it is not available to a beneficiary under a trust who is, of course, a person with a pure equitable title. Moreover, it must be clear that the claimant has retained legal title to the property. Given that title to money usually passes with possession, it is often easy to defeat a claim at law, as in *Box v Barclays Bank* (1998) where the legal title had passed from the claimants. On the other hand, some cases – for example, *Lipkin Gorman v Karpnale* (1991) and *Jones v Jones* (1996) – have sidestepped the claimant's *apparent* lack of title (that is, the claimants may have had title to a *'chose in action'*: a debt now representing the money) and allowed the claim to proceed. Thirdly, the personal nature of tracing at law may cause problems if the defendant has gone bankrupt because, in theory, the personal claim of the tracer will rank equally with other personal claims made on the bankrupt's estate. In practice, the defendant's trustee in bankruptcy may pay the tracer first – in order to avoid a personal claim against *him* as receiver of the claimant's property, although this is an incidental advantage rather than an inherent attribute of tracing at law. Fourthly, although there has been much debate, it seems that tracing at law is not available if the claimant's property has been mixed with that of another person and then passed on. Thus, although the claimant may trace her ownership into property no matter what its present form, the ability to trace legal title will expire if the property has been mixed with that of another person prior to coming into the hands of the defendant (*AGIP (Africa) Ltd v Jackson* (1992)). The essence of the matter is that mixing at law renders the legal title to the property unidentifiable, in much the same way as if the property had actually been destroyed. This is a serious practical drawback to the efficacy of common law tracing and is a major reason why successful actions are rare. Note, however, that this is an inability to trace against a recipient of the property after it has been mixed. There is nothing to stop the claimant tracing at law against the person who does the mixing because, prior to that person's possession, the property was identifiable. Fifthly, being traditionally regarded as a personal claim, an innocent defendant in an action supported by common law tracing should not normally be required to disgorge profits made by use of the property wrongfully received. The claim is for the value of the property, not *the* property (compare tracing in equity). However, in *Jones v Jones*, the Court of Appeal held, on general restitutionary principles, that if the defendant had no title to the money she had received, then she had no title to the profits she made by using it. In that case, the defendant was compelled to return the value of the initial sum plus the considerably greater profits she made by investing it in the futures market. This may well indicate the way ahead, although we should note that it involves seeing tracing at law as simply a device for reversing unjust enrichment. Finally, it may now be the case that a defendant may be able to plead 'change of position' as a defence to an action triggered by common law tracing (*Lipkin Gorman v Karpnale* (1991)). Although the precise details of this defence are not yet clear, its development by the House of Lords in *Lipkin* (and applied in *Bank Tejaret v HKSB* (1995)) clearly allows the court to mitigate the strictures of this remedy by an exercise of discretion in the defendant's favour (but not with respect to tracing in equity, where 'change of position' is not one of the defences: *Foskett*). For example, it may well provide a defence to a claim in money 'had and received' for a person who is a *bona fide* purchaser for value of the claimant's property and to other persons who, in all innocence, have received the claimant's property in circumstances where the court thinks they should not be held personally liable.

As noted already, the limits on common law tracing represent a practical limitation on the efficacy of the remedy. So, it remains unavailable to beneficiaries of trusts and will be defeated by a mixing of the trust property. Fortunately, tracing in equity does not suffer from these disadvantages and consequently is much more versatile. Importantly, tracing in equity is regarded as proprietary in nature, with the consequence that it attaches directly to the property in the hands of the possessor (no matter what its current form) and gives the claimant paramount rights to recover it, even if the defendant is bankrupt. The defendant has no right to the claimant's property and so it forms no part of the defendant's assets. Furthermore, the proprietary nature of the claim means that the claimant is entitled to any increase in the value of 'his' property while it has been out of his possession, as where shares are purchased with trust money and they rise in value (*Re Tilley* (1967); *Foskett* (2000)). The idea of equitable tracing as a claim having proprietary effect is further reinforced by the fact that the defendant in equitable tracing is not sued on a specific cause of action (not money had and received, etc), but is rather the object of specific orders designed to give concrete manifestation to the equitable right of ownership. These may include a charge over property in the defendant's hands if it represents the claimant's original ownership, or an order for the return of specific assets, or a charge over specific funds, or a charge over a specific portion of the property or funds. Indeed, in *Boscawen v Bajawa* (1995), the Court of Appeal indicated that equitable tracing should be regarded as a route to a defendant for all manner of remedies. So, in that case, once the defendant had been identified has having received the claimant's money (transferred in breach of trust), the claimant was subrogated to (that is, placed in the position of) the mortgagee whom the defendant had paid off with the money. So, it appears that equitable tracing – just like its counterpart at law – is developing a new restitutionary cloak.

The trigger for a claim of equitable tracing is that the claimant must have an equitable proprietary interest in property and *only* an equitable proprietary interest (*Re Diplock* (1948)). Consequently, a beneficiary under a trust may trace in equity, but a trustee (legal title only) and an absolute owner may not. Secondly, unlike the position at law, it seems that tracing in equity can occur only if there was in existence a fiduciary relationship between the equitable owner and some other person before the events giving rise to the tracing claim occurred (*Sinclair v Brougham* (1914); *AGIP (Africa) Ltd v Jackson* (1992); and confirmed in *Westdeutsche Landesbank Girozentrale v Islington LBC* (1996)). This will always be the case where the claim arises out of a trust and it is clear that courts may do their utmost to find the required fiduciary relationship in order to facilitate the tracing claim (*Chase Manhattan Bank v Israel-British Bank* (1981)), although it will not exist (and so will prevent tracing) where the relationship between the parties is purely contractual (*Box v Barclays* (1998)). However, the principle is that there must have been an initial fiduciary relationship; there is no requirement that the person actually committing the acts which give rise to the tracing claim must be in a fiduciary relationship to the claimants. For example, tracing in equity will lie in favour of beneficiaries when an agent of the trustees misapplies trust funds, even though the agent himself does not stand in a fiduciary relationship with the beneficiaries. It is enough that the trustees are in a fiduciary relationship to the beneficiaries. Indeed, *Chase* and *El Ajou v Dollar Land Holdings* (1994) suggest that the converse of the above principle is also true: that is, that while the act causing loss to the beneficiaries need not spring from a fiduciary relationship if one existed previously, it is enough if the act causing loss actually establishes the fiduciary relationship where none existed before. So, in *Westdeutsche,* Lord Browne-Wilkinson indicated that a thief holds stolen property on constructive trust for the rightful owner as the thief's conscience necessarily is bound. This means that the owner could trace the property through the hands of the thief into the hands of the ultimate recipient. It is an example of the 'act in breach' giving rise to both the claim and the fiduciary relationship necessary to support it. Clearly, this wide view would do much to reduce the practical obstacle placed in the way of tracing by the need to establish the fiduciary relationship.

Thirdly, it is inherent in the equitable tracing claim that the property of the beneficiaries must have been transferred to another person wrongfully. Otherwise, the equitable owner has no right or reason to claim its return. Fourthly, being a claim in equity, equitable tracing is not possible against a person who is a *bona fide* purchaser for value of the property, although it may still be possible to trace against the person who has sold the trust property to the purchaser (*Re Diplock* (1948)). Likewise, it appears that the court has a discretion to disallow tracing against an innocent volunteer (that is, a person who gives no value for the trust property but is innocent of wrongdoing), if to do otherwise would be inequitable in all the circumstances. This may well be the case where an innocent volunteer has received trust property and mixed it with his own, but in such a way that granting a charge over the mixed property would cause unwarranted hardship to the innocent volunteer. It is clear, however, that this is not (yet?) to be equated with a general change of position defence: Lord Millet in *Foskett*.

In conclusion, it is apparent that both tracing in law and tracing in equity can be powerful tools in the hands of persons wrongfully deprived of their property. At present, the conditions for the application of each are different and some would argue that they are fundamentally different in purpose. However, the object of tracing is quite limited: it is to restore to the claimant that of which he has been wrongfully deprived, often in breach of trust. For that reason, a tracing claim in equity may well be accompanied by a personal claim against the trustee for breach of trust and a claim that the defendant is liable as a constructive trustee because of their 'dishonest assistance' in a breach of trust or 'knowing receipt' of trust property. Finally, if it is true that tracing at law and tracing in equity are not logically different – that is, that they are both examples of a restitutionary claim used to restore to the claimantthat by which the defendant has been unjustly enriched at the claimant's expense – then, perhaps different considerations should not apply and the traditional view expressed at the outset of this answer should give way to a simpler question: has the defendant been enriched at the claimant's expense in circumstances where it would be unjust for him to keep the property?

Note

It is often difficult to describe and analyse the law of tracing in the abstract. The concept of following the ownership of property is metaphysical, but nevertheless very powerful if one happens to be the defendant in a tracing claim. The 'big' question is whether tracing at law and tracing in equity will survive as distinct classes of action in the face of the new restitutionary approach. Following *Foskett v McKeown*, it seems that they will for some time to come. However, in essays such as this, examples are always useful to illustrate difficult concepts. Note that this essay does not require discussion of the particular rules of equitable tracing (for example, *Re Hallett* (1880); *Re Oatway* (1903); *Clayton's Case* (1816), etc.).

Question 39

Charles was the trustee of a large private trust fund. He cashed a cheque for £26,000 drawn on the trust fund and gave the money to James, the trust's financial advisor, with directions to use half to purchase shares for the trust and to use half to invest in antique furniture. James used £7,000 of the money to purchase shares in X Co in the name of the trust, and he delivered the share certificates to Charles as promised. However, he used a further £10,000 to purchase shares in Y Co in his own name, although he has now given these to his daughter as a birthday present, much to her surprise. James puts a further £5,000 in his own bank account, in which he already has some £4,000 of his own money. Out of this account, he purchases shares in Z Co to the value of £3,000, and gives them to his son. He spends the rest of the money from this bank account on a family holiday. The final £4,000 of the trust money was used to purchase antique furniture at a local auction.

The shares in X Co have slumped in value; those in Y Co have remained constant; but those in Z Co have trebled in value. Unfortunately, James has disappeared, and the furniture turns out to be fake and is worthless. Advise Charles of any action he might take to recoup the losses to the trust fund.

Answer plan

- Tracing at law: existence of legal title and continuance of that title;
- appropriate remedy and defences, if any;
- the need to trace in equity: the beneficiaries;
- increase in value of trust property; and
- new restitutionary approaches.

Answer

This problem raises a number of issues concerning the remedies available to a trustee (Charles) and the beneficiaries for whom he holds the trust property when the trust property is misapplied in breach of trust. However, perhaps the first piece of advice that one may offer to Charles is to warn him of the possibility that he may be sued personally for breach of trust by the beneficiaries. Of course, the acts in breach were committed by James – Charles's agent – but it is clear that Charles might be held personally liable for losses to the trust estate through James's action if Charles did not fulfil his duties in respect of agents, under ss 1, 21 and 22 of the Trustee Act 2000, or otherwise delegated a function which he should have exercised personally (see s 11 of the Trustee Act 2000). Similarly, there is no doubt that James would have been liable for breaching his contract of agency and probably also as constructive trustee for knowingly dealing inconsistently with trust property (*Karak Rubber v Burden* (1972)).

Despite the availability of these other remedies, it seems that the law of tracing will offer the most hopeful path for recovery of the trust's assets. For example, it is not absolutely certain that Charles's acts or omissions are sufficient to found personal liability for breach of trust and James has disappeared. So, it is only if the trustee, or the beneficiaries on the advice of the trustee, can trace their respective legal and equitable ownership of the trust property that there is hope of substantial redress. In this regard, it is worth noting that the £7,000 worth of shares purchased in X Co in the name of the trust are safe and that the furniture purchased by James, according to his instructions, is also part of the trust estate, even though it is worth very little.

If at all possible, Charles should be advised initially to seek to trace the missing trust funds at law. The advantages of this approach are, first, that there is no need to prove an initial fiduciary relationship (although this would not be a problem for the beneficiaries); secondly, that an action to recover the property can be made against any persons who has received it, regardless of their state of mind or whether any of them still retains it (*AGIP (Africa) Ltd v Jackson* (1992)); and thirdly, that the defences available to the recipient of the property are fairly limited in scope, even though a change of position defence to a claim at law may now be accepted as valid (*Lipkin Gorman*). If Charles can establish that he – as trustee – retained legal title to the £10,000 which was passed to James, and which James improperly invested in Y Co, he may be able to maintain a tracing action at law against these assets which now lie in the hands of James's daughter. In this connection, Charles will have to establish that he has a legal right of ownership which has survived the transfers to James and subsequently to his daughter. This would not appear to be a problem in this case, especially since James received the money as agent (see *Lipkin Gorman v Karpnale* (1991)). Thereafter, James could not transfer the shares beneficially to his daughter under the equitable maxim *nemo dat quod non habet*. In addition, there is no doubt that a claim to trace at law will survive changes in the nature of the property, providing that it is not mixed with any other property (*Taylor v Plummer* (1815)). Thus, Charles will be able to trace his legal title to the property through James to his daughter. Charles will be able to maintain an action against James's daughter personally for wrongful interference with goods and can expect damages to the value of the property she has received. This liability will persist even if she has disposed of the shares and may be defeated only if she can rely on the defence of 'change of position', recognised in *Lipkin Gorman v Karpnale* (1991) and applied in *Bank Tejaret v HKSB* (1995). This is unlikely in the circumstances as there is no evidence that James's daughter has in any way acted to her own detriment in innocent reliance on her receipt of the shares.

The next issue concerns the £5,000 which James places in his own bank account, where there is £4,000 of his own money. James has mixed the trust money with his own money before purchasing the shares and giving them to his son. This is fatal to a claim of tracing at law against James's son because, as far as the common law, is concerned, the mixing of property before it is passed to the recipient makes it unidentifiable (*AGIP (Africa) Ltd v Jackson* (1992)). Despite much criticism of this rule and possible contrary authority (*Banque Belge pour L'Etranger v Hambrouk* (1921)), it appears to have been confirmed by the House of Lords in *Lipkin Gorman*. It is possible that Charles might be able to rely on *Trustee of the property of FC Jones v Jones* (1996) to establish a right to the money for, in that case, the Court of Appeal held simply that the claimant could recover on the ground that the defendant never had any right to the money, so had to return it. However, the survival of this claim when mixing had occurred was not addressed in that case, so reliance on it in our case, where mixing has occurred, might be unsafe. For example, the claim to trace at law was rejected in *Box v Barclays* (1998) because the claimant had lost legal title on payment to a bank account. It is possible that Charles could argue that James became a constructive trustee for *him* on the basis that James must have known that he was behaving in breach of trust and so became a trustee on the basis of conscience, following *dicta* in *Westdeutsche Landesbank Girozentrale v Islington LBC* (1996)). This would trigger a claim in equity by Charles – the trustee and now beneficiary, cf *Twinsectra v Yardley*. However, perhaps the best advice is that if the trust fund is to have a good chance of recovering the £5,000, the beneficiaries must be persuaded to pursue a tracing claim in equity against the shares now in the possession of James's son. In fact, there is every chance that an equitable tracing claim would be successful, at least in so far as the trust fund monies remain identifiable. For example, there is an initial fiduciary relationship and the beneficiaries undoubtedly have an equitable proprietary interest (*Re Diplock* (1948)). Moreover, as noted above, so long as the beneficiaries' equitable proprietary interest is identifiable, it is irrelevant that the property is no longer in its original form or that it has been mixed with other property (*Re Hallett* (1880); *Re Oatway* (1903)). The beneficiaries may trace the trust fund money into James's bank account and, following the rule in *Re Oatway* (1903), James will be presumed to have spent £3,000 of the trust money on the shares in Z Co (not following *Re Hallett* (1880) because there are no monies left in the bank account which could satisfy the beneficiaries' claim). Given that James's son is not a *bona fide* purchaser for value, he cannot resist the tracing claim against the shares and no change of position defence is available to a claim in equity (*Foskett*). It should also be noted that the beneficiaries are entitled to the increase in the value of Z Co's shares because tracing in equity gives the claimants a proprietary right to property and any increase in its value (*Foskett*). Had the claim been pursued at law – using *Jones v Jones* – this might also have been possible. Finally, as noted above and as *Re Diplock* (1948) makes clear, equitable tracing is unavailable when the property ceases to be identifiable. The money spent by James on a family holiday is lost and, following the traditional approach, the beneficiaries will be forced to rely on personal remedies (if any) against the trustee in order to recover the outstanding £2,000. Again, however, if it is now true that tracing in equity is merely a means to an end (*Boscawen v Bajawa* (1995)), then the fact that some of this property is no longer identifiable may not defeat the claim. Assuming – and it is an assumption that many would challenge – that equitable tracing is merely a means of finding a defendant against whom a claim in restitution can be made, the liability of the recipient will not cease on dispersal of the property but he (James) will be held accountable for its value, save only that he might plead change of position.

For the sake of completeness, it should also be noted that both James's daughter and son may incur the additional liabilities of constructive trusteeship if they have knowingly received trust property in breach of trust and, furthermore, the bank which cashed Charles' cheque could, in theory, be liable for assisting Charles in a breach of trust, provided they were dishonest (*Royal Brunei Airlines v Tan* (1995)). Again, both are unlikely on the facts as given (see *Lipkin Gorman v Karpnale* (1991)).

Note

This is a fairly gentle problem on the law of legal and equitable tracing. In theory, because the question asks one to advise the trustee, it might be possible not to consider equitable tracing at all – because, on one view, the trustee has no equitable title to trace. However, this would not be good *practical* advice given that a partially effective remedy in equitable tracing is available to the beneficiaries.

Question 40

Zebedee is the trustee of a trust fund, holding a large amount of money on trust for Dougal and Florence. At the same branch of the bank at which the trust account is held, Zebedee has his own current account which stands in credit at £500. The following events occur:

(a) Zebedee pays £5,000 of the trust fund into his own account;

(b) he then draws out £500 which he invests in the Roundabout Property Co;

(c) he draws a further £3,000 from his account and gives it to his son, Brian, an antique dealer, who uses his skill to make a very successful purchase of a painting at auction;

(d) he draws out a further £1,000, £500 of which he spends on making improvements to his house and the other £500 he gives to his daughter, Ermentrude, so that she can pay off her debt to Loanshark Co;

(e) he pays £500 to the local hospital appeal, which has used the money to purchase some much needed equipment; and

(f) he pays £500 into the current account of the Springboard Trust, of which he is also a trustee and which is in credit at £400. He then buys shares in Magic Co for £700 and entertains his family to dinner with the remainder.

Zebedee has gone bankrupt and the shares in Roundabout Property Co have halved in value. The painting is worth £10,000 and the shares in Magic Co have trebled in value. Advise Dougal, Florence and the Springboard Trust as to their remedies, if any.

Answer plan

- Breach of trust action is the first resort;
- in the event of an unsatisfied claim, tracing may be available;
- loss of the remedy – change of position;
- mixed funds: two trusts;
- replacement of trust funds; and
- innocent volunteers.

Answer

Although it is not absolutely clear from the facts of the problem, it is highly likely that Zebedee, the trustee, has committed a series of breaches of trust when disposing of the trust fund monies in the way indicated. Certainly, his mixing of the trust monies with his own may well be a breach of trust and it is highly unlikely that the trust instrument authorises him to make gifts to his children or other causes. Consequently, the first remedy of all the beneficiaries (Dougal, Florence and those of the Springboard Trust) will be to sue Zebedee personally for damages for breach of trust. Unfortunately, as we are told, Zebedee is bankrupt, and any damages awarded as a result of this personal claim will have to be abated in Zebedee's bankruptcy along with the claims of other creditors. In such circumstances, the beneficiaries will wish to pursue such proprietary remedies as they might have, as this will give them a right to their property *per se* in priority to those who are 'merely' creditors. Tracing in equity may well prove to be the route to the most effective remedy.

Fortunately, there is no doubt that Dougal and Florence are entitled to pursue equitable tracing. They will be attempting to pursue their equitable proprietary interest as beneficiaries under a trust and they stand in a fiduciary relationship with Zebedee (*Re Diplock* (1948)). Moreover, as is well known, it is possible in equity to trace ownership into, through, and out of a mixed fund, so the fact that the trustee has mixed the £5,000 of trust money with that of his own will not defeat the tracing claim. Likewise, although some of the final recipients of the trust money may well be innocent (thereby excluding the possibility that they are constructive trustees), none of them are *bona fide* purchasers of the property and so they are not free automatically from equitable tracing, although their status as innocent recipients may have some effect of the precise scope of the remedies granted to Dougal and Florence.

When Zebedee transfers the trust money into his account, it is likely that he is committing a breach of trust and it is immaterial that there has been no loss to the trust estate at this stage. Indeed, as is clear, subsequent events do deprive the beneficiaries of their property and so they will wish to trace their assets into the hands of the persons now possessing them. First, there is the £500 withdrawn from the mixed account and used to purchase shares in Roundabout Company Limited. The change in nature of the beneficiaries' equitable interest – from money into shares – is not an obstacle to equitable tracing, provided that the shares can be said to have been purchased with the beneficiaries' money in the first place, bearing in mind that Zebedee has £500 of his own money in the mixed bank account. In this regard, *Re Hallett* (1880) decides that a trustee making purchases from a bank account in which funds are mixed must be presumed to have spent his own money first, as there is always a presumption against a breach of trust. Yet, in our case, this would mean that the shares in Roundabout belonged to

Zebedee, even though, after all the events have taken place, there is no money left in the account to return to the beneficiaries. In these circumstances, when, in effect, there is nothing in the bank account to trace to, *Re Oatway* (1903) makes it clear that the beneficiaries can turn to property purchased out of the mixed fund as being the embodiment of their equitable interest, even if, at the time it was purchased there was enough money to satisfy their claim. Consequently, the Roundabout shares will belong in equity to Dougal and Florence, although the fact that they are now worth only half their original value means that they will have to rely on their personal claim against Zebedee to recover the balance.

In principle, the same considerations apply to the £3,000 which Zebedee then withdraws and pays to his son; this is trust money and capable of being traced. Again, the fact that it was then used to purchase an antique painting will not destroy the tracing claim. Moreover, the added complication that the property (as money, and then a chattel) is in the hands of Brian, a third party, is no bar. Brian is not a *bona fide* purchaser for value, although there is no indication that he knew the money was transferred to him in breach of trust and is unlikely to be a constructive trustee (*Westdeutsche v Islington LBC* (1996)). *Re Diplock* (1948) makes it clear that equitable tracing is perfectly possible against an innocent volunteer where the property is identifiable and, in our case, there is no suggestion that Brian has mixed the trust money with his funds before the painting was purchased. Moreover, because tracing in equity is a proprietary remedy, the court will not merely order Brian to repay £3,000 or charge the painting to the value of £3,000. The court is most likely to order the return of the painting itself as this is where the beneficiaries' equitable interest is to be found, especially since the proprietary remedy carries with it any increase in the value of the property (*Re Tilley* (1967); *Foskett v McKeown* (2000)). Brian's only hope is that the court will regard 'his skill' in purchasing the painting as either a reason why full restitution of the painting would be 'inequitable' (*per Re Diplock* (1948)) or as a ground for making a financial allowance for his skill and judgment (*Boardman v Phipps* (1967)). Note, however, that, following *Foskett v McKeown*, it seems unlikely that a 'change of position' defence is available to Brian in respect of the equitable tracing claim.

The issue of the identifiable nature of the trust property is quite pertinent when considering the next £1,000 which Zebedee withdraws, half of which he gives to his daughter and half of which he spends on his own house. In *Re Diplock*, it was stated that, in some circumstances, the beneficiaries' property could be regarded as unidentifiable and untraceable, or that it may have been used in such a way as to make recovery of it inequitable. In particular, the House of Lords was of the view that it was impossible to trace money that had been used to pay off a debt, both because the creditor could be regarded as a purchaser for value and because the money effectively ceased to exist as independent property. Consequently, at first, unless Zebedee's daughter (or Loanshark Co) has taken the money with knowledge of the breach of trust, and is thereby a constructive trustee, there appears to be no route to a successful recovery of this £500. By way of contrast, however, the Court of Appeal, in *Boscawen v Bajawa* (1995), allowed the claimant a remedy against a defendant who had used monies traced to him to pay off a mortgage. The rationale was, simply, that equitable tracing merely identified a defendant, and that, when identified, the defendant could be subject to any appropriate remedy; in *Boscawen*, the claimant was subrogated to the creditor who had been paid off. So, in our case, if we follow *Boscawen*, and similar reasoning adopted by the House of Lords in *Banque Financière de la Cité v Parc (Battersea) Ltd* (1998), the claimants will be subrogated to Loanshark Co, and may be able to recover the money by enforcing the debt against Ermintrude as creditors.

Turning to the £500 spent by Zebedee on his house, this might be recovered. It is perfectly possible to levy a charge for a specific amount on property owned by another if this would enable the beneficiaries' interest to be protected. Indeed, although *Re Diplock* suggests that it could be inequitable to levy such a charge on the property of an innocent volunteer where the bulk of its purchase price or improvement costs have been provided by the volunteer, there is no such objection to levying a charge on the property of the trustee who has actually committed the breach of trust. The beneficiaries will be able to take a first charge over Zebedee's house to the value of £500 (or as a proportion of its value) and, being proprietary, this should take precedence over the claims of other creditors. Conversely, however, there are doubts whether the £500 paid to the local hospital can be recovered by the beneficiaries. There is no doubt that the property is traceable *per se*; the facts suggest that the money has been used to purchase identifiable equipment and there is no suggestion that the innocent volunteer (the hospital) had contributed any of its own money to these purchases. Thus, the matter is not entirely within the *Diplock* defences referred to above because the innocent volunteer has not mixed its property with that of the beneficiaries. Yet, it is clear that the court has a general discretion to deny tracing where it would be inequitable to permit it and this may prevent recovery from the hospital. If the court does deny tracing of this £500, it may well take the view that it was, in any event, the £500 of Zebedee's own money which he had in his account prior to the mixing of the trust funds (*Re Hallett* (1880)), as the court may have done with the untraceable £500 given to his daughter but, on these facts, not both. This would ensure, at least, that the final £500 remaining in the account could be regarded as belonging to Dougal and Florence prior to its mixing with the trust money of the Springboard Trust.

If one follows the logic taken above – that is, that one of the untraceable £500 amounts was Zebedee's own money – the mixing of the final £500 with the £400 of the Springboard Trust raises the question of the ability to trace to an asset (the shares in Magic Co) when all claimants to it (Dougal, Florence and the beneficiaries of Springboard Trust) are innocent. In principle, unless the rule in *Clayton's Case* (1816) applies, the two sets of claimants will be able to trace and claim the shares in Magic Co in proportion to their money in the mixed bank account before the purchase took place: that is, in the ratio 5:4 (£500:£400). As before, both parties will be able to retain any increase in the value of their portion of the shares (*Re Tilley* (1967); *Foskett v McKeown* (2000)). The balance in the account would be shared on a similar basis. If, on the other hand, *Clayton's Case* does apply, then the beneficiaries of the Springboard Trust will be able to claim that the first £400 worth of Magic Co shares belongs to them, on a 'first in, first out' basis. However, even if it is clear that Zebedee's account is an 'active' bank account within the *Clayton* rule, *Barlow Clowes International Ltd (In Liquidation) v Vaughan* (1992) establishes that *Clayton's* rule is one of convenience only and should not be applied either where the property of the respective claimants is identifiable or where it would achieve an inequitable result. A similar view was echoed in *Commerzbank Aktiengesellschaft v IMB Morgan* [2004] EWHC 2771. It is suggested, therefore, that the proportionate share rule (*pari passu*, 5:4) should prevail.

In conclusion, it can be seen that Dougal and Florence are able to trace a significant amount of their property through the mixed account into the hands of the (presumably) innocent third parties. That which they cannot claim, and where they still suffer a loss, can be recovered only in a personal action against Zebedee or against any of the third parties who may have had such an awareness of the material facts as to make them liable as constructive trustees.

Question 41

By his will, Terrence appointed Edward and Edwina as his executors and trustees and bequeathed £500,000 to Lucy and £300,000 for the charitable purposes of the War Veterans

Association. Edward and Edwina took all proper steps to prove the will and, after making all proper enquiries, paid over the monies to Lucy and the charity. However, Terrence had provided for David and Dee, as his residuary legatees, and they claimed successfully that the will should be set aside on the grounds of Lucy's undue influence over Terrence. Likewise, it appears that the War Veterans Association is not entitled to charitable status, being merely a non-charitable association. It also transpires that Rack, a creditor of Terrence who had been abroad at the time of his death, is owed a large sum of money, and he now claims £300,000.

Unfortunately, the strain of this was too much for both Edward and Edwina: they turned to gambling and both are now bankrupt. Lucy, however, has spent £100,000 on completely renovating her house, £150,000 on shares in the stockmarket and £50,000 on a year of high living. The War Veterans Association has spent all the money on providing pensions for disabled servicemen.

Answer plan

- Tracing in equity;
- loss of the remedy;
- innocent and culpable defendants;
- *Re Diplock in personam* remedy – strict liability; and
- change of position.

Answer

In the law of trusts, there are many remedies by which a disappointed or defrauded beneficiary may seek to reclaim specific property from third parties, or at least seek damages by way of compensation for the loss they have suffered. The action for damages for breach of trust, the imposition of a constructive trust, the law of equitable tracing and the specialised *Re Diplock in personam* action are perhaps the most widely used. They form the subject matter of this problem.

It is clear that even innocent and honest trustees may be liable in damages for breach of trust if they have failed to carry out the terms of the trust or fulfil their fiduciary duties (*Tito v Waddell (No 2)* (1977)). Unfortunately for Edward and Edwina, it seems that they may have committed breaches of trust in paying the trust money to Lucy and the War Veterans Association, even though this may have been due to an understandable mistake as to law or facts (see, for example, *Re Diplock* itself). It may well be that the two trustees could mount a successful defence to such an action – perhaps under s 61 of the Trustee Act 1925 on the grounds that they have behaved honestly and reasonably and ought fairly to be excused (*Williams v Byron* (1901)). In any event, we are told that they are now bankrupt and so are unlikely to be able to satisfy the large claims of David and Dee for their losses of £800,000, even assuming they had no defence to the action. This means that the two claimants must seek alternative remedies.

As a first choice, it may be that David and Dee will wish to establish that Lucy should be regarded as a constructive trustee of the £500,000 she has received. If this proves to be the case, Lucy will be personally liable for this entire amount, whether or not she retains any of it. Of course, such liability is not easily established, and David and Dee will have to assert that Lucy has knowingly received trust property in breach of trust within the principles discussed in *International Sales Ltd v Marcus* (1982); *AGIP (Africa) Ltd v Jackson* (1992);

BCCI v Akindele (2000). Undoubtedly, the transfer was in breach of trust – because of the finding of undue influence – and Lucy has received the property for her own benefit, as witnessed by her subsequent use of it. The crucial question then remains whether she has a sufficient degree of knowledge to fix her with liability. Fortunately, whatever doubts there are as to the required degree of knowledge for knowing receipt – intention/recklessness and/or negligence (*Baden Delvaux and Lecuit v Société Génerale pour Favouriser le Développement du Commerce et de l'Industrie en France SA* (1983) or (if different) 'unconscionability' – the finding that Lucy procured the will by her undue influence is enough to establish her knowledge of the relevant facts. She will be a constructive trustee of the money she has received. As noted above, this imposes on her a personal liability to repay the £500,000. Of course, it is quite likely that she will be unable to find this amount of money and we are told that she has spent at least £300,000 on specific projects. In such circumstances, while David and Dee may well be able to recover the unspent £200,000 and perhaps even some of the balance out of Lucy's other assets, the beneficiaries would be well advised to resort to the proprietary remedy of tracing.

There is no doubt that David and Dee would be able to satisfy the preconditions for tracing in equity identified in *Re Diplock* (1948): as residuary legatees they have an equitable proprietary interest and there is a clear fiduciary relationship between them and Edward and Edwina. Moreover, although *Re Diplock* does indicate that recovery of property through tracing in equity might be refused if the property has been so mixed with that of an innocent volunteer that a successful action would be inequitable, Lucy is not 'innocent' and, therefore, there is every chance that David and Dee would be granted a charge over Lucy's house, either to the value of the money spent on it (£100,000) or in the proportion that £100,000 represents of the house's value after improvement (*Re Tilley* (1967); *Foskett v McKeown* (2000)). To some extent, whether the court chooses the fixed charge (£100,000) or the proportionate charge may depend on the value of the house and whether the court feels that the two claimants should benefit from any windfall profit arising from an increase in the house's value. The same considerations apply, *mutatis mutandis*, to Lucy's investment in the stockmarket. Presumably, the shares she has purchased are registered in her name and the beneficiaries will be entitled to recover them under equitable tracing. Moreover, as there is no suggestion that any of their purchase price was provided from Lucy's own funds, David and Dee will own the shares *per se*, at their current value, although if the shares stand at a loss at the time of their claim, they will have the normal personal action to recover the balance. Finally, it is unfortunately quite likely that the £50,000 spent on 'high living' will be untraceable, having been dissipated on unidentifiable purchases. This amount will have to be the subject of the personal claim against Lucy and/or the trustees.

David and Dee may also be able to maintain a tracing claim against the assets spent by the War Veterans Association. As before, there is no doubt about the nature of David's and Dee's equitable interest or the existence of their proprietary rights. Moreover, it is inherent in a tracing claim that the funds sought to be recovered have been transferred to the recipient in breach of trust: otherwise there is no ground of recovery. In this case, it is clear that the property should never have been distributed to the Association, since it is not a charity. The trust was for a non-charitable purpose, and therefore void, with the money resulting to the residuary legatees under the beneficiary principle (*Re Endacott* (1960)). In fact, these are similar facts to *Re Diplock* itself. Unfortunately, however, like *Re Diplock*, this tracing claim may run into difficulties. As noted above, *Re Diplock* suggests that tracing will not be permitted where it would be inequitable to force the return of the property from an innocent volunteer. It is highly likely that the court would regard it as inequitable to force the disabled war veterans to repay the funds which they have been given as pensions. The court might take the view that David's and Dee's claim should fail because of the identity of the defendants and the manner in which the property came to them.

However, that is not the end of the matter. In *Re Diplock*, the House of Lords expressly accepted the existence of a limited *in personam* action, available against the recipients of property, at the suit of unpaid or underpaid creditors or next of kin arising out of a wrongly administered testamentary estate. In our case, given that the estate of Terrence has been wrongly administered, David and Dee and Rack (the creditor) will have a personal action against Lucy and against the officers of the War Veterans Association, all of whom have received funds from the executors and trustees. Importantly, it was made clear in *Re Diplock* that this remedy exists against completely innocent recipients and while this is irrelevant for Lucy, who has personal liability on other grounds, it means that the officers of the Association cannot plead their good faith as a defence. Likewise, because the action is personal (*in personam*), it is irrelevant that the recipients no longer have the property and they must satisfy the claims of the three claimants out of their own funds. As is clear, this is a powerful remedy and this is one reason why currently it exists only in the context of a wrongly administered testamentary estate (and possibly after a wrongful distribution of the assets of a defunct company – *Re Leslie Engineers Co Ltd* (1976)). It is also true that the claimants must exhaust their personal actions against the executors before they can proceed further, although that is not a problem in our case. Finally, however, while at one time it was thought that there was no defence to this *in personam* action – that is, that the innocent recipients had to repay the amount transferred if the preconditions for the remedy were established – it is likely, following *Lipkin Gorman v Karpnale* (1991), that the officers of the War Veterans Association might be able to plead 'change of position' to minimise or deny their liability. This defence does, however, lie in the discretion of the court, and it may well be that, in the light of the bankruptcy of the executors, the court will admit the claim of Rack (who has little chance of a tracing claim being a 'mere' contractual debtor: *Box v Barclays* (1998)), and perhaps David and Dee to the extent that they have not recovered the funds from other sources.

Note

These two problem questions show the diverse range of issues that can arise in the law of tracing. Note how useful *Re Diplock* can be: it is authority for nearly every aspect of tracing in equity. Consider also the powerful nature of the *Re Diplock in personam* remedy. This is an invention of equity, limited in nature, but potentially ruinous for the innocent recipients of wrongly distributed funds. It remains to be seen whether *Lipkin Gorman* is authority for the existence of a general, strict liability restitutionary remedy – subject, as always, to the change of position defence.

9 Breach of Trust

Introduction

It is perhaps surprising that the last of the beneficiary's remedies to be considered is the personal action for breach of trust. After all, the attempt to fix a stranger with a constructive trust (Chapter 7) and the remedy of tracing (Chapter 8) are triggered by an initial breach of trust by the trustee. Moreover, even in situations where these other remedies are available, if the trustee responsible for the breach is able to satisfy the claims of the beneficiaries in full, a personal action for damages for breach of trust will be the normal course of action and the court may insist that it is pursued before other avenues are followed. As we have seen, the constructive trust and remedy of tracing are used principally against third parties, being persons who have meddled with the trust or who have come into possession of the trust property subsequent to the trustee. In contrast, the action for breach of trust is personal to the trustee in two senses. First, only those trustees who are responsible for the breach of trust may be sued for damages, although the extent of the 'personal responsibility' of a trustee for breach of trust is quite wide. Secondly, the action for breach of trust itself is a personal action and the successful claimant (usually the beneficiary) will become a normal judgment creditor. Consequently, in the event of the trustee's bankruptcy or death, the beneficiary will have to take her chance along with all of the other creditors and claimants and may not receive all of the damages awarded in the breach of trust action. This is why the proprietary remedies discussed in the two previous chapters are so useful when specific trust property is still in existence.

It would be a mistake to believe that the action for breach of trust is not important. It is the first weapon of the wronged beneficiary and one whose net can be cast particularly widely. In general terms, there are four areas of concern to the student although, as ever, this is a somewhat arbitrary classification. First, questions arise as to what actually constitutes a breach of trust and who is responsible for it. This is tied to the standard of care required of trustees and the measure of compensation for a proven breach. Secondly, there is much case law concerning the circumstances in which a trustee may be liable for breach of trust even though the 'act in breach' was committed by another person, such as an agent or co-trustee. This can be easily confused or interwoven with issues in the first category. Thirdly, the relationship of trustees with each other consequent upon a breach of trust can seem confusing, and hence questions concerning the liability of trustees *inter se* and any remedies they may have against each other are often asked in examinations. Fourthly, and perhaps less difficult, the student must have an awareness of the trustee's possible defences to an action for breach of trust. Once again, in all of these issues, case law is important although various provisions of the Trustee Act 1925 and the Trustee Act 2000 are relevant and must be examined with some care.

——— Question 42 ———

'A trustee may be liable to pay compensation for his own breach of trust and in some cases for those committed by others.'

Analyse the concept of 'a breach of trust' and assess whether the above is an accurate statement of the law relating to liability for breach of trust.

—Answer plan

- Nature of liability for breach of trust;
- distinction between primary liability and vicarious liability: the Trustee Act 2000.

——— Answer ———

It is perhaps the most fundamental duty of a trustee that he should manage the trust in accordance with the terms of the trust. Any deviation from this paramount obligation, or from the obligations of trusteeship imposed by the general law, will constitute a breach of trust for which the trustee will be liable personally. Necessarily, this liability can arise in many different situations, but it may be triggered by either a positive act of commission on or a failure to act when action was required (an omission). Examples of the former include distribution of the trust property to the wrong people or at the wrong time, investment of trust funds contrary to a restriction in the trust instrument and, of course, the use of the trust property for personal gain. Examples of the latter include failure to distribute the trust property, failure to exercise a discretion, failure to have the trust funds transferred into the trustee's name and failure to review properly the actions of those persons employed to act on behalf of the trust (such as stockbrokers and solicitors). Any act or omission which violates the high standard of stewardship required of trustees (under either the common law or under the duty of care imported for certain powers by s 1 of the Trustee Act 2000) or which is in contravention of the terms of the trust, or which amounts to an inadequate performance of the powers and duties of a trustee, is a breach of trust.

This liability is generally strict in the sense that it is enough that the trustee has committed the act or omission which amounts to a breach of trust. It is irrelevant for liability whether the trustee knew he was committing a breach of trust and did so for his own benefit, was reckless as to the possibility of a breach occurring, was negligent of the same or was entirely innocent and honest. Thus, it remains a breach of trust for even if he believed he was acting in conformity with the terms of the trust (as in *Re Diplock* (1948)) and did so in the belief that his action was in the best interests of the beneficiaries (*Harrison v Randall* (1852)). Indeed, although the entirely innocent trustee can ask the court to relieve him from the full consequences of liability (s 61 of the Trustee Act 1925), it is clear that the obligations of trusteeship are far reaching and powerful and that even the most judicious and careful of trustees may not escape an action for breach of trust. The only possible exception to the strict nature of the liability for breach of trust is where the breach was entirely technical, was undertaken for the benefit of the beneficiaries and was such that the court would have authorised it had the trustee sought its permission in advance (*Lee v Brown* (1798)).

The very powerful nature of this liability is the main reason why professional trustees insist on the inclusion, in the trust instrument, of a clause excluding liability for certain types of breach of trust. As *Armitage v Nurse* (1997) illustrates, an exemption clause can be effective to exclude liability for negligence and 'equitable fraud' (that is, deliberate and honest breaches believed to be in the interests of beneficiaries), although it cannot exclude liability for dishonesty. Despite some fierce criticism of *Armitage v Nurse*, the Trustee Act 2000 leaves the existing law on exclusion clauses and touches and, further, permits the exclusion of the statutory duty of care imported by s 1 (see Sched 1 and s 7 of the Trustee Act 2000).

Once the liability of a trustee for breach of trust is established, the trustee is under an obligation to make good such loss as flows from the breach of trust, although the loss is not limited to that which is reasonably foreseeable (*Target Holdings Ltd v Redferns* (1996)). In this sense, the essential quality of the trustee's obligation is restitutionary and, not being limited by considerations of foreseeability and remoteness of damage (see, for example, *Re Dawson (Decd)* (1966)), can be more extensive than damages for breach of contract or those which lie in tort. Of course, that does not mean that the trustee is liable for all loss that flows directly or indirectly from his breach of trust, for there must still be a causal link between the breach of trust and the loss to the claimant (*Swindle v Harrison* (1997)). The essential question is, then, whether it could be shown that the loss would not have occurred but for the breach (*Target Holdings*) and no liability for the total loss will arise if the trustee can show that the loss, or part of it, would have occurred in any event – as where the beneficiaries lose money because of a fall in the value of property rather than because of the admitted misapplication of trust funds (*Target Holdings*) or where the claimant would have acted in the same way had the breach not occurred (*Swindle*). While this seems a sensible and obvious conclusion, it does mean that, in some circumstances, a trustee in breach may escape liability because of some fortuitous event that would have caused the loss anyway. Of more concern is whether Lord Browne-Wilkinson is correct to suggest in *Target Holdings* that the rules on causation and breach could be applied differently in 'commercial' and 'traditional' trust cases.

Finally in this survey of the nature of liability for breach of trust, two further supplementary rules can be noted. First, if there is no loss, or no provable loss (*Nestlé v National Westminster Bank* (1992)), the trustee's liability is limited to account for any profits he has received (*Vyse v Foster* (1874)). Secondly, in general, the losses occasioned by a breach of trust in one transaction cannot be set off against any profits made by them in another (*Dimes v Scott* (1828)), save in the exceptional case where the loss making transaction and the profit making transaction can be regarded as essential ingredients of the same activity (*Bartlett v Barclays Bank Trust Co (No 2)* (1980)).

It is also important to appreciate that it is inherent in the concept of breach of trust, as with other forms of liability, that only those trustees responsible in law for the breach will be liable to the beneficiaries. This is self-evident. However, because it is perfectly possible for a trustee to commit a breach of trust through omission as well as commission, the extent of a trustee's personal responsibility for breach is more extensive than might first be imagined. In simple terms, a trustee will be liable for a breach of trust in the following situations, even though some other person may have committed the acts or omissions that constitute the *actus reus* of the breach.

First, and most obviously, a trustee will be liable for a breach of trust where he has actually committed the acts in breach, as where a trustee pays money to the wrong persons (*Re Diplock*) or makes off with the trust fund. Secondly, a trustee may be liable for failing to perform a duty imposed on him by the trust instrument or general law, as where a trustee fails to safeguard the trust's assets. Thirdly, a trustee (A) may be liable for a breach of trust even if the act or omission in breach was committed by a co-trustee (B), but only if A can be said to have failed in his duty to supervise the trust's affairs, which failure facilitated the breach of trust by B: see, for example, *Bahin v Hughes* (1886). This is not liability for B's actions (it is not vicarious), but rather A's primary liability because of his failure to monitor the trust in accordance with his own duty. This duty may spring from the common law, or be an aspect of the statutory duty of care imposed on trustees in respect of their powers under the Trustee Act 2000 (s 1 and Sched 1). An example is where a co-trustee pays away money to the wrong beneficiaries and was allowed to do so by the inattention of his colleagues. Fourthly, a trustee may be liable even if the act or omission in breach of trust was committed by an agent employed to act on the trust's behalf, but only if it can be shown that the trustee failed in his duty in one of two ways: (a) by falling below the standard of care required by trustees in the appointment of agents, etc (for example, stockbrokers), s 1 and Pt IV of the Trustee Act 2000; or (b) by failing to review the exercise of the delegable functions of agents as required by s 22 of the Trustee Act 2000. Again, this liability is not vicarious (it is not for the agent's acts), but arises because the trustee has failed in his or her own duty of selection or supervision. Importantly, whatever may have been the position prior to the Trustee Act 2000 with respect to vicarious liability for the acts of agents (see the now defunct ss 23 and 30 of the Trustee Act 1925), s 23 of the Trustee Act 2000 makes it clear that a trustee is not liable for acts amounting to a breach committed by an agent *per se*: that is, liability is triggered only by the trustee's failure in appointment or supervision as indicated above and not because of the agents acts *per se*. This is a welcome and overdue reform and much simplifies this area of the law.

Finally, it should be noted that once the liability of particular trustees for a breach of trust has been established, that liability is, between them, joint and several. In other words, a beneficiary may sue any one of the trustees who has been held liable for the entire amount of the recoverable loss, irrespective of whether any action is taken against any of the others. As against the beneficiaries, those trustees in breach of trust are 'as one' and this is particularly important if some are missing or bankrupt. Of course, in practice, one liable trustee may be more culpable than another and, as a matter of principle, it is unfair that only one of the trustees should be made to bear the entire liability. Consequently, a contribution may be sought from other liable trustees under the Civil Liability (Contribution) Act 1978. Further, in limited circumstances, a liable trustee may be required to pay a complete indemnity to the trustee who has been required to make restitution to the beneficiaries under the principle of joint and several liability. This occurs where the indemnifying trustee was a solicitor on whose advice the other trustees relied (*Re Linsley* (1904)), where the trustee has committed fraud (*Re Smith* (1896)), where the trustee has received the trust property and made use of it for his personal benefit (*Bahin v Hughes* (1886)) and where the trustee is also a beneficiary (*Chillingworth v Chambers* (1896)).

The above principles illustrate the powerful nature of liability for breach of trust. However, although it may appear that a trustee is being held responsible for an act or omission in breach committed by another person – such as a co-trustee or agent – this is not the case. Although the rules are complicated, the new s 23 of the Trustee Act 2000 has ruled out this pure vicarious liability and has ensured that a trustee is liable only where the breach occurs because of a failure to perform some duty imposed on that particular trustee.

Note

Reference could also be made to the potential liability of a trustee who retires: first, for a breach of trust committed while he was a trustee; and secondly, for breach of trust committed by his successors, if the retirement was designed to facilitate such a breach (*Head v Could* (1898)). The Trustee Act 2000 has, at last, brought some clarity and certainty to this area of the law.

Question 43

In what circumstances may a trustee successfully plead a defence to an established breach of trust?

Answer plan

- Participation/consent to a breach of trust by the beneficiary;
- release/acquiescence by the beneficiary;
- s 61 of the Trustee Act 1925;
- s 62 of the Trustee Act 1925;
- statutory limitation and laches; and
- the joint and several liability of trustees: although a trustee may be liable, an indemnity may be obtained from co-trustees who are more culpable.

Answer

The personal liability of a trustee for breach of trust extends to all loss which can be causally linked to the breach (*Target Holdings v Redferns* (1995)) and it is generally no defence to the imposition of liability that the trustee was innocent, honest or was acting in the best interests of the trust. Furthermore, as we shall see, although the liable trustees may have rights of contribution against each other, the liability of the co-trustees in breach is joint and several such that a beneficiary may sue any one or all in order to recover the full amount of compensation (*Jackson v Dickinson* (1903)). Liability for breach of trust, extensive and in all material respects operates firmly in favour of the beneficiaries. This is as it should be for the trust obligation is an obligation of conscience that must be upheld. However, it is equally apparent that the powerful nature of liability for breach of trust can, in some circumstances, produce unfairness, especially if a trustee is morally innocent or if real culpability lies with a co-trustee. Consequently, in order to ensure that liability for breach of trust is not entirely overpowering, and to protect trustees from unscrupulous or culpable beneficiaries, there are a recognised number of defences to a claim of breach of trust. It should be noted, however, that these are 'defences' in a peculiar sense. They do not prevent the liability of the trustee from arising but may, if certain conditions are satisfied, relieve the trustee of the full consequences of that liability. In this way, the strict nature of breach of trust liability is preserved, but some protection is offered to trustees.

Before considering the defences proper, note should be made of two preliminary points. First, according to *Lee v Brown* (1798), a trustee who has innocently committed a technical breach of trust which has turned out to be for the benefit of the beneficiaries will not be held liable if the action was one which the court would have authorised if application for permission had been made in the normal way (and see, also, *Nestlé v National Westminster Bank* (1993)). However, this is of only limited comfort to an innocent trustee, as there is no clear definition of what amounts to a 'technical' breach. In any event, the court needs to be persuaded of the merits of the trustee's action before it will relieve him of liability. Secondly, it follows from this that a trustee contemplating a course of action which may or may not amount to a minor or technical breach of trust, but which he thinks would be for the advantage of the beneficiaries, should seek the authority of the court before proceeding. This may be granted for a variety of reasons, often under the court's inherent or statutory powers to vary the terms of the trust in favour of the beneficiaries (*Chapman v Chapman* (1954); Variation of Trusts Act 1958).

We must look now to the general issue of what defences are available to a trustee to relieve him from the consequences of liability for breach of trust. These can be found in both statute and common law. As indicated previously, they are designed to relieve the trustee from the full extent of his liability, but they do not go to establish that there has not been a breach of trust. It will also be apparent that certain defences are available only against certain claimant beneficiaries. Consequently, a trustee may be relieved from liability in an action for breach of trust brought by one beneficiary but may well have to make full restoration to other beneficiaries suing in respect of the same set of circumstances. Many of the defences to an action for breach of trust are relative, not absolute, as befits a relationship springing from the conscience of the parties.

First, a trustee may rely on the principle that a beneficiary who participates in, or consents to, a breach of trust by the trustee will thereafter be barred from bringing an action for breach of trust (*Life Association of Scotland v Siddal* (1861)). The essence of the matter is that that particular beneficiary has so involved himself with the breach that he should not thereafter be able to deny it and, consequently, it is irrelevant whether the beneficiary actually benefits from the breach or not (*Fletcher v Collis* (1905)). Whether the beneficiary has become so involved will be a question of fact, although it is clear that the beneficiary must be aware of all the relevant facts and understand fully the nature of the transaction which is proposed, although it is not necessary that he also understands that it does, in fact, amount to a breach of trust (*Re Pauling* (1964)). Similarly, the consent must be freely given and it has been said that a beneficiary who consents or participates without independent advice may not be so aware of what is proposed as to bar him from a later action for breach of trust (*Holder v Holder* (1966)). Again, the personal nature of this defence, operating as it does against particular beneficiaries, means that the trustee may still face claims arising from his activities from other beneficiaries not implicated in the breach.

In similar vein, a beneficiary's conduct after the breach may be such as to amount either to a release of the trustee or acquiescence in the breach sufficient to protect the trustee from later suit by that beneficiary (*Farrant v Blanchford* (1863); *Stafford v Stafford* (1857)). The essential point here is that the beneficiary's conduct after the breach has occurred may be such that it amounts to a personal bar against pursuing an action. As with cases of consent, whether there has been a release or acquiescence is a question of fact and, again, the state of knowledge of the beneficiary is decisive. For cases of release, the classic judgment in *Farrant v Blanchford* emphasises that a release is effective only if the beneficiary was of full age and capacity and had full knowledge of all the circumstances and of his claims against the beneficiary. This seems to suppose that, unlike cases of consent (and possibly *ex post facto* acquiescence), a release can be effective only if the beneficiary realised he was releasing a trustee from a breach of trust. At first, this seems quite logical yet, as discussed above, cases of prior consent require knowledge of the facts and circumstances, but not that they amount to a breach, and this is sometimes said to be the position with *ex post facto* acquiescence also (*Holder v Holder* (1966)). It would be unfortunate if there was a distinction between consent/acquiescence on the one hand and release on the other and so it is submitted that the general test put forward in *Re Pauling* should be adopted.

The matters just discussed give a trustee limited protection against an action by certain of the beneficiaries. They do not prevent liability to the other beneficiaries and, of course, where liability is not barred, the trustee is obliged to make restoration out of his own funds. However, there are circumstances when beneficiaries may be compelled to use their beneficial interests to indemnify the trustees for monies paid out in restoration of a breach of trust. Although the trustee is under a personal obligation to make restoration for loss flowing from the breach of trust, he may recover all or part of that sum from certain beneficiaries. This may be achieved in either of two ways. First, a court of equity has an inherent and discretionary jurisdiction to impound (that is, confiscate) a beneficiary's equitable interest in order to indemnify the trustee when the beneficiary has instigated or requested a trustee to commit a breach of trust (*Chillingworth v Chambers* (1896)) or when the beneficiary had consented to a breach of trust out of which he had received a personal benefit, such confiscation being limited to the benefit received (*Fletcher v Collis* (1905)). Secondly, this equitable jurisdiction has been extended by s 62 of the Trustee Act 1925 which gives the court a discretionary power to indemnify a trustee out of the beneficiary's interest if the breach of trust was committed 'at the instigation or request or with the consent in writing' of the beneficiary. Once again, the court will not exercise its statutory discretion unless the beneficiary knew and understood all the relevant facts which thereafter amounted to a breach of trust (*Re Somerset* (1894)), although it is only in respect of consent that the trustees' claim to indemnity under s 62 must be supported by writing.

In addition to these defences, all of which rely to one extent or another on the actions of other persons, a 'stand alone' defence is available irrespective of the actions of individual beneficiaries and which can afford a defence to an action by them all. According to s 61 of the Trustee Act 1925, the court has a discretionary power to relieve a trustee of liability for breach of trust, in whole or in part, if it appears that the trustee 'has acted honestly, reasonably, and ought fairly to be excused'. It is clear that, despite the general words of this section, this is not a statutory modification of the strict liability of trustees. The statute does not give the court a general power to exempt all honest trustees but is for those exceptional occasions when there is simply no justification in conscience for the imposition of liability despite the fact that a breach has occurred (*Williams v Byron* (1901)). Moreover, the section is to be read disjunctively so that a trustee must establish that he has acted honestly *and* reasonably *and* ought fairly to be excused (*Davis v Hutchings* (1907)). Consequently, there may be situations, such as the reduced or special circumstances of the beneficiaries, where an entirely honest trustee who has acted reasonably ought *not* to be fairly excused for his breach of trust. Other factors, such as whether the trustee has taken proper advice and whether the trustee had previously undertaken the disputed course of action without any legal difficulties, will be relevant (*Ward-Smith v Jebb* (1964)).

Finally, mention must be made of three further matters. First, the general principles of limitation of actions applies to the action for breach of trust in much the same way as to other personal actions. Thus, except in the case of fraud or where the trustee has possession of trust property or had possession of trust property and converted it to his own use (s 21(1)(a) and (b) of the Limitation Act 1980; and see *Armitage v Nurse* (1997)), no action for breach of trust can be brought after six years have expired from the date the action accrued. There is no period of limitation for cases within s 21(1)(a) and (b), and liability for dishonesty endures without limitation of time (*Armitage*). Secondly, the liability of trustees *inter se* may be adjusted by a claim for a contribution by those trustees who have been required to make entire restoration against those who have not paid or who are more culpable. This jurisdiction now resides primarily in the Civil Liability (Contribution) Act 1978 (see, for example, *Dubai Aluminium Co v Salaam* (2000)), although there are three situations outside of the Act where one trustee may be made to indemnify completely any others who have actually made restoration to the beneficiaries: where a trustee has received trust money and made use of it (*Bahin v Hughes* (1886)); where the trustee at fault was a solicitor trustee on whose advice the other trustees relied

(*Re Linsley* (1904)); and where a trustee is also a beneficiary of the trust (*Chillingworth v Chambers* (1896)). Thirdly, a trustee in breach may escape liability by relying on an exemption clause. These are popular with professional trustees as they mitigate the strict liability of trusteeship. Further, as *Armitage v Nurse* (1997) illustrates, an exemption clause can be effective to exclude liability for negligence and 'equitable fraud' (that is, deliberate but honest breaches believed to be in the interests of beneficiaries), although it cannot exclude liability for dishonesty. Such is the effect of these clauses in relieving liability for a proven breach that the Court of Appeal in *Armitage* made a point of encouraging Parliament to intervene to limit their effect. As yet, this has not been done (there is no restriction on such clauses in the Trustee Act 2000), but it is possible that the matter will be referred anew to the Law Commission.

Note

This is a general question that should be answered with full reference to case law. The distinction between defences available against particular beneficiaries, those available against all beneficiaries and those 'quasi-defences' available to one trustee against another is of considerable importance.

Question 44

Sam and Samantha are trustees of a trust established by George in 2003, under which they are directed to hold the trust property on trust for Zeus for life, thereafter for his children, Hermes and Hector absolutely. The trust property comprises some UK government stock, some shares in Goldco plc and a freehold property. An investment clause authorises the trustees to invest only in UK government securities and public companies quoted on the London stock exchange. The following events occur:

(a) In 2004, with the oral consent of Zeus, the trustees sold the shares in Goldco plc to themselves for their market value (£50,000) and re-invested the capital in Bloomsbury Limited, a speculative property development company;

(b) in 2005, the freehold property was sold to Bloomsbury Limited and the money used to purchase shares in Silverco plc; and

(c) at the instigation of Hermes and Hector, Sam and Samantha sold the government stock on the open market and invested money in an overseas stock market.

The shares in Silverco have lost half of their value and the overseas stock market has crashed to an all time low. The shares in Goldco have doubled in value and Bloomsbury Limited has gone into liquidation. Advise the beneficiaries of the extent to which they may be able to recover the value of the trust fund through an action for breach of trust.

The trust instrument contains no clause excluding the liability of trustees for innocent or negligent breach of trust and states that:

> The general power of investment contained in s 3 of the Trustee Act 2000 is hereby excluded under s 6(1)(b) of the Trustee Act 2000.

Answer plan

• Personal liability for breach of trust: standard of care (Trustee Act 2000), breach of terms of trust and wrongful investments (Trustee Act 2000);

- trustees' duty not to profit from the trust;
- joint and several liability; and
- defences and measure of damages.

— Answer —

For generations, courts of equity have acted swiftly and powerfully to ensure that persons accepting the office of trustee carry out their duties to the fullest degree. The beneficiaries of a trust have many remedies at their disposal to trigger the court's intervention although, most often, it is the personal action for breach of trust that is the remedy of first resort. In the problem under consideration, the beneficiaries seek advice specifically on whether an action for breach of trust against Sam and Samantha will succeed and this, in turn, necessarily depends on the scope of the trustees' duties and whether the facts disclose any breach of those duties.

By way of introduction, it should be noted that it is generally enough if the trustees have breached their duties *per se* and it is immaterial for the purpose of establishing liability whether they acted recklessly or negligently, innocently and honestly or fraudulently and dishonestly. Liability is strict (*Harrison v Randall* (1852)) and may be established either by a positive act or failure to act where action was required (*Grayburn v Clarkson* (1868)). Similarly, once liability is established, the trustees must account by way of restitution for all loss causally linked to the breach (and/or for any profits thereby made) and the court is not limited in this regard by considerations of remoteness of damage or causation found in the law of contract and tort (*Target Holdings v Redferns* (1996)).

In order to assess accurately the liability of our trustees in a breach of trust action, it is necessary to consider each of the events in turn and whether the trustees' actions violate their duties under the trust instrument, exceed their powers or contravene a general rule of equity governing the conduct of trustees.

(a) The sale of shares - Goldco plc and investment in Bloomsbury Limited

There is every reason to believe that the trustees may have exposed themselves to liability for breach of trust and to an obligation to make restitution when considering their dealings with the shares in Goldco. First, the trustees appear to have placed themselves in a position where their duty and self-interest conflict, contrary to the principle of *Bray v Ford* (1896). In particular, the trustees have contravened the 'self-dealing' rule which, as explained in *Tito v Waddell (No 2)* (1977), establishes that a trustee cannot be both vendor and purchaser of property which they are holding for the benefit of another (*Ex p Lacey* (1802)). So, trustees may not purchase the trust property, no matter how fair the transaction may have been and regardless of whether this was done in all innocence. Such a breach of the duties of a trustee enables the beneficiaries to have the transaction set aside, irrespective of the fact that the market price was paid for the shares (*Campbell v Walker* (1800)). In principle, the beneficiaries acting together may require the re-conveyance of the shares in Goldco, and necessarily this would enable them to enjoy the increase in value that Goldco shares attain subsequently. However, as one of the beneficiaries (Zeus) has consented to this sale, there is some doubt whether the transaction can be set aside, even though Hermes and Hector may have so wished. Consequently, Hermes and Hector may find that their remedy is limited to a resale by the trustees of the shares (*Holder v Holder* (1966)). This means that the non-consenting beneficiaries would be deprived automatically of the later increase in the value of the shares in Goldco and, as such, they may well be advised to pursue the trustees for breach of trust on the ground that an authorised investment was sold (Goldco shares) and was replaced by an unauthorised investment (the shares in the private company, Bloomsbury Limited, the general power of investment under the Trustee Act 2000 having been excluded). There is little doubt that this is a breach of trust and the measure of damages is either an account of the proceeds of sale (which would encompass the now worthless Bloomsbury shares) or the cost of replacing the investment at its current value, whichever is the greater (*Phillipson v Catty* (1850)).

Obviously, Hermes and Hector will choose to sue for breach of trust and will adopt the second measure of compensation, for this more truly represents their loss caused by the breach. For Zeus, the matter may be different because of the fact that he had consented to the breach disqualifies him from pursuing the remedy and he will not be entitled to share in the restitution that the trustees must provide (*Fletcher v Collis* (1905)). In this connection, it is not relevant that Zeus may have been unaware that what he had consented to was actually a breach of trust, so long as he was aware of the nature of the transaction and its general legal effect (*Re Pauling* (1964)). So, Zeus may come under a personal bar, preventing him from bringing an action, although the fact that his consent is not in writing means that s 62 of the Trustee Act 1925 (whereby a beneficiary's interest may be confiscated in order to satisfy the claims of other beneficiaries) is not applicable. Nevertheless, Zeus may still find his interest impounded under the common law if he has received personal benefit from the breach (*Fletcher v Collis* (1905)). As such, Hermes and Hector's rights are not affected, save that their measure of damages may be adjusted to reflect the fact that they are entitled in remainder.

(b) The sale of freehold property and subsequent investment in Silverco plc

The facts indicate that the trustees had no power or duty to invest in freehold property (Trustee Act 2000 excluded) and, in consequence, there is no breach of trust when the freehold property is sold. In fact, this sale is in fulfilment of their duties as trustees for they are not permitted to retain unauthorised investments. Likewise, the purchase of shares in Silverco plc is a permitted investment within the express investment clause, since that company appears to be a public company quoted on the London Stock Exchange. It is now the case that the shares in Silverco have lost half their value and the beneficiaries may feel that this investment was such an unwise choice that it amounted to a breach of trust. It is true that just because an investment is permitted does not mean that every actual investment is proper and in conformity with the duty of care owed by the trustees under s 1 of the Trustee Act 2000 in respect of their investment powers. For example, they must exercise reasonable care and must apply the standard investment criteria laid down in s 4 of the Act and may well have to seek advice under s 5 of the Act. (These obligations apply to any investment power, not merely the general power specified in the act itself.)

Unfortunately, however, aside from whether the trustees have sought advice when required to do so, it is notoriously difficult to prove a breach of trust from an investment in a permitted investment which subsequently turns out to be loss making or which performs unsatisfactorily (see *Nestlé v National Westminster Bank* (1992)). The duty of care laid down in s 1 of the Trustee Act 2000 applies and probably equates to the old common law test in *Learoyd v Whitely* (1887), that the trustee must take such care as that exercised by an ordinary prudent man of business who is considering making an investment for the benefit of others. The statutory standard of care requires the trustees to take such care as is reasonable in the circumstances, having regard to any special knowledge and experience of the trustees. There is insufficient evidence in this case to determine whether

Sam and Samantha have fallen below this standard of care. Likewise, we do not know whether Sam and Samantha sought advice and, although they could be obliged to do so by s 5 of the Trustee Act 2000, this may well be a case under s 5(3) where the obtaining of advice can be dispensed with because the trustees reasonably believed that such advice was not necessary. All in all, subject only to the uncertainty over the need to obtain advice, this may well be a case like *Nestlé v National Westminster Bank* (1992), where the fact that an investment has not performed as the beneficiaries had hoped is not itself a breach of trust.

(c) At the instigation of Hermes and Hector, Sam and Samantha sold the government stock on the open market and invested the proceeds in an overseas stock market

The sale of the government stock and purchase of other assets is, like the sale of shares in Goldco, a breach of trust. It amounts to a sale of a permitted investment and its replacement by an investment outside the terms of the express investment clause (the Trustee Act 2000 not applying, compare *Phillipson v Catty* (1850)). Again, the measure of damages for this breach of trust is an account of the proceeds of sale or the value of restoring the original investment, whichever is the greater, subject to credit being given for any gains by the beneficiaries, such as from a subsequent sale of the shares in the overseas stock market. Therefore, the trustees are *prima facie* liable to make restitution.

Yet, as the facts of the problem make clear, while Zeus has remained ignorant of these activities and is able to pursue his action for breach of trust, Hector and Hermes have 'instigated' the sale and purchase. Apart from statute, this instigation could well mean that Hector's and Hermes's own equitable interests could be impounded (confiscated) to satisfy the claims of the other beneficiary (*Sawyer v Sawyer* (1885)). Although the trustees *prima facie* will be responsible for making restitution to Zeus, according to the measure of damages noted above, Hector and Hermes may be required to meet these costs out of, and to the extent of, their equitable interests (*Chillingworth v Chambers* (1896)). Such a possibility now also exists under s 62 of the Trustee Act 1925 although, as under the general equitable jurisdiction, the impounding of Hector and Hermes's interest is at the discretion of the court (*Re Pauling* (1961)). It is also imperative, if the trustees are to succeed in their attempt to plead this limited defence, that Hermes and Hector can be said to have acted in full knowledge of what they were instigating. They must have appreciated the significance of their actions and, according to one view, must have been aware that the proposed action would amount to a breach of trust (*Re Somerset* (1894)), although other cases suggest that this extended degree of knowledge is not required (*Re Pauling* (1964)). It is not clear from the available facts whether Hector and Hermes had the relevant degree of knowledge and much will depend on their awareness of Sam and Samantha's powers of investment and the nature the companies they have promoted. Should it not be possible to impound the beneficiaries' interests under the equitable or statutory jurisdiction (for example, because their level of understanding was not sufficient), it is reasonably clear that neither Hector nor Hermes will be able to sue for breach of trust, having at least acquiesced in and, in all probability, consented to, the breach of trust (*Brice v Stokes* (1805)). It is true that 'knowledge' on the part of the beneficiaries is also required in order that the trustees may make out this defence, but it is clear that an appreciation of the nature and consequences of their action will suffice, and not the higher standard of realising that a breach of trust contemplated (*Re Pauling* (1961)). This lower standard is entirely appropriate given that under the 'consent/ acquiescence' defence, the beneficiaries lose their right to sue but do not lose their equitable interests.

Finally, we should note that it is unlikely, in relation to any of these events, that the trustees will be able to rely on the court's statutory discretionary power to relieve them of liability on the ground that they have acted 'honestly, reasonably and ought fairly to be excused' (s 61 of the Trustee Act 1925). Both Sam and Samantha should have been aware of the extent of their powers of investment and their duty to place the interests of the trust above their own. These breaches were not trivial or obscure, and although ignorance of the law is not of itself a reason to refuse relief, there is little here that would justify the court in exercising its discretion in their favour (*Chapman v Browne* (1902)).

Note

The question is designed to test general principles concerning breach of trust and trustee defences. Consequently, the trustees' powers of investment are artificially limited (that is, the trust instrument excludes the Trustee Act 2000 investment powers) in order to make the breaches more obvious. In reality, it is unlikely that the Trustee Act 2000 powers would be excluded. Also, if this trust was professionally drafted, there may well be a clause excluding liability of the trustees for negligence or honest error: see *Armitage v Nurse* (1997).

Question 45

Alex and Bernard are trustees under the will of Klondyke, who died in 2002. Under the terms of the trust, the trustees are to hold various items of furniture, some family heirlooms and cash in Klondyke's deposit account on trust for Perky for life, thence absolutely for such of his children then living. In 2003, Alex approached James, a stockbroker, to seek his advice on the investment of the money, and although James was only recently authorised by the Stock Exchange, he confidently recommended several investments. Alex paid over half the trust monies to James in order to carry out the recommended investment policy after telling Bernard that this was 'purely a matter of form'. James invested the money as agreed but, due to his inexperience of high tech stocks, all the investments made a substantial loss. In response to James' further requests, Alex paid over the rest of the monies, this time failing to consult Bernard. Due to good fortune, the second batch of investments on old fashioned 'blue-chips' made a substantial profit and the eventual sum repaid to the trust was far in excess of the original sums invested. Meanwhile, Perky has persuaded both trustees to sell the furniture and family heirlooms and to purchase a sports car for him with the proceeds of the former and to donate the rest to charity.

In 2004, Perky dies and his two living children become aware of how the trust has been administered. Have they any cause for complaint and, if so, what are their remedies?

Answer plan

- Breach of trust: on whom does the liability fall;
- standard of care, delegation, and liability for acts of a co-trustee: Trustee Act 2000;
- defences;
- tracing remedies; and
- *Re Diplock* remedies.

On the face of it, one might think that Perky's children had little to complain about. As the problem makes clear, the sum held by the trust at Perky's death was 'far in excess' of the original sums and the investment policy seems to have been successful. However, the essential nature of liability for breach of trust is that it is restitutionary: it should restore to the trust fund all the loss causally linked to any breach of trust and it matters not that certain activities of the trustees have brought considerable gains to the trust (*Dimes v Scott* (1828); *Bartlett v Barclays Bank Trust Co (No 2)* (1980)). Likewise, where investment powers are in question, the possibility of a breach is measured against the duty of care laid down in s 1 of the Trustee Act 2000 viz, that a trustee 'must exercise such care and skill as is reasonable in the circumstances', having regard to any special knowledge or experience that the trustee has, or holds himself out as having, and with regard to any special knowledge and skill acquired by the trustee acting in the course of business. As under the law before the Act, it is likely that fulfilment of the trustee's duty in regard to investments is not to be measured in terms of absolute results, be they gains or losses (see, also, *Nestlé v National Westminster Bank* (1992)), but in terms of the care exercised on reaching the gain or loss. Seen in this light, this problem raises a number of issues concerning the trustees' potential liability for breach of trust. In particular, it is necessary to determine, first, whether there have been any breaches of trust which have caused loss to the trust fund; secondly, who has caused these breaches and who is responsible in law for them; thirdly, whether the trustees may raise any defences in an action by the beneficiaries; and, fourthly, whether there are any other remedies the beneficiaries might pursue if the action for breach of trust proves insufficient to meet their claims.

The first matter to examine is whether Alex or Bernard, or both, can be said to have committed a breach of trust when the initial investments recommended and effected by James result in a substantial loss. There is no breach of trust simply because investments make a loss or only a little profit. That risk is in the nature of investment (*Nestlé v National Westminster Bank* (1992)). However, there are a number of reasons why Alex and Bernard might be liable. It will be remembered that Alex is the 'active' trustee in this matter and it is he who initiates these events. So, focusing on his position, it is clear that when exercising investment powers, he must meet the duty of care specified in s 1 of the Trustee Act 2000. This is to take reasonable care in all the circumstances (taking account of any particular skills he has or professes). The exact scope of this duty remains to be elucidated by the courts, but because Alex is not, and does not purport to be, an investment professional (who, after the Act may owe higher duties), his duty may well equate to the old common law standard of having to take such care as an ordinary prudent man of business would exercise when considering making an investment for the benefit of others (*Learoyd v Whitely* (1887)).

Moreover, in exercising this power, it is perfectly in order for Alex to employ an agent (s 11 of the Trustee Act 2000), provided that, because this is an asset management function (that is, investment), such delegation is either in writing or evidenced in writing (s 15 of the Trustee Act 2000).

Applying this law to our case, it appears that Alex is in breach of trust because even if he believed that James was a suitable person to act in this capacity (that is, assuming that Alex has discharged his duty of care with respect to the appointment: query James' inexperience), the appointment is not in writing or evidenced in writing. In consequence, all loss caused by the breach can be recovered from Alex and possibly from Bernard (see below) (*Target Holdings Ltd v Redferns* (1996); *Swindle v Harrison* (1997)). Note, however, that Alex (and possibly Bernard) is liable because of his failure to properly appoint. He is not liable because James has made a poor choice of investment because, even if such a poor choice amounted to a breach of trust, s 23 of the Trustee Act 2000 makes it clear that a trustee is only liable for the acts of agents (such as James) if the appointment was effective (as in our case) or if the trustee failed in his duty to review the actions of the agent (of which in our case there is no evidence).

Assuming then that Alex has committed a breach of trust, what is the position of Bernard? Clearly, Bernard is not vicariously liable for Alex's actions (see s 23 of the Trustee Act 2000), but it may well be that Bernard has failed in his own duties to supervise the trust properly by failing to question Alex about his proposed dealings (*Styles v Guy* (1849)). A so called 'passive' trustee cannot escape liability for breach of trust if that passivity itself amounts to a neglect of duty breaching the duty of care of the Trustee Act 2000. This could be the case in respect of the first amount of money paid to James and, if so, Alex and Bernard are jointly and severally liable to the beneficiaries. It seems unlikely that Bernard can be held responsible for the second payment of money to James unless he was so inattentive of the trust's affairs so as to fail in his duty. There is no evidence to support this and consequently Bernard should be able to claim a contribution from Alex under the Civil Liability (Contribution) Act 1978.

This brings us to the measure of loss. As is made clear, the second transaction actually makes a profit for the trust and, without doubt, this profit must be held for the beneficiaries, whether deriving from a breach of trust or not (*Vyse v Foster* (1874)). The real issue is whether the trustees will be able to set off the gains made by the second transaction against the losses made in the first (*Dimes v Scott* (1828)). The general principle from *Dimes* is that this is not permitted unless the 'two' transactions are so interdependent that one follows inextricably from the other (*Bartlett v Barclays Bank Trust Co (No 2)* (1980)). That limited exception is unlikely to apply here, leaving Alex (and possibly Bernard) liable to compensate for the loss caused to the beneficiaries by the breach in respect of the first investment (there being no loss with respect to the breach over the second set of investments).

It is also clear that a breach of trust is committed when Perky persuades the trustees to sell the furniture and heirlooms and to use the money for his personal benefit and for donations to charity. Such instigation of a breach of trust by the beneficiary will not only prevent Perky claiming against the trustees for any loss arising out of these breaches (*Life Association of Scotland v Siddal* (1861)), it may also result in his interest being confiscated to indemnify the trustees in so far as they are required to make restitution to the trust estate (*Chillingworth v Chambers* (1896) and s 62 of the Trustee Act 1925). In this connection, it is quite possible (even likely) that Perky is aware that his request amounts to a breach of trust (so satisfying *Re Somerset* (1894)) and his chances of avoiding the impounding of his interest are slim. However, any loss not covered from the use of Perky's interest will have to be met by the two trustees and it is unlikely in the circumstances of this case that they will have a defence under s 61 of the Trustee Act.

Finally, if the personal actions against the trustees fail to recover the full loss to the trust estate, there is the possibility that the beneficiaries could trace the funds from the sale of the furniture to Perky's sports car (Perky not being a *bona fide* purchaser for value) and possibly also trace the heirlooms to the person now possessing them. Note, however, this may well prove impossible if the current possessor is a purchaser in good faith (*Re Diplock* (1948)).

Questions involving the liability of co-trustees and the liability of trustees for acts of agents can be complicated. It is always important to identify the primary liability of trustees for wrongful appointments and failure to review an agent's activities. The Trustee Act 2000 has brought much needed simplicity to this area, replacing the complicated ss 23 and 30 of the Trustee Act 1925. The defences to an action for breach of trust are easier to grasp. Not surprisingly, whether a liable trustee has a defence is controlled by the facts of each case.

10 The Office of Trustee and its Powers and Duties

Introduction

This chapter represents something of a 'sweeping up' of several issues that have not been dealt with so far. Necessarily, in the subjects considered in previous chapters, much has been said about the responsibilities of trustees, their duties towards the beneficiaries and the powers they enjoy in respect of the trust property. Many of these responsibilities are of a general nature – such as the duty to respect the terms of the trust and the power to choose beneficiaries under a discretionary trust – and they should not be forgotten in any general discussion of the nature of trusteeship and the extent of the trustee's powers and duties. In particular, in Chapter 6, we examined the trustee's duty not to make a profit from the trust and this forms an integral part of any discussion of trustee's duties. Thus, it must not be thought that the specific matters considered in this chapter are the only attributes of trusteeship nor, indeed, should it be assumed that there is any essential thread that ties together the matters dealt with below in a way that excludes consideration of other issues.

The questions considered in this chapter cover several areas: first, the trustee's duty not to delegate any of his essential responsibilities under the trust; secondly, the appointment and removal of trustees; thirdly, the trustee's power of maintenance and advancement; fourthly, the trustee's power of investment; and fifthly, the variation of trusts, being the extent to which the duty to carry out the terms of the trust as originally conceived can be altered by application to the court.

The duty not to delegate is another example of the powerful nature of the trust obligation. It is for the trustee to discharge his specific duties and to exercise any discretionary powers. Any unauthorised delegation of these responsibilities is itself a breach of trust. Indeed, even if a trustee legitimately delegates some administrative function connected with the trust (such as the purchase of shares), that trustee still may be liable for breach of trust even though the act which gives rise to the breach was committed by the person to whom the task was entrusted. Secondly, although the appointment and removal of trustees may seem a technical matter, it is of considerable practical importance. Trustees die, retire, or simply desire to have nothing more to do with the trust and it is imperative that the good administration of the trust fund does not suffer because of a lack of new or suitably qualified trustees. The relevant principles are to be found primarily in statute, albeit supplemented by case law. Thirdly, the power of maintenance and advancement refers to an attribute enjoyed by trustees of certain kinds of trust. In outline, such powers allow the trustee either to use the income from trust property for the benefit of an infant beneficiary before the infant is actually entitled to it (power of maintenance) or to pay a proportion of the trust's capital sum to a potential beneficiary before he or she becomes absolutely entitled to it (power of advancement). These powers may be either expressly included in the trust instrument or implied under ss 31 and 32 of the Trustee Act 1925. Fourthly, the investment of trust property is one of the most important of the trustees' responsibilities, for it ensures that the trust fund generates the maximum benefit for all the beneficiaries. Consequently, it is vital that the trustees invest the capital monies lawfully, securely and competently, bearing in mind the need to provide a good income for those immediately entitled and to preserve the capital value of the fund for those entitled in remainder. Most professionally drafted trusts include express powers of investment but a trustee may also take advantage of the provisions of the Trustee Act 2000. Finally, the court's power to sanction a change in the nature or extent of the powers and duties of a trustee (and, indeed, other aspects of the trust) falls within the general law on variation of trusts. As we shall see, this jurisdiction is both inherent and statutory although, because it often involves amending the settlor's or testator's original intentions, the court exercises its power with considerable care and in limited circumstances only. This is particularly so where it is not only the trustees' powers and duties that may be varied but also the nature and extent of the beneficiaries' equitable interests.

 ——————— **Question 46** ———————

The Trustee Act 2000 has clarified the circumstances in which a trustee may delegate his responsibilities under the trust. The Act is a vast improvement on the complexities of the law which it replaced where reform was long overdue.

Discuss.

—Answer plan

- The trust obligation is vested in the trustees, along with the responsibility to exercise the powers and fulfil the duties of the trust;
- moral or legal necessity or business usage;
- the old law: ss 23 and 30 of the Trustee Act 1925;
- s 9 of the Trusts of Land and Appointment of Trustees Act 1996;
- ss 11–16 of the Trustee Act 2000.

 ——————— **Answer** ———————

It is inherent in the very nature of a trust that the settlor or testator has 'trusted' certain chosen individuals to carry out his wishes in relation to the trust proper in so far as this may be lawful. Had the settlor or testator wished the powers and duties of the trustee to be exercised by another, he would have chosen a different person. Consequently, it is upon the trustee, however appointed, that the burden of carrying out the trust falls (*Turner v Corney* (1841)). In simple terms, a trustee may not delegate his responsibilities to another unless authorised to do so by either the trust instrument itself, some equitable rule or by statute. Any unauthorised delegation will be a breach of trust and the trustee will be responsible for any loss to the trust estate caused by the unlawful delegation (*Fry v Taps* (1884); *Target Holdings v Redferns* (1996)).

Necessarily, however, it is also recognised that such an absolutist approach to the exercise of the trustee's powers and duties might actually cause more harm to the trust fund than the mischief which the non-delegation rule is designed to prevent.

For example, an ordinary trustee might do irrevocable harm to the trust's investments by acting personally in the stockmarket and it would be positively foolish for a trustee with no previous experience to attempt to negotiate leases or the purchase of freeholds on behalf of the trust. Consequently, as was recognised in *Speight v Gaunt* (1883), a trustee might delegate certain functions to agents if this was within 'moral' or 'legal necessity' or ordinary business usage. This rather elastic exception to the non-delegation rule effectively meant that a trustee might delegate such functions to an agent as would be so delegated by an ordinarily prudent man of business acting on his own behalf (*Fry v Tapson* (1884)). So, a trustee could employ a stockbroker to advise on and execute the purchase of investments and a solicitor to carry out legal transactions on behalf of the trust. Moreover, if the agent was properly employed, the trustee was not to be held liable for any loss to the trust estate arising from the agent's actions (*Tapson*). Not surprisingly, there were limitations to this limited power of delegation, the violation of which resulted in the trustees themselves being in breach of trust. So, a trustee could delegate a function to an agent only if that function was within the agent's normal course of business, and the choice of specific agents had to be made according to the standard of care discussed in *Speight v Gaunt* (1883). Likewise, a trustee had to supervise an agent when undertaking acts in connection with the administration of the trust, and the trustee would be liable to the beneficiaries if the agent caused a loss to the trust through inattention by the trustee (*Speight*). Most importantly, this common law power of delegation authorised only the delegation of managerial and administrative functions to agents, such as buying shares and acting in legal affairs. So, where the trust instrument or statute gave the trustees a power or discretion, it was for the trustees to exercise that power or discretion, albeit after considering the advice offered by their lawfully appointed agents. For example, the trustee had to exercise the power of choice inherent in a discretionary trust and it was for the trustees to decide upon an investment policy after considering all relevant advice. As will be apparent from this brief analysis, the common law power of delegation was for legal or moral necessity or business usage, and it did not permit the trustees to transfer any of their primary responsibilities under the trust: it merely facilitated the fulfilment of those responsibilities.

This common law position was altered significantly by the enactment of the Trustee Act 1925, but even these provisions proved to be inadequate as well as largely incomprehensible. According to the now defunct s 23(1) of the 1925 Act, a trustee could have employed and paid an agent 'to transact any business or any act required to be transacted or done in the execution of the trust' and was not to be responsible for 'the default of any such agent if employed in good faith'. Thus, s 23 authorised the employment of an agent to carry out the business of the trust whether or not this was necessary or usual business practice. However, this apparently wide power was circumscribed. According to *Re Vickery* (1931), a trustee would be in breach of trust if he appointed an agent to carry out a task outside the normal scope of the agent's expertise and, moreover, there was nothing in the section that absolved the trustee from primary liability should he fall below the standard of care when selecting the agent or supervising the agent in the execution of his (the agent's) duties. Again, there was nothing in s 23(1) to suggest that a trustee might have delegated his primary powers under the trust. In this sense, the enactment of s 23(1) brought about a quantitative change in the ability of trustees to delegate (that is, by removing the common law limitation that delegation had to be necessary for normal business usage), but not a qualitative change. We should note, however, that this limited reading of s 23(1) was not unchallenged (at least academically), for it did appear that s 23(2) of the Trustee Act 1925 gave trustees the power to delegate even their primary responsibilities under the trust.

A further aspect of s 23(1) which was obscure, was the meaning of the proviso that a trustee was not to be 'responsible for the default of any such agent if employed in good faith'. Clearly, this offered some form of protection to a trustee when the agent committed an act or omission that amounted to a breach of trust. In this sense, it was close to the (also now defunct) s 30 of the Trustee Act 1925, which offered a similar protection: viz, that a trustee should 'be answerable and accountable only for his own acts, and not for those of ... any person ... nor for any other loss unless the same happens through his own wilful default'. Unfortunately, the relationship between these two statutory provisions was unclear, save that both exempted the trustee from some liability when an agent had been lawfully employed. There were, indeed, many attempts to explain the relationship between these two statutory provisions, both judicially (for example, *Re Vickery* (1931); *Re Lucking* (1968)) and academically, but in reality it was probably an error of draftsmanship in the 1925 legislation that generated all the complexity and uncertainty.

Alongside these now defunct statutory provisions, there also existed (and still exist) more precise powers of delegation of a clearer ambit. For example, the Trustee Delegation Act 1999 permits a trustee individually to delegate functions in limited circumstances, and trustees of land may delegate any of their functions as trustees to the beneficiaries of the trust under s 9 of the Trusts of Land and Appointment of Trustees Act (TOLATA) 1996. Nevertheless, the difficulties surrounding ss 23 and 30 of the Trustee Act 1925 and the limitations on the common law power to delegate meant that the law was ripe for reform. That reform is now provided by comprehensive provisions of the Trustee Act 2000.

Under s 11 of the Trustee Act 2000, a trustee may authorise any person to exercise any or all of their delegable functions. Apart from charitable trusts, these delegable functions are any function relating to the distribution of trust assets; any power to decide whether payments should be made out of income or capital; any power to appoint; and any other power made delegable by another enactment or the trust instrument. For charitable trusts, s 11(3) limits the delegable functions to, essentially, acts carrying out the decisions of trustees, investment functions and fund raising functions. Evidently, this is a wide power to delegate and permits the trustees to delegate administrative and management functions (as before), but also some fiduciary powers. It represents a significant change in the law. Moreover, apart from beneficiaries and restrictions imposed by s 9 of TOLATA 1996 in respect of a trust of land, any person can be an agent for the purpose of exercising the delegable functions (s 12) and, under s 14, the trustees have a wide discretion to decide the terms of the agency. Of course, along with such sweeping powers come responsibilities. First, the exercise of the power to delegate is subject to the statutory duty of care (s 1 and Sched 1) and this will ensure that trustees take all necessary and reasonable caution in both their choice of agent, terms of agency and in respect of which delegable functions actually to delegate. Secondly, there are special rules under s 15 of the Trustee Act 2000 in relation to 'asset management' functions, being largely concerned with investment powers. Such delegation must be in, or evidenced in, writing, and the agent must comply with a 'policy statement' which the trustee must prepare concerning their investment strategy. Thirdly, in dealing with the *Re Vickery*, ss 23–30 of the Trustee Act 1925 fiasco, s 23 of the Trustee Act 2000 makes it clear that, so long as the trustee has fulfilled his obligations with respect to the appointment of the agent and in respect of review of the agent's activities, then there can be no liability for the trustee if the agent then commits an act which is in breach of the terms of the trust. Again, this is a welcome and timely clarification of a difficult area of the law.

All in all, the Trustee Act 2000 has provided a simple, comprehensive and intelligible set of principles concerning the ability of trustees to delegate their responsibilities under the trust. Such delegation is no longer limited to purely administrative matters, nor is it confined to certain types of persons. The liability of trustees in respect of the acts of agents is clarified, but is balanced by the imposition of clear duties on trustees in respect of their own responsibilities. Once again, judicial interpretation of the new Act will show us conclusively whether it is a success, but, at present, the outlook is good.

Note

The provisions of the Trustee Act 2000 are quite detailed and only a general outline of their effect can be given in such an essay. Reference could also be made to s 16 (power to appoint nominees), s 17 (power to appoint custodians) and s 22 (trustees' duty to review acts of agents, nominees and custodians).

Question 47

David is a solicitor to a trust. The trustees are Margaret and Norman and the beneficiaries Edward and Francis. The trust instrument contains a clause excluding the trustees from liability for any loss or damage to the income or capital of the fund 'unless such loss or damage shall be caused by their own actual fraud'. The assets of the trust included a painting which David wished to buy. David informed the trustees of his wish and, upon David's suggestion, the trustees approached a valuer, Tony, from whom they sought a valuation of the painting. David was aware that Tony had previously been convicted of an offence involving fraud but did not reveal that fact to the trustees. The trustees themselves made no inquiry as to Tony's character and merely accepted David's nomination of him.

Having been told by David of his wish to buy the painting, Tony put its value at £100,000, approximately one half of its true market value, and David bought it from the trustees at that price. He has just sold it for £210,000.

Discuss the possible liabilities of Margaret, Norman, David and Tony to the beneficiaries.

Answer plan

- Trustees' duty of care
- Extent of exclusion clause
- Fiduciary duties
- Dishonestly receiving property for one's benefit
- Accessory liability

Answer

Liability of Margaret and Norman

Margaret and Norman are the express trustees under the settlement. They are required to exercise a duty of care. The standard of care as laid down by s 1 of the Trustee Act 2000 is such care and skill as is reasonable in the circumstances:

(a) having regard to any special knowledge or experience he has or holds himself out as having; and

(b) if he acts as a trustee in the course of a business or profession, to any special knowledge or experience that it is reasonable to expect of a person acting in the course of that kind of business or profession.

Thus, the section has created an objective/subjective test of the standard of care required from the trustees. The minimum degree of care and skill expected from a trustee is to be determined purely objectively by the court. But this standard of care may be increased by reference to the trustees' special knowledge or experience acquired personally or held out by him. Schedule 1 of the Trustee Act 2000 lists the occasions when the duty of care arises. This includes occasions when trustees enter into arrangements in order to delegate functions to agents, nominees, custodians as well as the review of their actions. On the facts of the problem the trustees were aware that David, a fiduciary to the trust, wished to purchase the trust property, a sale was made to David, the trustees relied on David's recommendation of a valuer, Tony, the trustees made no inquiries as to Tony's character who turns out to have had a previous conviction for a crime involving fraud, did the trustees review the actions of the agent, Tony with any degree of care? These factors are strong indications that the trustees may not have exercised the appropriate degree of care necessary in the execution of their office.

However, the trustees may be entitled to rely on the exclusion clause that exists in the trust instrument. Assuming that the clause had been validly inserted in the instrument the issue concerns the extent to which such a clause may protect the trustees from a claim for breach of trust. Such clauses are not, without more, void on public policy grounds. Moreover, provided the clause does not purport to exclude the basic minimum duties of the trustees, it may not be construed as being void for repugnancy to the trust. Some of the minimum duties which may not be excluded are the duties of honesty, good faith and acting for the benefit of the beneficiaries, see *Armitage v Nurse* [1997] 3 WLR 1046. In this case the court decided that the expression 'actual fraud' conjures up the notion of dishonesty and is not capable of protecting trustees. In the problem breach of duties owing to actual fraud is not excluded by virtue of the clause, for such breach is expressly inserted in the proviso. In effect, the settlor intended to protect the trustees from breaches owing to 'constructive fraud' or breaches of fiduciary duties. On this basis the clause may be sufficient to protect the trustees from a claim by the beneficiaries.

David's liability

Firstly, David may not be able to claim protection from the exclusion clause, even as a constructive trustee. The clause is intended to protect express trustees and in any event there may be actual fraud involved in David's conduct.

In order to establish the liability of David, the beneficiaries are required to establish the following three cumulative propositions:

(a) the defendant holds a fiduciary position towards the claimant; and

(b) the defendant obtained a benefit; and

(c) a causal connection exists between the relationship and the benefit.

A fiduciary is an individual who is aware that his judgment and confidence is relied on, and has been relied on, by the claimant.

A definition of a fiduciary was offered by Millett LJ in *Bristol and West Building Society v Mothew* [1996] 4 All ER 698, as one who has undertaken to act for or on behalf of another in a particular matter in circumstances which give rise to a relationship of trust and confidence. The distinguishing obligation of a fiduciary is the obligation of loyalty. In *Boardman v Phipps* [1966] 3 All ER 721, a solicitor to a trust was treated as a fiduciary. In like circumstances, David is a solicitor to the trust and would be treated as a fiduciary.

Has David obtained a benefit? This is a question of fact and the issue seems clear that he obtained a benefit, namely a profit of £110,000. Alternatively, he had obtained trust property namely, the painting valued at £200,000 approximately. Did he obtain this benefit as a result of his fiduciary relationship to the trust? Again this is a question of fact. Did David become aware of the painting by virtue of being a solicitor to the trust? There is no conclusive evidence on the facts of the problem. However, David informed the trustees of his desire to purchase the painting, he recommended a valuer who was unsuitable to give an independent valuation of the chattel, he failed to disclose material facts to the trustees. The cumulative effect of these facts suggest that David was in breach of his fiduciary duties to the beneficiaries.

There is an additional basis of liability as David purchased the trust property – has he knowingly received trust property for his own use? The basis of liability under this head is that a stranger who knows that a fund is trust property transferred to him in breach of trust, cannot take possession of the property for his own benefit, but is subject to the claims of the trust. He is not a *bona fide* transferee of the legal estate for value without notice. The elements of the cause of action were stated by Hoffman LJ in *El Ajou v Dollar Land Holdings* [1994] 2 All ER 685. The types of knowledge for these purposes were laid down in *Re Baden Delvaux* [1983] BCLC 325, as including all types of knowledge, including constructive knowledge.

Alternatively, Megarry VC in *Re Montagu's Settlement* [1987] Ch 264, reviewed the basis of liability under this head and decided that the test is 'want of probity' or 'dishonesty' which requires subjective knowledge of wrongdoing on the part of David. This view was affirmed by the Court of Appeal in *BCCI v Akindele* [2000] 4 All ER 221. In this case, Nourse LJ declared that the categories of knowledge are best forgotten. The test is whether it would be unconscionable for David to retain the property. This is a question of law for the courts to decide. Dishonesty on the part of David may have this effect. In *Twinsectra v Yardley* [2002] 2 All ER 377, the majority of the House of Lords adopted the criminal law test for dishonesty (as laid down by Lord Lane CJ in *R v Ghosh* [1982] QB 1053) namely, the defendant's conduct is dishonest by reference to the ordinary standards of reasonable and honest people *and* that he himself realised that his conduct was dishonest by those standards. On the facts of the problem it is clear that David is aware that the painting is trust property transferred to him in breach of trust. He will therefore become a constructive trustee. As David has sold the painting to a third party, possibly a *bona fide* transferee of the legal estate for value without notice, the remedy available to the beneficiaries is to recover the profit from David.

Liability of Tony

Tony's liability may be based on the fact that he was an accessory in the breach of trust or dishonestly assisting in a fraudulent breach of trust. The liability here was stated in the classic case of *Royal Brunei v Tan* [1995] 3 All ER 97. The test of dishonesty was stated above by reference to the *Twinsectra* decision. On the facts of the problem Tony was aware that he was undervaluing the property with a view to assisting David in acquiring the same at an undervalue. It would seem that the test of dishonesty is satisfied and he will become liable for a breach.

The final point concerns Tony's status. Millett LJ in *Paragon Finance v Thakerar* [1999] 1 All ER 400, opined that the liability of an accessory is strictly not as a constructive trustee because he does not acquire the trust property. His liability is to account to the beneficiaries for any benefits received.

Question 48

A trustee's power of maintenance and power of advancement are essential for the good administration of family trusts, especially if unforeseen circumstances and mere technicalities are not to thwart the intentions of the settlor or testator. Unfortunately, the statutory powers found in the Trustee Act 1925 are so complicated and restrictive that their usefulness is greatly diminished.

Discuss.

Answer plan

- Power of maintenance, being the power to apply the income of a trust for the maintenance, education or benefit of an infant beneficiary;
- power of advancement, being the power to give immediately a beneficiary part of the capital sum under a trust which he or she would receive in the future;
- express powers;
- s 31 of the Trustee Act 1925: maintenance; and
- s 32 of the Trustee Act 1925: advancement.

Answer

It is a cardinal principle of the law of trusts that a trustee must carry out the terms of the trust according to the letter of the trust instrument, at least in so far as this is consistent with the general law. However, as well as imposing duties on a trustee, a trust instrument might well give the trustee certain powers, usually those which are necessary for the good administration of a trust, being such that they *allow* the trustee to do certain things without imposing a requirement that they must be done. This has the further advantage of providing much needed flexibility. The existence of powers of all kinds is particularly important for trusts that are expected to endure for a reasonable period, as the settlor or testator cannot be expected to foresee all future events and must leave certain matters to the discretion of the trustees. For family trusts, two of the most common powers are the 'power of maintenance' and the 'power of advancement'. Indeed, as we shall see, such is the importance of these two powers that the Trustee Act 1925 provides that a statutory version of the power shall be available to trustees of certain kinds of trust.

The power of maintenance is a power given to the trustees to use the income generated by an infant's real or potential beneficial share of a capital fund in order to provide for the maintenance or benefit of that infant during his or her minority (childhood). It might be thought that the use of power to achieve this was superfluous – after all, a share of the capital fund may be vested in the infant already or he may become entitled to it. The point is, however, that an infant with a vested (that is, confirmed) share of the capital fund is not competent to give a valid receipt to the trustees for any income to which he is entitled, and an infant with a contingent share (that is, a potential share dependent on circumstances, such as reaching maturity) may not be entitled to any income at all. In such cases, the power of maintenance allows trustees to distribute income both for the benefit of an infant earlier than otherwise might be the case and even if the infant's share of the capital fund from which the income derives is not confirmed.

Prior to the Trustee Act 1925, it was common for express powers of maintenance to be inserted into trust instruments. These commonly allowed the trustees to apply the income for the 'maintenance or benefit' of the infant and, as such, they gave the trustees a considerable discretion to pay money for the advantage of the infant, even if this also benefited the infant's parents (*Re Lofthouse* (1885); *Fuller v Evans* (1999)). Now, s 31(1) of the Trustee Act 1925 contains an extensive power of maintenance that is available to trustees of qualifying trusts (see below), unless an express or implied contrary intention appears (s 69(2) of the Trustee Act 1925; *Re Ransome* (1957)). Specifically, s 31(1) provides that, where a person has a vested or contingent interest in a trust, then, during that person's infancy, the trustees may pay to his parent or guardian (if any), or otherwise apply the income, for his 'maintenance, education or benefit'. Necessarily, what amounts to the maintenance, education or benefit of the infant will be a matter of construction in each case, and s 31(1)(i)(b) makes it clear that the power may be exercised even if 'any person is bound by law' to provide for the infant. Unfortunately, however, the matter is not as simple as this, and the statutory power is subject to some important and confusing restrictions (*Re Vestey's Settlement* (1951)).

First, an exercise of the statutory power of maintenance cannot affect any prior interests or charges over the trust property (s 31(1)). This is clear enough and is a necessary restriction on the power. However, by virtue of s 31(3), in the case of contingent interests, the statutory power of maintenance is available only if the trust 'carries the intermediate income'. A contingent gift 'carries the intermediate income' if the income generated while waiting for the contingent interest to become vested (that is, for the condition – for example, maturity – to be satisfied) is carried forward with the capital sum rather than being made available for something (or someone) else. The rules to determine whether this is the case are, unfortunately, quite complicated. In general terms, a contingent interest will carry the intermediate income in three sets of circumstances:

(a) if it has been established by a parent (or a person *in loco parentis*) and the capital gift is with interest (s 31(3) of the Trustee Act);

(b) under testamentary gifts if s 175 of the Law of Property Act applies, viz, where there is a contingent specific gift of real or personal property, a contingent residuary gift of freehold land, or a gift of freehold land (specific or residuary) to trustees on trusts of land; and

(c) under a testamentary contingent residuary gift of personalty (*Re McGeorge* (1963)). Moreover, although a contingent pecuniary legacy does not usually carry the intermediate income, it will do so in the three special cases identified in *Re Raine* (1929), being cases where the testator is *in loco parentis* and no other maintenance is available; where there is an intention in the will to maintain the infant; and where income is expressly set aside until the contingency occurs.

It is apparent that these rules are not easy to come to grips with, even though they are essential if the statutory power of maintenance is to be exercised validly. In family trusts administered by non-professional trustees, these provisions can be daunting and a trap for the unwary. Any wrongful application of income by way of maintenance will amount to a breach of trust for which the trustees must make restoration. Consequently, there is a premium on clarity and experience when exercising these powers, and if the trustees are in any doubt they should seek the approval of the court before acting.

Fortunately, the power of advancement is not as complicated. The power of advancement is the power to give a beneficiary part of the capital sum to which he or she may be entitled under the trust, but in advance of the time the capital sum actually becomes payable (if at all). The idea is simply that the trustees may wish to pay over part of the capital to a beneficiary who is entitled in the future or only entitled if certain events occur (that is, a contingency). As stated in *Pilkington v IRC* (1964), use of the power will accelerate a beneficiary's entitlement to capital, even if that entitlement is not certain, providing that to do so would be for the benefit or maintenance of that person. Consequently, such powers may be used to pay capital so that a young adult beneficiary might establish herself in business, or further her education, or even so that a general benefit can be achieved by the avoidance of tax (*Re Garrett* (1934); *Pilkington*).

The statutory power of advancement is to be found in s 32(1) of the Trustee Act 1925, which gives trustees the power to pay or apply capital money 'for the advancement or benefit' of any person entitled to that capital either absolutely or contingently, immediately or in the future. As with the statutory power of maintenance, the power can be excluded by contrary intention (s 69(2) of the Trustee Act) and no payment may be made which prejudices the rights of a person with a prior interest unless that person is of full age and consents in writing (s 32(1)(c)). Again, no more than one half of the beneficiary's actual or potential share can be advanced (s 32(1)(a)), and any advance is then deducted from the beneficiary's share when his interest in the capital falls into possession (that is, becomes payable) (s 32(1)(b)). However, even taking account of these restrictions, which are of an obvious and essential kind and do not seriously impede the exercise of the power of advancement, there is no doubt that the statutory power of advancement is easier to comprehend than the equivalent power of maintenance.

All in all, the exercise of the power of advancement has become less fraught with danger after the Perpetuities and Accumulations Act 1964 introduced the 'wait and see' principle. This effectively ensures that most proposed advancements will not be void for perpetuity. Likewise, in *Pilkington v IRC* (1964), the House of Lords emphasised the very wide discretion given to trustees under the power (with the exercise of which they would not lightly interfere) and confirmed that it was perfectly in order to advance half the capital on completely new trusts if this would be for the 'benefit' of the beneficiaries – as was usually the case when the advancement was made with fiscal objectives in mind, especially the legitimate avoidance of tax.

There are few who would dispute that the statutory powers of maintenance and advancement are useful, especially in family trusts where the settlor or testator would not wish an infant or adult beneficiary to suffer deprivation because sufficient express powers had not been included in the trust instrument. As is obvious, however, the statutory power of maintenance is hedged with restrictions and complications that make it very difficult for the layman trustee to decide whether the power is exercisable or not. Fortunately, the power of advancement does not suffer from the same difficulties.

Note

It can be quite difficult to explain on paper how and when the power of maintenance may be exercised. A genuine exercise of the power has the same characteristics as an elephant: difficult to define, but easy to spot. Advancement is much more comprehensible, although the meaning of 'advancement or benefit' can generate serious litigation if a person with a contingent interest asks for an advance and the trustees know that the contingency is never likely to happen.

Question 49

The repeal of the Trustee Investment Act 1961 and its replacement by the 'general power of investment' and related provisions of the Trustee Act 2000 is greatly to be welcomed.

Discuss.

Answer plan

- The duty to invest;
- express investment clauses;
- the purpose of the Trustee Investment Act, the original scheme and its limitations;
- s 3 of the Trustee Act 2000 – general power of investment;
- s 4 of the Trustee Act 2000 – standard investment criteria;
- s 5 of the Trustee Act 2000 – the duty to obtain advice.

Answer

In many trusts, the role of the trustees is to act as custodians of the capital value of the trust fund – whether represented by money, land or other property – and to hold the same on trust for various persons, some entitled to the income immediately and some entitled to the capital or the income in remainder. Obviously, the trustees will be responsible both to maintain (or increase) the real value of the trust fund and to ensure that a balance is achieved between the interests of the person immediately entitled to the income from the trust property (for example, the life tenant) and those to whom the property will eventually fall in its entirety. Such a balance requires both the production of sufficient income from the capital fund to satisfy the reasonable needs of the life tenant and a sufficient capital gain so that the trust fund is not eroded by inflation or other factors (*Hume v Lopes* (1892)). These goals are achieved by granting the trustees a power, now usually a duty, of investment.

Today, in most professionally drafted trusts, the trustees will be given an express power of investment by the trust instrument. The exact scope of this power will, of course, depend on the terms of the investment clause and the construction placed upon it by the court. It is clear following *Re Harari's Settlement Trusts* (1949), that express investment clauses must not be artificially restricted by imposing a narrow construction on the words used, although the trustees will be empowered only to make those dispositions that can properly be regarded as 'investment' (see, in another context, *R v Clowes (No 2)* (1994)). Moreover, consequent upon the entry into force of the Trustee Act 2000, a trustee must, when exercising such an express power of investment have regard to the statutory duty of care (s 1 and Sched 1) and must have regard to the standard investment criteria (s 4) and the need in some circumstances to take advice (s 5). These are discussed more fully, below, in connection with the new general power of investment but the broad effect is to bring consistency to the exercise of all investment powers, whether statutory or express.

There are, however, many trusts which contain no investment clause – or no satisfactory clause – and then resort must be made to the legislation which provides trustees with a statutory power of investment in default (or in addition to) an express power. Previously, such a power was found in the Trustee Investment Act 1961 and it was the shortcomings of this scheme that led to the new power found in the Trustee Act 2000.

The Trustee Investment Act 1961 was passed in order to meet the then serious deficiencies in the statutory provisions relating to the investment of trust funds and to provide trustees with the capacity to act in a rapidly changing investment climate. The Act applied to trusts established before or after 1961 and its application was not limited by any words in such settlements. For trusts created after 1961, the Act applied in so far as the trust instrument disclosed no contrary intention. When it was enacted, the Trustee

Investment Act did indeed mark a significant increase in the powers of investment of trustees who lacked an express power, but it soon became obvious that the power was hampered by a mandatory scheme for investment that was both complicated and unwieldy. It placed limitations on the exercise of the power that rapidly became obstructive and unduly restrictive. In general terms, the Act permitted trustees to invest the capital funds in a number of different investments, provided that the trust fund was administered according to the stipulations of the Act. This meant that the trustees first had to divide the trust fund into two equal parts: the 'narrower range' part and the 'wider range' part, although these proportions were later changed. The 'narrower range' of investments were specified in Pts I and II of Sched 1 to the Trustee Investment Act and generally comprised those investments which entailed a low level of risk and gave as close to a guaranteed return as is possible. Part I of the 'narrower range' included those investments which the trustees could undertake without advice and included very safe investments such as National Savings Certificates and deposits at the National Savings Bank. Part II 'narrower range' investments were also safe, but could be undertaken only after the trustees had sought the advice of a qualified adviser. They included investment in fixed interest securities issued by the UK government, government of a Commonwealth country or government of an EU/EFTA State; deposits in building societies; debentures issued by a company incorporated in such states; and mortgages of freehold property or of leasehold property with more than 60 years unexpired in such States. The advice required to invest in Pt II of the narrower range had to come from a person who the trustees reasonably believed to be qualified to give such advice. Additional provisions applied if the trustee wished to protect himself against a charge of breach of trust when the investment was by way of mortgage over land. Clearly, these restrictions had some merit, for example, to protect the beneficiaries from over enthusiastic investment activity by the trustees, but there is no doubt that they prevented a trustee from having access to the considerable investment opportunities provided by the investment in stocks and shares on the stock exchange in respect of a large proportion of the capital fund.

As to the 'wider range' investments, these were specified in Pt III of Sched 1 to the Trustee Investment Act 1961 and included shares of companies incorporated in the UK and other States, shares in building societies and unit trusts. They were thought to be more speculative investments than those within the narrower range and so trustees were required to seek professional advice before such investment. Moreover, according to Pt IV of Sched 1 to the 1961 Act, certain investments although within the parameters of Pts 1, II and III of the Act were not permitted at all. These included any securities where payment was not to be in sterling, securities of companies whose capital share value was less than £1 m, and shares of companies that had not declared a dividend in each of the last five years before the proposed investment. Again, these limitations were unduly restrictive and closed off many avenues of beneficial investment.

Obviously, the 1961 Act, even after its partial amendment, imposed significant restrictions on the power of the trustees to invest in the absence of an express investment clause. These were both procedural (fund splitting, seeking advice, etc) and substantive (limitations on types of investment). In particular, the range of companies that could be chosen was limited and, originally, there was no power to invest in foreign companies quoted on an overseas stock exchange, despite the fact that this had been a very productive sector of the investment market. Likewise, there was no power to invest by way of the purchase of land (as opposed to granting mortgages over land), even though land offers long term protection against inflation. Indeed, the very heart of the Act, in that it required a portion of the original fund to be placed in certain forms of investment, was unduly restrictive.

Consequently, after much debate and some piecemeal reforms (for example, by virtue of s 6 of the Trusts of Land and Appointment of Trustees Act (TOLATA) 1996, trustees of land were given the power to purchase a legal estate for investment or other purpose), a new scheme was introduced by the Trustee Act 2000. Under s 3 of the Act, trustees are given a general power of investment, and this is in addition to any express powers they may be given and subject only to express limitations in the trust instrument. Under this general power, a trustee may make any kind of investment that an absolute owner could make, except that an investment in land must be made in accordance with s 8 of the Act. The power does not apply to the special types of trusts known as pension funds and unit trusts and certain funds established under the Charities Acts, as these are already subject to sensible investment regimes. Evidently, this represents a very welcome deregulation of trustees' investment powers and frees them to make investment decisions based on sound management of the trust rather than prescriptive limitations. Of course, the Act also provides safeguards. First, all powers of investment, including this statutory power, are subject to the statutory duty of care.

Section 1 of the Trustee Act 2000 reformulates the duty of care applicable to powers exercisable by trustees under the Act. This provision replaces the common law standard of care as indicated above. The section enacts that the trustees are required to exercise such care and skill as is reasonable in the circumstances:

(a) having regard to any special knowledge or experience he has or holds himself out as having; and

(b) if he acts as a trustee in the course of a business or profession, to any special knowledge or experience that it is reasonable to expect of a person acting in the course of that kind of business or profession.

Thus, the section has created an objective/ subjective test of the standard of care required from the trustees. The minimum degree of care and skill expected from a trustee is to be determined objectively by the court. This standard of care may be increased by reference to the trustees' special knowledge or experience acquired personally or held out by him. This provision echoes the view of Brightman J in *Bartlett v Barclays Bank* [1980] Ch 515.

Schedule 1 of the Trustee Act 2000 lists the occasions when the duty of care arises. These are in the *exercise* of the statutory and express powers of investment, including the duty to have regard to the standard investment criteria and the duty to obtain and consider proper advice. In addition the duty applies to the trustees' power to acquire land. Moreover, the duty of care applies when trustees enter into arrangements in order to delegate functions to agents, nominees, custodians as well as the review of their actions.

Secondly, in exercising any power of investment (express or statutory), the trustees must have regard to the 'standard investment criteria': s 4 of the Trustee Act 2000. This criteria will ensure that trustees have regard to the suitability of any type of investment for the particular trust and the need for diversification (s 4(3)(a) and (b)). Thirdly, under s 5, before exercising any power of investment (express or statutory), the trustee must obtain and consider proper advice from a person who is reasonably believed by the trustee to offer relevant advice, save only that advice need not be sought unless it is reasonable for the trustee to conclude in all the circumstances that such advice is not necessary (s 5(3) and (4)).

Clearly, this new power of investment, which may be exercised in default of or in addition to any express power, is simpler and more malleable than that contained in the now defunct Trustee Investment Act 1961. Of course, its simplicity and breadth might be thought to bring dangers for the beneficiaries, but the imposition of statutory duties and controls, that are themselves clear and precise, should ensure that an appropriate balance has been struck between the need for trustees to protect the trust fund through investment and the need to protect the beneficiaries from over zealous investment practices.

Note

The 1961 Act was all but useless before its repeal. The Trustee Act 2000 has created a streamlined and simpler mechanism. We shall not know just how effective the new Act is until it has had some judicial interpretation through case law. Importantly, the safeguards of the new Act also apply to express investment clauses.

Question 50

In what circumstances may the court sanction a variation of the terms of a trust?

Answer plan

- The need for a power to vary trusts;
- intervention of the court where consents cannot be obtained;
- inherent jurisdiction;
- s 57 of the Trustee Act 1925;
- s 53 of the Trustee Act 1925;
- s 64 of the Settled Land Act 1925; and
- Variation of Trusts Act 1958.

Answer

It is intrinsic in the nature of a trust that the trustees are under an obligation to carry out the terms of the trust according to the trust instrument, as modified or superseded by the general law. However, there may be many reasons why the details of the trust, the powers and duties of the trustees, or even the nature and extent of the beneficiaries' interests as originally specified, prove impossible to implement in practice. Likewise, the testator or settlor cannot be expected to foresee all possible future contingencies and no amount of expansive or open ended drafting can hope to cover all possibilities. So it is that there must be some method by which the terms of a trust may be varied, in detail and in substance. Today, the great majority of proposed variations of trust arise because of a desire to minimise the tax liabilities of the trust (see *Re Weston* (1969)), although applications to vary can have other, more altruistic motives, such as a desire to protect the trust property from wayward beneficiaries (*Hambro v Duke of Marlborough* (1994)).

As a matter of principle, it is open to all of the beneficiaries under a trust, providing they are of full age and capacity, to consent to any proposed reordering of the trust (*Saunders v Vautier* (1841) and related powers under s 6 of the Trusts of Land and Appointment of Trustees Act (TOLATA) 1996)). However, many of the trusts where a variation would be most beneficial are precisely those where the beneficiaries are either unwilling or unable to consent – for example, because they are infants or members of a hypothetical class, such as future children. In these cases, a variation of the terms of the trust can be achieved only with the aid of the court exercising its inherent or statutory jurisdiction.

The court's inherent jurisdiction to order a variation of trust on the application of either the trustees or interested beneficiaries was examined in detail by the House of Lords in *Chapman v Chapman* (1954). Effectively, this decision limited the court's power to approve a variation to four sets of circumstances only. First, in cases of genuine emergency or necessity where the trustees request the authorisation of the court to enter into a transaction which is not permitted by the trust instrument (*Re New* (1901)). The essence of this jurisdiction is that the court will authorise some otherwise impermissible dealing with the trust property – such as a sale of protected assets – if this is necessary to meet an emergency facing the trust estate. It is not enough that the proposed action would benefit the estate *per se*; there must be real necessity caused by unforeseen events which the requested transaction would remedy (*Re Montague* (1987)). Secondly, the court will authorise a variation of trust in the sense of consenting on behalf of those who are unable to consent, if this is required to settle a *bona fide* dispute as to the terms of the trust, as discussed, but not permitted, in *Chapman* itself (where there was no genuine dispute). Thirdly, the court will authorise a variation of the beneficial interests of a settlement if this is needed to provide for the maintenance of a tenant for life who is otherwise unprovided for (*Re Collins* (1886)). Fourthly and finally, the court will act in the now largely redundant situation where a change in the nature of an infant's property (from personalty to realty and vice versa) is desired for the purposes of testamentary disposition.

It will be obvious from the preceding discussion that the inherent jurisdiction of the court to authorise a variation of trust is very limited. There is nothing here that allows the variation of a trust because it is expedient or generally beneficial, and such statutory powers as the court possessed at the time of *Chapman v Chapman* (1954) were limited to specific kinds of property or specific circumstances (see below). In fact, such was the concern at the restrictive nature of the inherent jurisdiction revealed in *Chapman* and the limited nature of the existing statutory jurisdiction, that the Law Reform Committee proposed the enactment of a general statute granting the court a greater jurisdiction to authorise variation of trusts. The result was the Variation of Trusts Act 1958.

Before considering the Variation of Trusts Act (VTA) 1958 in detail, brief mention should be made of three other forms of statutory jurisdiction to vary trusts. Under s 57(1) of the Trustee Act 1925, the court is given the jurisdiction to vary the powers of the trustees so as to enable them to achieve transactions connected with the administration of the trust that would otherwise be impermissible. Importantly, this jurisdiction is limited to varying the *administrative* powers of the trustees (such as the power of investment) and does not enable the court to sanction a change in the nature or extent of the beneficiaries' equitable interests (*Re Downshire* (1953); *Mason v Fairbrother* (1983)). Further, the court will only grant an application to vary trustees' administrative powers if it believes this to be 'expedient' for the management of the trust (*Re Craven* (1937)) and the statutory power does not apply to trusts of settled land. Secondly, the court has a limited jurisdiction to authorise certain otherwise impermissible transactions under s 53 of the Trustee Act 1925 in cases where this is necessary to provide for 'the maintenance, education or benefit' of any infant beneficially entitled to trust property (*Re Gower* (1934)), and this can include making the trust more tax efficient (*Re Meux* (1958)). Thirdly, and of real significance, s 64 of the Settled Land Act 1925 gives the court power to authorise the tenant for life to undertake any transaction affecting settled land which 'in the opinion of the court would be for the benefit of the settled land, or any part thereof'. Obviously, this jurisdiction applies only to land within a settlement, and no new settlements may be created after 1 January 1997 (s 7 of TOLATA), but it does permit the court to vary both the administrative provisions of the trust and the beneficial entitlements of the equitable owners (*Re Downshire* (1953)). Indeed, as *Hambro v Duke of Marlborough* (1994) illustrates, s 64 may be used to alter the beneficial entitlements of an equitable owner against his wishes and may even result in the transfer of the land to completely new trusts (see, also, *Raikes v Lygon* (1988)).

In similar fashion to s 64, the VTA also allows changes to be made to both the administrative powers of trustees and the beneficial interests of the equitable owners, although the court's jurisdiction under this statute is of a general and wide ranging nature and was entirely novel (*Re Steed* (1960)). However, the Act does not simply empower the court to authorise any variation to the terms of a trust as it thinks fit. Rather, the Act builds upon the *Saunders v Vautier* principle that all of the beneficiaries, if of full age and capacity, can consent to a variation of their trust. Thus, under s 1, the court is empowered to give its consent to a variation or arrangement of the trust on behalf of any of four classes of person who are incapable of consenting for themselves. These are:

(a) infants with a vested or contingent interest (s 1(1)(a));

(b) persons who may become entitled to an interest as being a member of a specified class on the happening of a future event, except if that person would be a member of the class if the future event happened on the date of application to the court (s (1(1)(b));

(c) persons unborn (s 1(1)(c)); and

(d) persons with an interest under a discretionary trust arising in consequence of a protective trust, where the interest of the principal beneficiary has not failed (s 1(1)(d)).

Although these provisions appear complicated (and s 1(1)(b) has caused difficulties – see *Knocker v Youle* (1986)), the essential point is that the court will consent for these people – who may be adults or infants respectively – but may only do so if it is satisfied (for classes (a), (b) and (c)) that the variation is for those persons' benefit. Moreover, although the 'benefit' will usually be financial in the form of fiscal advantages (*Re Sainsbury* (1967); *Re Robertson* (1960)), the court can consent to a variation that is of moral or social benefit to the beneficiaries (*Re Weston* (1969); *Re CL* (1969)), and, in exceptional circumstances, this benefit can outweigh any financial disadvantage caused by the variation (*Re Holt* (1969)). In *D (a child) v O* [2004] 3 All ER 780, the court accepted jurisdiction under the VTA 1958 to increase the amount subject to the statutory power of advancement under s 32 of the Trustee Act 1925. Likewise, the court will consider the proposed scheme as a whole and may even consent to a variation that contradicts the settlor's original intentions (*Re Remnant* (1970)) (but see, *contra*, *Re Steed* (1960)). There is some doubt, however, whether a completely new scheme which undermines the essential basis of the trust can amount to a 'variation' or 'arrangement' that the court could approve. In *Re T* (1964), it was held that an alleged variation which in fact attacked the very substratum of the trust could not be approved, as it was not a variation but the substitution of completely new trusts. Yet, as *Re Ball* (1968) illustrates, there is a fine line between a substantial variation that leaves the 'substratum' intact and one that does not.

In principle then, the court now has an extensive jurisdiction to order the variation of trusts and this is in addition to the very specialised jurisdictions under the Matrimonial Causes Act 1973 (see, for example, *Brooks v Brooks* (1996)) and the Mental Health Act 1983. The court's jurisdiction under the VTA is, however, of a special kind, for in theory, the variation is effected by action of the parties, the court merely consenting on behalf of those beneficiaries who cannot consent for themselves (*Re Holmden* (1968)). This is despite the problems then arising under s 53(1)(c) of the Law of Property Act 1925 when equitable interests are transferred under a variation in the absence of signed writing (see, also, *Re Holt* (1969)). Nevertheless, this theoretical obstacle has not prevented widespread use of the VTA. Nor has the passing of this general statute affected the powers of the court under the other statutes discussed above. In particular, provided that the beneficial interests are not in issue, s 57 of the Trustee Act is generally thought preferable for a proposed variation giving wider investment powers (*Anker-Petersen v Anker-Petersen* (1991)).

Note

Case law is important when discussing the Variation of Trusts Act as it adds much needed life to the bare bones of the statute. A similar question could ask the student to discuss the meaning of 'benefit' under the VTA when, obviously, considerable case law should be cited.

——— Question 51 ———

Does the law of trusts have a future?

Answer plan

- The peculiar nature of the trust concept;
- original use of trust concept;
- trusts to achieve certain goals: charities, purposes, fiscal advantages;
- trusts as remedies; and
- trusts as vehicles for investment: pensions, life assurance, savings schemes.

——— Answer ———

The 'trust' concept is a peculiar creation of English common law. In isolation, the idea of property being 'owned' by two persons concurrently, each with different rights and duties in respect of it, seems slightly absurd. The whole idea appears even stranger when it is realised that the 'legal' owner, the person with the formal, provable title, has, in effect, no claim to the beneficial use of the property for this is reserved for the person with the informal, possibly unwritten, equitable title. Originally, the trust was used to achieve a certain measure of protection for the property of an absent lord of the manor or, more deviously, as a device to avoid feudal dues or certain statutes restricting the devolution of property. The formal passing of property to a 'trustee', while placing 'beneficial' ownership elsewhere, was well suited for this. However, in modern times, the basically simple idea at the heart of the trust – division of ownership, with one person holding property for the benefit of another or others – has assumed far greater significance. Nowadays, such is the sophistication of some modern trusts that the law of equity has had to develop rapidly and flexibly to keep pace.

It would be foolish to attempt a categorisation of the many different roles to which the trust concept can be put without sounding a note of caution. In one sense, each trust is individual and unique for the duties, powers, beneficial interests and administrative provisions of each settlement will vary according to the express words of the testator or settlor. No two trusts are entirely the same and the precise scope of each will depend on the trust instrument as supplemented by the law of equity and statutory provision. That said, it is true that one can identify general categories of trust, usually by reference to the purposes which they are intended to serve. Of course, these categories are not mutually exclusive and the settlor or testator may have had a combination of motives in mind when establishing his trust.

Perhaps the most obvious use of the trust is to establish a scheme for the future regulation of the settlor's property, usually with the intention of maintaining certain assets for the use and enjoyment of future generations of the settlor's family. Examples include the family trusts discussed in *Re Montague* (1987) and *Hambro v Duke of Marlborough* (1994). Necessarily, the use of trusts to provide for future generations is circumscribed by the rule against perpetuities, itself an expression of social and economic policy. Nevertheless, the trust concept is ideal for this purpose as it allows the settlor to provide for many beneficiaries (such as spouses and children) secure in the knowledge that the trust property will be managed even handedly under the control of the court of equity for the benefit of all. In similar vein, and often as a concomitant to dispositions of property among family members, a trust can be used to minimise the tax liabilities of both the settlor and his immediate successors. However, as cases such as *Grey v IRC* (1960) and *Pariny (Hatfield) v IRC* (1997) illustrate, the use of the trust as a tax avoidance device must be approached with some care, especially if the establishment of the trust was not wholly motivated by fiscal considerations. Where trusts are established solely for fiscal advantages (for example, as in certain kinds of discretionary trust), there are usually well established procedures and provisions which the Inland Revenue will accept as being appropriate and lawful for this purpose. Again however, care must be taken not to overstep the line between lawful tax avoidance and unlawful tax evasion and courts are not shy of striking down schemes that fall on the wrong side of the boundary (*Furniss v Dawson* (1984); *LM Tenancies v IRC* (1998)).

Similarly, note should be made of those forms of trust which serve as a vehicle for general investment purposes, including unit trust and investment trust schemes. These very specialised uses of the trust concept are established for the sole purpose of providing easy and convenient access to investment opportunities for members of the public, usually accompanied by fiscal advantages. The person acting as manager of the subscribers' monies will be in the fiduciary position of trustee, and the investors usually retain some form of beneficial interest in the investments or general investment fund. Not only may such a form of investment be tax efficient and convenient, it also provides the beneficiaries with additional protection should the trustee become bankrupt or abscond with their monies (see, for example, the civil and criminal litigation culminating in *R v Clowes (No 2)* (1994) and the claim in *Foskett v McKeown* (2000)). Finally in this connection, the trust concept is also used as the primary vehicle for the management of pension funds, as in *Mettoy Pension Trustees Ltd v Evans* (1990). Unfortunately, there has been a number of *causes célèbres* involving the misapplication of pension fund monies and the ability of the trust to protect the persons with an interest in the fund (that is, the pensioners) has been questioned. Likewise, as the *Mettoy* case and *Davis v Richards and Wallington Industries Ltd* (1990) illustrate, the substantive law of trusts may not always serve well the particular and peculiar requirements of pension funds. This led to a wide ranging review of pensions law (The Goode Committee Report) which, while accepting the role of 'the trust' in pensions management, proposed additional statutory safeguards and tighter regulation for the administration of pension funds. It remains to be seen whether the trust is the most suitable vehicle for this particular purpose, even with additional statutory safeguards.

Another crucial function of the trust concept in the modern law is the role it plays in the financing of charities. As is well known, the extent to which a trust may be used to achieve a non-charitable public purpose is limited (*Re Endacott* (1960)), and this has been the subject of considerable criticism. However, the elastic and malleable definition of 'charity' does permit the achievement through trust law of a considerable number of beneficial purposes. This is especially important in an age where governmental financial support for 'public' causes is decreasing and no doubt the role of the trust in charitable giving is likely to increase. Likewise, the law's different approach to charitable trusts, at least in terms of their validity, susceptibility to perpetuity rules and fiscal liabilities, indicates the importance with which these trusts are regarded by the legislature and judiciary.

Lastly in this brief survey of the role of the trust in the modern world, there is a significant body of law that identifies the trust as a powerful remedy in the hands of the court against those guilty of inequitable conduct. This may take many forms, and perhaps the greatest strength of this use of the trust is that the law is constantly developing to meet new challenges. Thus, the use of the resulting or constructive trust to recognise the beneficial ownership of a person living in shared premises which belongs formally at law to another is one of the great achievements of the post war era (*Pettitt v Pettitt* (1970) and *Lloyds Bank v Rosset* (1991)). Not only has the development of this equitable jurisdiction had a profound effect on the substantive rights of ordinary citizens, it has also prompted and required a change in the lending practices of banks and building societies, with much greater care being taken to ensure that the rights of occupiers of domestic property are respected (*Williams & Glyn's Bank v Boland* (1981) and *Barclays Bank v O'Brien* (1993)). Similarly, the imposition of a constructive trust on persons who are already trustees (*Keech v Sandford* (1726)) and persons who are not (*Karak Rubber v Burden* (1972); *International Sales Ltd v Marcus* (1982); *El Ajou v Dollar Land Holdings plc* (1994)) illustrates the breadth of this remedial jurisdiction when it is activated to meet actual or intended inequitable conduct. Indeed, these are but a few examples of the use of the trust as a substantive remedy, and that is without consideration of cases arising under the law of secret trusts (*Bannister v Bannister* (1948)) or the principle that 'equity will not permit a statute to be used as an instrument of fraud' (*Rouchefoucauld v Boustead* (1897)).

Whether the trend towards using the 'trust' as a remedial institution continues is one of the most interesting questions in the modern law of trusts. While the House of Lords in *Westdeutsche Landesbank Girozentrale v Islington LBC* (1996) indicated that English law is not *yet* ready for the use of the trust purely as a remedial institution – that is, the 'traditional' rules concerning the circumstances in which a person can be held to be a constructive trustee must still be respected – it is clear that pressure is mounting for the recognition of a wide remedy by way of constructive trusteeship. Likewise, the deconstruction of some aspects of the law of trusts – for example, the law of knowing receipt – and their reformulation (or perhaps discovery?) as aspects of a general restitutionary remedy is arousing much comment. This is certainly one area where the story is not yet written and where, in the end, there may be no future for the law of trust as such.

This takes us back to the question of whether the trust concept has a future. This brief look at the role of trusts in the modern world has, if nothing else, illustrated that without it there would be a lacuna in the law that would be difficult to fill. However, we can be more positive than this. The trust is not only useful, it is an ingenious creation of equity. The division of ownership, the separate yet related rights of the legal and equitable owners, the remedies for inequitable conduct and the founding of legal obligation on the conscience of a freely accepted moral obligation are, of themselves, powerful reasons why the concept of the trust will survive and continue to develop in English law.

Note

With such a general question, the student may range across any number of issues. The above answer simply presents some of the more obvious ones. In fact, this could be a thesis title rather than an essay.

Index